Unnamed Desires

Unnamed Desires

A SYDNEY LESBIAN HISTORY
REBECCA JENNINGS

© Copyright 2015 Rebecca Jennings
All rights reserved. Apart from any uses permitted by Australia's Copyright Act 1968, no part of this book may be reproduced by any process without prior written permission from the copyright owners. Inquiries should be directed to the publisher.

Monash University Publishing
Matheson Library and Information Services Building
40 Exhibition Walk
Monash University
Clayton, Victoria 3800, Australia
www.publishing.monash.edu

Monash University Publishing brings to the world publications which advance the best traditions of humane and enlightened thought.

Monash University Publishing titles pass through a rigorous process of independent peer review.

www.publishing.monash.edu/books/ud-9781922235701.html

Series: Monash Studies in Australian Society.

Design: Les Thomas

Cover image: Maureen, Brenda and their dog Geronimo, Wyee, early 1960s, photo by Zita Deaves / courtesy the Australian Lesbian and Gay Archives

National Library of Australia Cataloguing-in-Publication entry:

Creator:	Jennings, Rebecca, author.
Title:	Unnamed desires : a Sydney lesbian history / Rebecca Jennings.
ISBN:	9781922235701 (paperback)
Subjects:	Lesbians--New South Wales--Sydney--History.
	Lesbians--New South Wales--Sydney--Social conditions.
	Lesbianism--New South Wales--Sydney--History.
Dewey Number:	306.7663099441

Printed in Australia by Griffin Press an Accredited ISO AS/NZS 14001:2004 Environmental Management System printer.

CONTENTS

Acknowledgements ix

Introduction xi

Chapter 1.   Constructing the Lesbian as 'Unacceptable' 1

Chapter 2.   Concealment and Isolation 26

Chapter 3.   A Room Full of Women: Lesbian Bars and
               Social Spaces in Postwar Sydney 50

Chapter 4.   Lesbian Politics 75

Chapter 5.   Cultures of Intimacy 101

Afterword 129

Bibliography 137

Index 147

For Sandra and Leonie, whose beautiful garden in Marrickville, with its veggie beds, chooks and bees, will always be the heart of lesbian Sydney for me.

ACKNOWLEDGEMENTS

I would like to acknowledge the support of Macquarie University, who funded this research through a Macquarie University Research Fellowship. In particular, I am grateful to my then head of department, Angela Woollacott, whose sponsorship of the project and generous encouragement of my work in its early stages was invaluable. My fellow MQ Research Fellows, Lisa Featherstone and Tanya Evans, provided intellectual stimulation, advice and friendship throughout as have more recent colleagues, Shirleene Robinson, Julia Miller and Robert Reynolds and I am very grateful to them all. At Macquarie, I would also like to thank Hsu-Ming Teo, Bridget Griffen-Foley, Mary Spongberg, Margaret Sampson, Michelle Arrow, George Parsons and Jackie Anker, who variously suggested possible leads, commented on my work or provided advice, encouragement and assistance.

However, this book has been framed, more than anything else, by the lesbian and gay communities of Sydney and beyond, and would not have been written without the help and enthusiasm of many people in the Pride History Group in Sydney, the Older dykes network, and the Australian Lesbian and Gay Archives in Melbourne. I am grateful to John Witte, Ken Davies and Di Minnis for welcoming me into the Pride History Group, and to John Witte especially, for recognising the importance of research into lesbian history at a time when the group included very few lesbians. Sandra Mackay helped shape this book through our collective adventures in oral history interviewing and by sharing her own experiences of lesbian feminist Sydney, which have forever changed my views of lesbian feminist culture. The women of the Older dykes network generously passed on word of my project and I am very grateful for their support. I would also like to thank Gary Jaynes, Liz Ross, Graham Willett, Nick Henderson and many others at the Australian Lesbian and Gay Archive, who kindly gave up their time to make the archive accessible and shared their immense knowledge of Australian lesbian and gay history with me.

Oral histories and personal memories are at the heart of this book, and it could not have been written without the courageous and generous contributions of those women who kindly agreed to share their experiences and memories of lesbian Sydney with me. A huge thank you to you all.

Finally, I would like to thank my family, and in particular my partner, Vicky, who has shared every stage of this and many other journeys with me, debating every point, making invaluable suggestions, reading endless drafts and reminding me, when necessary, why it is so important that we continue to research our lesbian history.

INTRODUCTION

Reflecting on her life as a young woman who desired other women in 1960s Sydney, Kris explained:

> If you even looked at a woman, you had to be really careful because … there was a lot of silence … it was a secret … You would just, you would be rejected … it wasn't right. You weren't – you just weren't healthy. You were a queer. That was the main thing. You're a bloody queer. You weren't accepted. People would shun you.[1]

Kris' account of a life of secrecy and deception echoed the stories of many lesbians in mid-twentieth century New South Wales. For the majority of women in this period, acknowledging their same-sex desires meant living a double life in which feelings for, or relationships with other women were kept hidden from family, friends and work colleagues. Women who were exposed as lesbians were at risk of losing their jobs or their homes and being rejected by family and friends. Many women responded to the cultural idealisation of marriage and motherhood by getting married, but this could exacerbate feelings of isolation or, if women subsequently had relationships with other women, could lead to marital breakdown and loss of custody of their children. Others, however, forged social networks with other lesbians, sustained loving same-sex relationships, and developed successful careers as teachers, nurses, secretaries and in many other occupations. In the 1960s, small numbers of women began to participate in a mixed public bar scene; and in the 1970s, new political movements opened up spaces in which to debate lesbians' experiences – as women and as lesbians. This book explores lesbian life and culture in mid-twentieth century NSW, unpicking the experiences both of those women who led 'double lives' and those who did not.

---

1 Interview with Kris Melmouth, 25 August 2011.

The existing literature

In 1991, Garry Wotherspoon prefaced his history of Sydney's gay subculture, *City of the Plain*, with this assertion:

> This book also deals solely with the male sub-culture and touches only peripherally on life for lesbians. The history of life for lesbians in Sydney – and indeed in Australia – is more properly part of women's history, since what has happened to the lesbian community has far more to do with the situation of women in our society than it has to do with male homosexuality. Their non-inclusion (except incidentally) in this book is not intended then as a slight, rather it reflects a proper recognition of the fact that the forces that have gone to shape their lives are different to the forces that have shaped the lives of homosexual or gay men.[2]

Wotherspoon's claim that gender was central in defining lesbians' experience in the past constituted both a justification of the focus of his own book on gay men and an implicit call for a distinct 'history of life for lesbians in Sydney' to be written. Nearly 25 years after the publication of *City of the Plain*, however, an urgent need still remains for a detailed examination of lesbian life in mid-twentieth century New South Wales. This book aims to fill that gap. In the intervening period, a number of important studies of lesbian and gay culture and identity in the second half of the century have appeared, but while this literature has demonstrated the extent to which lesbians and gay men shared certain experiences and concerns in common, it is also clear that any attempt to examine male and female homosexuality together inevitably obscures many of the crucial differences between the two.[3] Graham Willett's carefully researched account of the development of gay and lesbian activism across Australia from the 1950s to the 1990s has had a major impact on the field but fails to consider the specific insights of feminist and lesbian politics in this period.[4] Similarly, Robert Reynolds' *From Camp to Queer* offers a nuanced analysis of the ways in which emerging political notions of sexuality reshaped models of gay identity, but also tends to assume a gay

---

2 Garry Wotherspoon, *City of the Plain: History of a Gay Sub-Culture* (Sydney: Hale and Iremonger, 1991).
3 Clive Moore, *Sunshine and Rainbows: The Development of Gay and Lesbian Culture in Queensland* (St Lucia: University of Queensland Press, 2001); Graham Willett, *Living Out Loud: A History of Gay and Lesbian Activism in Australia* (St Leonards NSW: Allen & Unwin, 2000).
4 Willett, *Living Out Loud*. See Baird, Barbara, 'Review of Living Out Loud, by Graham Willett', *Australian Humanities Review* (2001), http://www.australianhumanitiesreview.org/archive/Issue-April-2001/baird.html.

male subjectivity as the norm, concentrating analysis of feminist perspectives in a single chapter towards the end of the book.[5] The extent to which notions of gender impacted on lesbians' access to employment, their economic status, freedom of movement and access to public spaces, as well as the ways in which these ideas shaped social and familial expectations about their potential roles as wives and mothers, needs careful and detailed consideration distinct from discussions of the difficulties faced by homosexual men.

However, it would be a mistake to assume that such a discussion would fit as comfortably into the field of women's history as Wotherspoon implies. Since the emergence of second wave feminism in Australia in the late 1960s, a significant body of historical work exploring women's lives and women's political engagements has appeared.[6] However, much of this work touches only briefly on lesbian experience, while those studies which devote more space to the subject tend to focus on the marginality of lesbians to the mainstream experience of women. Gisela Kaplan's examination of the Australian women's movement, for example, frames her chapter on lesbianism in terms of conflict, emphasising the dissension between lesbian and heterosexual feminists, and the extent to which lesbians were ignored or marginalised in the movement.[7] More recent work on the 1970s has attempted to incorporate lesbian perspectives more productively into a broader picture of the diversity of women's experience, but inevitably only limited space can be accorded to a discussion of these issues. The specific impact of attitudes toward female sexuality in shaping the experience of lesbians in the past tends to be obscured.[8]

If we are to approach a more nuanced understanding of lesbian history, therefore, we must remain mindful of the interconnections between gender and sexuality in shaping lesbian experience. The work of Ruth Ford, Sylvia

---

5   Robert Reynolds, *From Camp to Queer: Remaking the Australian Homosexual* (Melbourne: Melbourne University Press) 2002.
6   Marilyn Lake, *Getting Equal: The History of Australian Feminism* (Sydney: Allen & Unwin, 1999); Jan Mercer, ed., *The Other Half: Women in Australian Society* (Melbourne: Penguin, 1975); Norma Grieve and Patricia Grimshaw, eds, *Australian Women: Feminist Perspectives* (Melbourne: Oxford University Press, 1981); Anne Summers, *Damned Whores and God's Police: The Colonization of Women in Australia* (Melbourne: Penguin, 1975); Ann Curthoys, 'The Women's Movement since 1970' in Kay Saunders and Raymond Evans, eds, *Gender Relations in Australia: Domination and Negotiation* (Sydney: Harcourt Brace Jovanovich, 1992), pp. 425–447; Ann Curthoys, *For and Against Feminism: A Personal Journey into Feminist Theory and History* (Sydney: Allen & Unwin, 1988).
7   Gisela Kaplan, *The Meagre Harvest: The Australian Women's Movement 1950s–1990s* (Sydney: Allen and Unwin, 1996).
8   Michelle Arrow and Mary Spongberg, eds, *Australian Feminist Studies* vol. 22, no. 53 (July 2007).

Martin and Lucy Chesser has laid the foundations of this project, significantly increasing our understanding of lesbian identity in Australia, particularly in the first half of the twentieth century. Through a series of case studies of notorious passing women such as Eugenia Falleni and Harcourt Payne, as well as more discreet female companions, Ruth Ford has demonstrated that the cultural meanings attached to same-sex desire were in flux in Australia in this period, influenced by a range of discourses from the newly emerging medical language of sexology to older moral discourses of sin and the carnival 'freak'. Contemporary understandings of gender and sexuality were complicated in these discourses by the language of class and ethnicity. Working from official records such as court transcripts, medical records and press accounts, Ford has pieced together a nuanced picture of mainstream and dominant discourses on female same-sex desire in the first half of the twentieth century.[9] However, in the absence of personal records, the self-understandings and experiences of the women concerned are more difficult to pinpoint, and Ford faced the perennial difficulty of lesbian historians in attempting to reconstruct a history of emotion and physical intimacy in the face of a pervasive silence maintained by, and about, her subjects. Sylvia Martin has encountered similar challenges in her biographical studies of several Australian literary women, whose passionate friendships, forged in a culture of silence about same-sex desire, resisted historians' attempts at definition.[10]

Defining 'silence'

Silence – as a methodological problem, a conceptual paradox, and a definitional premise – has been widely discussed by lesbian historians. In her exploration of female homosexuality and modern culture, *The Apparitional Lesbian*, Terry Castle refers to women who desired other women in the past as ghosts. She observes:

---

9   Ruth Ford, 'Speculating on Scrapbooks, Sex and Desire: Issues in Lesbian History', *Australian Historical Studies*, vol. 27, no. 106 (1996), pp. 11–26; Ruth Ford, '"The Man-Woman Murderer": Sex Fraud, Sexual Inversion and the Unmentionable "Article" in 1920s Australia', *Gender and History* vol. 12, no. 1 (2000), pp. 158–196; Ruth Ford, 'Lady-Friends and Deviationists: Lesbians and the Law in Australia 1920s–1950s', in Diane Kirkby, ed., *Sex, Power and Justice: Historical Perspectives on the Law in Australia, 1788–1990* (Melbourne: Oxford University Press, 1995), pp. 33–49.

10 Sylvia Martin, *Passionate Friends: Mary Fullerton, Mabel Singleton and Miles Franklin* (London: Onlywomen Press, 2001); Sylvia Martin, *Ida Leeson: A Life* (Sydney: Allen & Unwin, 2006); Sylvia Martin, '"These Walls of Flesh": The Problem of the Body in the Romantic Friendship/ Lesbianism Debate', *Historical Reflections/Réfléxions Historiques*, vol. 20, no. 2 (Summer 1994), pp. 243–265.

Introduction

> The lesbian is never with us, it seems, but always somewhere else: in the shadows, in the margins, hidden from history, out of sight, out of mind, a wanderer in the dusk, a lost soul, a tragic mistake, a pale denizen of the night. She is far away and she is dire. (She has seldom seemed as accessible, for instance, as her ingratiating twin brother, the male homosexual.)[11]

Castle's primary aim in her own work is to 'bring the lesbian back into focus', and this has been the implicit or explicit goal of much lesbian historiography in recent decades. Influenced by the gay liberation rhetoric of visibility, historians of sexuality have tended to focus on and value those forms of same-sex desire which can be seen or heard. Less scholarly attention, however, has been devoted to analysing the meanings and nature of the silence surrounding lesbianism.

Anna Clark considers the operational mechanisms of silence in her recent work on 'twilight moments'. Clark suggests that the concept of 'twilight' might be employed by historians of sexuality 'as a metaphor for those sexual practices and desires that societies prohibit by law or custom but that people pursue anyhow, whether in secret or as an open secret.'[12] In relation to nineteenth-century lesbian history, she argues:

> In contrast to male homosexuality, which was frequently subject to hostile stereotypes, legal sanctions, and medical discourses, allusions to lesbianism were vague and often confused, although not uncritical. As Vicinus writes of desire between women, 'recognition and denial went hand in hand.' The Victorians' inability to define or articulate lesbianism did not prevent their regarding it through this twilight haze as shameful desires.[13]

Silence in this context, then, articulated a need for secrecy and a sense of shame surrounding same-sex desire between women. As Isabel Hull has argued in her work on late eighteenth- and early nineteenth-century German sexuality, 'one should be wary of confusing silence with tolerance'.[14]

---

11   Terry Castle, *The Apparitional Lesbian: Female Homosexuality and Modern Culture* (New York: Columbia University Press, 1993), p. 2.
12   Anna Clark, 'Twilight Moments', *Journal of the History of Sexuality*, vol. 14, nos. 1/2 (January/April 2005), p. 140.
13   Clark, 'Twilight Moments', p. 156.
14   Isabel Hull, *Sexuality, State, and Civil Society in Germany, 1700–1815* (Ithaca, New York: Cornell University Press, 1996), p. 48.

Clark notes that while Michel Foucault influentially demonstrated the mechanisms by which discourse shaped sexual identities in the past, he failed to fully consider the operations of silence:

> The twilight metaphor can help refine our understanding of sexual discourses. Foucault rightly revealed how the nineteenth-century proliferation of legal, medical, psychiatric, and sexological discourses shaped sexual identities. But his stress on the power of discourse overshadowed another dynamic of sexual language – the power of silence and secrecy. To be sure, he acknowledged that some words could not be spoken, but he did not fully explore the power relations of sexual discourse: who had the authority to deploy sexual discourses.[15]

Graham Willett also draws attention to the difficulties of analysing the sexual repression apparent in 1950s' Australia through a Foucauldian lens. Referring to the work of Ruth Ford and Garry Wotherspoon on this decade, Willett claims:

> Both Ford and Wotherspoon rely explicitly upon the Foucauldian notion that, as Ford puts it, 'discourse and mechanisms of repression are prohibitive and generative at once, as repression produces the object it aims to deny.' In this chapter, I wish to argue, on the contrary, that, far from witnessing the emergence of a new, public, homosexual subject, the 1950s saw, instead, a period of repression and silencing and that this actually prevented the emergence of a public homosexuality until well into the 1960s.[16]

Willett rightly notes that, in certain circumstances, repression does not inevitably produce the prohibited subject. For the generative mechanism to operate, the subject must be produced through a prohibitive discourse, but if that prohibition is articulated through silence, a new discursive subject cannot be formed. In order to make sense of this process, therefore, we must consider silence as a disciplinary mechanism in itself.

Silence is a central concern of this book. I am interested both in defining and giving shape to silence in a specific historic period and location, and in exploring the impact of silence on individual women's lives. I will ask:

---

15 Clark, 'Twilight Moments', p. 151.
16 Graham Willett, 'The Darkest Decade: Homophobia in 1950s' Australia', in John Murphy and Judith Smart, eds, *The Forgotten Fifties: Aspects of Australian Society in the 1950s* (Melbourne: Melbourne University Press, 1997 [a special issue of *Australian Historical Studies*, vol. 28, no. 109]), p. 121.

what was the extent of the silence surrounding female same-sex desire in mid-twentieth century New South Wales? How did silence function as a disciplinary mechanism to articulate the unacceptable nature of female same-sex desire, and how were attitudes toward and understandings of lesbianism shaped in the context of silence? But also, crucially, how did women negotiate that silence to construct meaningful, productive and – in some cases – emotionally fulfilled lives?

The silence surrounding female same-sex desire had a very distinct quality in mid-twentieth century NSW. While British and US lesbian historians have noted the taboos surrounding discussion of female same-sex desire in their respective countries, a rich literature in both national contexts attests to the occasional outbursts of debate which framed the subject – for example during the obscenity trials surrounding the publication of Radclyffe Hall's lesbian novel *The Well of Loneliness* in 1928, or the McCarthyite witch-hunts in the United States in the late 1940s and 1950s.[17] However, stricter censorship laws, press conventions and the pervasive cultural influence of the Catholic Church (amongst other factors) created a very different climate in Australia, in which no such scandals reached the public ear. In 1969, academic and literary critic RF Brissenden noted that until recently there had been a tacit agreement amongst the press not to mention homosexuality, and this assertion is supported by press surveys which demonstrate the almost complete silence of the Australian press on the subject of female homosexuality.[18] To a certain extent, this reflects a common experience of male and female homosexuals in Australia. However, the different legislative frameworks which governed male and female homosexuality – explicitly penalising sexual acts between men while policing desire between women in subtler ways – created different contexts for the discussion of lesbianism and male homosexuality. Graham Willett has argued that, in the case of lesbians in the 1950s, 'the silencing regime was, if anything, even more rigorous and around which there seems to have been very little popular "common sense" discourse'.[19] This silence has been interpreted by contemporaries, and to

---

17 There is an extensive literature on both these debates. See, for example, Laura Doan, *Fashioning Sapphism* (New York: Columbia University Press, 2001); Lillian Faderman, *Odd Girls and Twilight Lovers: A History of Lesbian Life in Twentieth-Century America* (New York: Penguin, 1991).

18 R F Brissenden, 'Censorship in Australia', in Ian Edwards, ed., *A Humanist View* (Sydney: Angus & Robertson, 1969), p. 125; Robert French, *Gays Between the Broadsheets: An Annotated List of Australian Media References on Homosexuality, 1948–1980* (Darlinghurst, New South Wales: Gay History Project, Sydney, 1986).

19 Willett, 'The Darkest Decade', p. 124.

some extent by historians, as evidence of greater tolerance toward female homosexuality. Reflecting on the lack of research into female homosexuality in Australia, a contributor to *The Medical Journal of Australia* argued in 1969:

> This fact may be related to the lesser social stigma attached to sexual attraction between females, plus the lack of restrictive legislation on lesbian behaviour, a fact which renders the field of operation of the sensationalist, blackmailer and busybody a barren one.[20]

This contributor expressed a widely held misconception that in the absence of legal penalties lesbians were free to express their desires openly without fear of repercussions. However, the mechanism of silence policed lesbianism in different ways, preventing the formation of lesbian subcultures and identities and forcing women, through lack of choice, into acceptable patterns of femininity such as conventional marriage and motherhood.

Methodologies

The silence surrounding female same-sex desire in mid-twentieth century New South Wales also poses methodological obstacles for the historian. The paucity of sources pertaining to desire between women has become a truism in lesbian history and the absence of a public discourse around lesbianism in NSW between the 1930s and late 1960s renders archival research particularly frustrating. In recent decades, however, the silencing of lesbian and gay experience in the past has been challenged by the practice of recording personal testimonies. Oral histories have provided historians of sexuality with invaluable insights into the experience and subjectivity of women who desired other women in the past, and have been utilised in Australia by Ruth Ford and Lucy Chesser in their respective research into women in the armed services and lesbian identity in 1960s Melbourne.[21] This book draws on the interviews they, and others, have recorded. However, no such interviews had been conducted with lesbians residing in NSW. Therefore, a series of new oral history interviews were conducted by the author with self-identified lesbians in NSW for this book. Interviewees were recruited

---

20 'A Study of Lesbianism', *The Medical Journal of Australia*, 24 May 1969, p. 1095.
21 Ruth Ford, 'Disciplined, Punished and Resisting Bodies: Lesbian Women and the Australian Armed Services, 1950s–60s', *Lilith: A Feminist History Journal*, no. 9 (1996), pp. 53–77; Ruth Ford, 'Lesbians and Loose Women: Female Sexuality and the Women's Services During World War II', in Joy Damousi and Marilyn Lake, eds, *Gender and War: Australians at War in the Twentieth Century* (Melbourne: Cambridge University Press, 1995), pp. 81–104.

through advertisements in the lesbian and mainstream press across NSW, by contacting lesbian social and activist organisations and through word-of-mouth. Although efforts were made to avoid assuming a monolithic lesbian identity category in participants, nevertheless all those women who agreed to participate currently identified as lesbians, and it was difficult to reach those women who may have engaged in same-sex relationships at one or more stages in their lives but did not currently identify as 'lesbian'. Similarly, although recruitment efforts were made across NSW, all participants resided in Sydney at the time of the interview. Some narrators had previously relocated from country or small-town NSW, so their interviews provided some insight into non-urban lesbian experiences, but the project is nevertheless Sydney-centric in focus and in particular does not fully explore the experiences of those same-sex attracted women who chose to remain in or moved to country NSW in this period. Further research is needed to trace this history.

Both the process of recruitment and the narrative which was constructed in each interview were also inevitably shaped by my own identity as a white British middle-class lesbian historian, employed by a Sydney university. A sense of shared gender and sexual identity undoubtedly facilitated the recruitment of narrators, many of whom stated that they would not have agreed to participate if the interviewer had not been a lesbian. However, my identity as a British woman who had only recently migrated to Australia impacted more significantly on the interviews, prompting narrators to reflect on previously taken-for-granted aspects of Australian culture, draw out narratives of migration and make transnational comparisons in their interviews. While this enriched many of the interviews, my racial identity as white British was surely a factor in the failure of the project to attract narrators of non-European ethnic origin. Ultimately, 22 interviews were conducted with women from working- and middle-class backgrounds, ranging in age from their 40s to their 90s. All the women interviewed were of British or European descent, with the result that it has not been possible to theorise the ways in which sexual and racial identities intersected in shaping women's experience.[22] The oldest narrator was born in Wellington, New Zealand in 1914 and the youngest in Sydney in 1960. Unfortunately, however, identifying potential narrators who reached adulthood between the 1930s and 1950s proved difficult and the majority of narrators were born in the 1950s. While we have a rich and detailed picture of lesbian life in NSW in the 1960s and 1970s, therefore, sources for the earlier

---

22 Despite attempts to recruit a diversity of women by advertising in a range of different media, respondents were all of European descent.

decades are relatively scarce. To a certain extent this reflects the continued impact of a culture of silence in discouraging women who became aware of their own same-sex desires in the 1930s, '40s and '50s from openly discussing them. It is also, however, a factor of old age and infirmity and acts as a reminder of the urgent need to collect the memories of older generations of lesbians before our history is lost. The interviews each tell powerful and emotional stories of individual women's struggles to make sense of their own same-sex desires in a hostile cultural climate. Some offer bleak accounts of decades of loneliness and self-doubt, battles with depression and suicide, and the pain of losing lovers or being unable to find them. They speak of a sense of loss at what might have been, and of anger at the need for a daily struggle for survival. Many, however, also describe the joy of being in love, the strength and support they drew from tight-knit networks of lesbian and gay friends, maintained for a lifetime, and the pride they felt in building successful careers or participating in political activism. This book is shaped by their stories.

The telling of stories has been at the heart of the lesbian and gay history project since its origins in the 1970s and, indeed, Ken Plummer has argued that the proliferation of sexual stories has been a defining characteristic of late modernity. 'Sexual stories', he argues, are:

> [P]robably as old as human time. But in this late modern world – at century's end, at the *fin-de-siecle*, at the turn of the millennium – they seem to have gained an unusual power and prominence. It is curious, perhaps, that they should have become so celebrated. When I grew up as a child in the late 1940s and 1950s such stories resonated a deafening silence. But now the time has certainly come for personal sexual stories to be told.[23]

The telling of personal stories was crucial to the development of a politics of women's and gay liberation in the 1970s, when women told each other of their personal experiences in consciousness-raising groups, and 'came out' as lesbians to family, friends and society. Individual stories exploring what it meant to be a woman or a lesbian were shared in activist journals and in anthologies, helping to build a sense of community encompassing both contributors and readers. Building on these practices, historians of lesbian, gay and queer history found, in common with historians of other minority groups, that oral history offered an invaluable route into the lives of sexual

---

23 Ken Plummer, *Telling Sexual Stories: Power, Change and Social Worlds* (London: Routledge, 1995), p. 6.

Introduction

minorities in the past, people whose experiences were often not a matter of public record. Oral history was initially regarded with some suspicion in the academy, being considered a dubious source for social scientific research. In the ensuing decades a wealth of literature has explored the methodological challenges of oral history. In response to the critique of oral sources as lacking objective truth, some oral historians have advocated the use of triangulation to test oral evidence against other, printed sources. Others such as Elizabeth Kennedy and Madeline Davis noted (for example in their ethnographic study of the lesbian community in Buffalo, New York in the mid-twentieth century) that frequently no printed sources existed to corroborate oral evidence. They argued that narrators' accounts could be trusted if they belonged to a cohort of between five and ten other interviews verifying a similar version of events.[24]

The more recent cultural turn in history has produced a broader questioning of the search for objective truth, suggesting that historians might more productively explore the cultural meanings ascribed to experiences and identities in the past. Reflecting this development, oral historians such as Alessandro Portelli and Graham Dawson have suggested that personal narratives are valuable to historians by virtue of their very subjectivity. Portelli argues that 'misremembering' or factual inaccuracies can be an important indicator of cultural meaning in oral history interviews. In his analysis of the death of Luigi Trastulli, a steel worker from Terni, Portelli noted: 'The oral sources used in this essay are not always fully reliable in point of fact. Rather than being a weakness, this is however, their strength: errors, inventions and myths lead us through and beyond facts to their meanings.'[25] Graham Dawson has considered the relationship between personal narratives and wider culture in his concept of 'composure', suggesting that the attempt to achieve composure – both in terms of 'composing' the narrative and of finding a 'sense of composure' by constituting oneself as the subject of one's own account – is at the heart of a narrator's attempt to construct a personal narrative. For narrators, the composition of an account that draws on existing cultural models, and hence fits established notions of identity and behaviour, is essential in achieving composure.[26] Historians of sexuality have noted a similar process at work in the construction of sexual stories, with lesbian

---

24　Elizabeth Lapovsky Kennedy and Madeline D Davis, *Boots of Leather, Slippers of Gold: The History of a Lesbian Community* (New York: Routledge, 1993), p. 23.
25　Alessandro Portelli, *The Death of Luigi Trastulli and other stories: Form and Meaning in Oral History* (New York: State University of New York Press, 1991), p. 2.
26　Graham Dawson, *Soldier Heroes: British Adventure, Empire and the Imagining of Masculinities* (London: Routledge, 1994).

and gay narrators typically structuring their narratives around an account of 'coming out' and claiming a sexual identity. As Nan Alamilla Boyd has argued, while the claiming of a subject position as a lesbian is typically the basis from which a narrator claims the authority to speak, this insistence on framing a stable sexual identity is problematic for the lesbian, gay or queer historian. 'It is difficult to escape the trap of subjectivity', she claims, 'because it is through coherent and intelligible subject positions that we learn to speak, even nonverbally, about desire.'[27] Further, this discourse of identity limits the types of history we can tell. The prioritising of explicit identity categories such as lesbian or gay in the post-Stonewall era impacts on the questions raised in oral history interviews and the ways in which narrators structure their stories. As a result, some of the complexities of sexual desire and practice can be lost in narratives structured by questions of identity, while the stories of those individuals who elude categorisation can be silenced altogether.

However, as Penny Summerfield has demonstrated, collective cultural models are not discrete: narrators frequently move between different identity models at different stages in their account and, at others, fail to achieve 'composure' at all.[28] Thus, in lesbian life-history interviews, when contemporary interpretations of an event did not allow for the articulation of a lesbian identity or when individual women did not possess a coherent understanding of their own sexuality as 'lesbian' at a given point in their past, narrators were unable to produce a coherent lesbian narrative and suffered discomposure. These moments of 'discomposure' were expressed in a variety of ways: through emotion, contradiction and silence. These moments of slippage or dislocation in a narrative can be of particular value to the oral historian, providing a sense of individual women's subjective interpretation of their own sexual and gender identity and demonstrating the disjunctures between desires or expectations and lived experience.

Questions of identity

The thorny question of identity has been debated continuously by historians of sexuality since the 1970s. While the activism that inspired much of the early interest in lesbian and gay history in the 1970s and '80s was predicated on essentialist understandings of lesbian and gay identity as fixed and inborn,

---

27 Nan Alamilla Boyd, 'Who Is the Subject? Queer Theory Meets Oral History', *Journal of the History of Sexuality*, vol. 17, no. 2 (May 2008), p. 189.
28 Penny Summerfield, *Reconstructing Women's Wartime Lives: Discourse and Subjectivity in Oral Histories of the Second World War* (Manchester: Manchester University Press, 1998).

INTRODUCTION

sociologists and historians began to explore the ways in which individuals' sexual identities were constructed by wider cultural discourses. In the preface to his historical survey, *Sex, Politics and Society*, first published in 1981, British sociologist Jeffrey Weeks argued that his book's 'working premise ... is that "sexuality" is not an unproblematic natural given, which the "social" works upon to control, but is, on the contrary, an *historical* unity which has been shaped and determined by a multiplicity of forces, and which has undergone complex historical transformations.'[29] As influential theorists such as Michel Foucault argued, sexual identities, as cultural constructs, were shaped differently in different historical periods and locations, and the notion that an individual's sexual identity is a defining aspect of their being is a fundamentally modern concept.[30] Reflecting on her seminal work of lesbian history, *Boots of Leather, Slippers of Gold*, published in 1993, Elizabeth Kennedy noted:

> Our research was informed by the powerful intellectual framework, initiated in part by John D'Emilio's *Sexual Politics, Sexual Communities: the Making of a Homosexual Minority in the United States, 1940–1970*, that assumed that while homosexual acts have existed throughout history, homosexual identities as the core of a person's subjectivity and as the basis for a consciousness of kind and pride are a modern phenomenon. This framework, which conceptualised gay/lesbian history as documenting and analyzing the development of gay/lesbian identities and their connection to the growth of gay/lesbian politics, dominated the first 20 years of lesbian/gay history.[31]

In recent decades, queer theorists have problematised notions of identity further, emphasising the fluidity of identity categories and the ways in which historical subjects have deployed shifting, multiple and sometimes contradictory identities. Challenging Foucault's notion of a historical succession of coherent sexual identity models, Eve Kosofsky Sedgwick argued that widely held beliefs about gay identity are fundamentally incoherent and contradictory.[32] Judith Butler has developed this critique further in her work, arguing that an individual is assigned a social identity by cultural discourse and 'performs' that identity. For Butler, the impossibility of any

---

29 Jeffrey Weeks, *Sex, Politics and Society: The Regulations of Sexuality Since 1800* (London: Routledge, 2014), p. x.
30 Michel Foucault, *The History of Sexuality, Volume 1: An Introduction*, trans. R Hurley (New York: Vintage, 1978).
31 Elizabeth Lapovsky Kennedy and Madeline D Davis, *Boots of Leather, Slippers of Gold: The History of a Lesbian Community* (New York: Routledge, 2014), pp. xiii–xiv.
32 Eve Kosofsky Sedgwick, *Epistemology of the Closet* (New York: NAL Books, 1989).

individual ever fully inhabiting their assigned identity rendered identity categories intrinsically unstable and opened up the possibility of individuals performing a variety of identities simultaneously.[33]

These insights draw our attention to the fact that a focus on lesbian and gay identities in the past has tended to obscure the experience of those whose sexual identities were more fluid or who resisted categorisation as 'lesbian' or 'gay'. In his work on same-sex desire between men in the American South, John Howard adopts a queer approach in an attempt to move beyond questions of sexual identity and explore the experiences and desires of men who did not build an identity around their same-sex sexual activities. In unstructured interviews with 'men like that', Howard sought from his narrators secondhand stories of 'men who liked that' but whose experiences had been silenced from the historical record by a privileging of gay identity.[34] Drawing on Howard's approach, I have similarly attempted to read the silences of the interviews to uncover the stories of those women whose experience is lost in an emphasis on visible lesbian identity. This book's reliance upon interviews with women who self-identified as lesbians in the early 2000s has inevitably resulted in a prioritisation of certain experiences and narratives of identity formation and community-building. However, many other women in this period acted on desires for other women and formed intimate same-sex relationships without explicitly identifying as lesbian, either at the time or subsequently. Their stories are often elusive, but glimpses of them can be traced through the interviews of women they related to, such as in Margaret's account of her 'seduction' of, and two-year-long relationship with fellow secretary, Jann, and Sandra Willson's description of her affair with Barbara. Both Jann and Barbara had apparently no previous experience of same-sex encounters, and subsequently went on to form heterosexual marriages, but Margaret and Sandra's accounts paint both of these women as desiring sexual agents and committed participants in their respective same-sex relationships.

The need to be alert to the experiences of women such as Jann and Barbara, and to recognise the fluidity and historical specificity of sexual identities, raises issues around the language of same-sex desire. Women who desired other women in mid-twentieth century Australia deployed a variety of words to name themselves, while other terms were used by others to describe them. Prior to the 1970s, the sexological term, 'homosexual' was used by medical

---

33   Judith Butler, *Bodies That Matter: On the Discursive Limits of 'Sex'* (London: Routledge, 1993).
34   John Howard, *Men Like That: A Southern Queer History* (Chicago: The University of Chicago Press, 1999).

and legal professionals and by some women themselves. In the mixed-gender communities which emerged around bars and coffee shops in the 1950s and 1960s, the word 'camp' was used by both men and women, alongside (although with less frequency) more specific terms such as 'butch' or 'dyke'. 'Lesbian' emerged as the most popular term amongst the feminist and activist women of the 1970s, while 'dyke' was redeployed by some lesbian feminists in the 1970s as a term indicating the radical and transgressive potential of female same-sex desire. For many women, however, particularly in the decades prior to the 1970s, the culture of silence surrounding same-sex desire resulted in an absence of any language with which to describe their feelings. Some narrators struggled to name themselves or their relationships, while others described the process of laying claim to a language of sexual subjectivity as a painful and protracted experience. This book attempts to reflect the fluidity of language around same-sex desire, wherever possible using the terms used by women in the given historical context. Where no such term seems appropriate, I have used either the descriptive phrase 'same-sex desire between women' to indicate desires and practices which went unnamed, or 'lesbian' as the generic term most frequently adopted by women at the time of interview.

Organisational structure

Chapter 1 considers the function of silence as a disciplinary mechanism which constructed same-sex desire between women as taboo. Analysing legal, medical and religious discourses of female homosexuality alongside personal narratives, this chapter suggests that a sense of lesbianism as unacceptable was conveyed primarily through the silence of these mainstream discourses on female same-sex desire rather than through their prohibition. In the absence of explicit condemnation, individual women developed an awareness that there was 'something wrong with them' due to their failure to conform to conventional models of feminine heterosexuality, rather than their attraction to other women. Chapter 2 examines the ways in which women who had recognised their same-sex desires began to build lives for themselves in the context of a culture of silence. For many, the threat of exposure to family and friends carried with it a risk of rejection, loss of employment and even a fear of legal penalties. Such women lived double lives, constructing alternative, socially acceptable identities and accounts of themselves for the benefit of those around them, which enabled them to conceal their desires for, or relationships with, other women. Cultural media depicting female same-sex desire offered some alleviation of the sense of isolation produced by the practice of secrecy, but such representations were limited and often reinforced a notion of lesbians as socially marginal. In the 1950s and 1960s, some women were able to participate in overseas lesbian networks without risking exposure at home by reading and contributing to US and British lesbian magazines.

Chapters 1 and 2 focus on the ways in which individual women made sense of their same-sex desires and attempted to negotiate the culture of silence and secrecy. The remaining chapters consider women's collective experiences, from the forging of social networks to the emergence of a common political identity. Chapter 3 focuses on lesbian bars and social spaces. Sydney's lesbian scene changed significantly between the 1930s and the 1970s, from mixed private social networks to a more gender-segregated public scene. For many lesbians in the early part of this period, private friendship networks defined patterns of socialising, and this impacted on the development of lesbian identity, limiting the scope for the emergence of distinctive lesbian subcultures and styles. Larger numbers of women joined camp men on the commercial scene in the 1960s but the increasing influence of feminism in the 1970s prompted the development of new women-only spaces and encouraged increasing gender segregation on the commercial scene.

Chapter 4 analyses the development of lesbian politics in New South Wales in the 1970s. The development and impact of a lesbian and gay political movement in Australia in the 1970s has been widely discussed by historians, but a focus on the organisation of particular groups, or on gay male experience, has resulted in a lack of attention to its impact on lesbian culture and identity. This chapter argues that lesbian politics in Sydney in the 1970s was heavily gendered and that feminist groups and ideas had a much more pervasive impact both on notions of lesbian sexuality and identity and on lesbian cultural practices than the lesbian and gay political movement did. Chapter 5 traces the shifting ways in which individual women and couples imagined and experienced same-sex relationships over the course of the mid-century. This final chapter explores what women looked for in a relationship with another woman and the roles they adopted both in domestic organisation and sexual practice. Between the 1930s and the 1960s, lesbian relationship models tended to mirror earlier turn-of-the-century patterns of passionate friendship or reflect notions of intimacy circulating in wider society. However, the emergence of a new lesbian feminist ideology in the 1970s profoundly reshaped notions of lesbian sexuality and the potential of female intimacy as an engine of social change; the impact of these ideas on individual women's experiences in this decade is examined.

Chapter 1

CONSTRUCTING THE LESBIAN AS 'UNACCEPTABLE'

In the late 1930s, Beverley, a young New Zealand woman, embarked on a visit to her cousins in Sydney, which was to transform her life. At the time, Beverley was in her early 20s and was working as a secretary for General Motors. Despite having received an offer of marriage from her sister-in-law's brother, she remained single and lived at home with her family. Her life followed the conventional patterns of respectable lower middle-class life before the war: she visited an Anglican church with her parents on a Sunday and went to local dances with boys in her leisure time. However, something in this life did not feel quite right to Beverley and when she started talking to one of her cousins' housemates in Sydney, her doubts began to crystallise:

> I knew there was something wrong with me, but I didn't know what it was … Well I didn't know, I just, I don't know, I've no idea. I used to go out with boys, dancing, but I would never let them make any sexual advances towards me. And I used to wonder: 'Why do I prefer going out with girls?' I can't remember, well of course I knew when I came over here on holidays to stay with my cousins and this woman said to me, 'Do you know you're a homosexual?' I said 'I don't know what you're talking about' … She stood in front of me in her flat, put her hands on my shoulders and … she explained things. And I knew then, well I'd never heard of homosexuality, never! Didn't know what it was.[1]

---

1   Interview with Beverley, 22 December 2008.

Beverley's recollection that she 'knew there was something wrong with me, but I didn't know what it was' was typical of many women who experienced same-sex desire in this period. Aware that her feelings did not quite match the conventional narrative – that she was more emotionally drawn to her own sex than perhaps she should have been, and less interested in the opposite sex than expected – Beverley was nevertheless unable to make sense of this difference. Lacking knowledge of the concept of same-sex desire, Beverley was made aware of her difference by the absence of 'proper' feelings for men, rather than the presence of 'improper' feelings for women.

This narrative of confusion and lack of knowledge is echoed in the experience of Lee, 30 years later. Growing up in the 1950s and '60s on a farm in country New South Wales and attending a nearby girls' boarding school, Lee experienced a number of intense emotional attachments to her own sex:

> [There were probably] two who really spring to mind in terms of adults that I had a crush on, without realising because you know, I had no idea what a dyke was, I mean I'd never, I'd never been confronted with the phenomenon. And to me, heterosexuality was the only thing that there was.[2]

By the age of 16, Lee had encountered the word 'homosexuality', which she looked up in a dictionary, but applied it only to men. Her understanding of the concept was extremely negative and she 'thought that homosexuality was filthy, depraved, absolutely you know, bad, bad'. Her attitude was confirmed when she developed a passionate devotion to a 20-year-old woman she met at her summer job, who had recently separated from her homosexual husband. She recalled:

> Oh, I fell head over heels in love with Evelyn! Oh! I just, I thought she was wonderful! Again, no idea about lesbianism, not, no idea at all, but at this stage I knew that homosexuality existed, but homosexuality to me was men, right, didn't, didn't touch women, it was just filthy, dirty men.[3]

A couple of years later, Lee became aware of the possibility of female homosexuality for the first time when a young boy called her a 'lezzo' as a term of abuse. She recalled:

---

2   Interview with G J Lee, 31 July 2008.
3   ibid.

> And I had no idea what the word was, I'd never heard the word in my life before, but the way he said it, I knew it was a really derogatory statement. So that was my first ever contact with the word 'lesbian' and he was calling me a lesbian. And when I found out what a lesbian was, I was horrified! How could he think that of me? That wasn't me at all, I wasn't a lesbian.[4]

It was not until she was at university in the early 1970s that Lee connected her own feelings with the broader concept of homosexuality:

> All my adolescent years I knew I was different and I thought of it as something being wrong with me. I mean the matron saw that there was something wrong with me: 'You shouldn't talk to the juniors!' You know, this sort of something wrong with me, something didn't quite fit and I realised that I was a dyke. I just, I knew it! I absolutely knew it. And I didn't think back to being in love with you know, students or teachers, it just, it was an absolute: 'That's it, I am a dyke, I am a lesbian' … And it was with total horror, because to me, lesbianism was like homosexuality, it was filthy, it was perverted, I was unclean. I shouldn't even be alive. You know, it was the most horrendous thing to realise. I was devastated.[5]

These accounts reflect the experience of many women in the mid-twentieth century, who struggled to make sense of same-sex desire in the context of a complete cultural taboo around the subject of lesbianism. Separated by 30 years, both Beverley and Lee experienced passionate feelings for other women without possessing any awareness of a broader cultural context of homosexuality. Their vague sense of unease was articulated simply as a perception that 'something was wrong'. This chapter will explore the ways in which this implicit social judgement of lesbianism as unacceptable was conveyed to individual women in mid-twentieth century Australia. Historians have frequently identified legal, medical and religious discourses as the three pillars of homophobia in this period. Graham Willett, for example, argued: 'The notions of homosexuality as crime, sin or bio-medical disorder were the dominant ways in which the problem was discussed'.[6] However, Willett's research, like much of the

---
4   ibid.
5   ibid.
6   Graham Willett, 'From Vice to Homosexuality: Policing Perversion in the 1950s', in Shirleene Robinson, ed., *Homophobia: An Australian History* (Sydney: The Federation Press, 2008), p. 114.

literature in the field, focuses on male homosexuality, and this chapter will re-examine these three cultural discourses in light of the deeper cultural silence which surrounded female same-sex desire. Notions of the lesbian as unacceptable in this period were shaped through a complex interplay of condemnation of male homosexuality, silence around female same-sex desire and the promotion of a narrow definition of normative female sexuality, centred on marriage and motherhood. While social condemnation of male homosexuality was explicitly defined through its construction as criminal, sick or immoral in legal, medical and religious discourses, the unacceptability of lesbianism was conveyed primarily by its absence from these and other discourses.

Legal attitudes toward lesbianism

Cultural attitudes toward homosexuality in mid-twentieth century Australia were shaped in part by the strong legal stance on the issue. Male homosexual activity was legally proscribed under the Crimes (Amendment) Act 1924, but lesbianism was never explicitly criminalised in New South Wales. Official concern over female same-sex desire appears to have been extremely limited and there is no evidence that the question of legislating against lesbianism was even debated in government circles. Some cultural commentators were critical of this apparent oversight. Dr McGeorge, member of a special committee appointed by the NSW government in 1955 to examine problems associated with homosexuality, complained: 'No investigation into the lesbianism aspect of it has been suggested. It should have been. The investigation is overdue.'[7] Claiming that 'ordinarily normal and healthy' young girls were being seduced into the practice by subtle, older lesbians, McGeorge argued: 'The authorities, unfortunately, seem to regard this as too delicate a question to be tackled openly. Because of its increase, it must be brought into the open and fought in the open.'[8] For McGeorge, lesbianism was a social evil which posed a threat to young women and needed to be both publicly debated and legally proscribed.[9] However, his

---

7   Vince Kelly, *Rugged Angel: The Amazing Career of Policewoman Lillian Armfield* (Glebe: Fast Books, 1995 [originally published by Angus & Robertson, 1961]), p. 83.
8   ibid., pp. 83, 82.
9   Similar views were expressed by John Catarinch in 'Medical Aspects of Responsibility in Homo-Sexuals', *Australian Journal of Psychological Research* 1.1 (October 1959), p. 32, cited in Naomi Cranenburgh, 'From Invisibile to "Menace": Lesbians in Australia from 1939 to 1965' (Honours thesis, Monash University, October 2010), pp. 45–46.

views did not find support amongst legislators and the special committee of which he was a member was never to publish a report.[10]

While the political will to tackle the issue at government level was limited, concern was apparently greater in the police force. In her autobiography, NSW's first woman police officer, Lillian Armfield, suggests that female homosexuality was a matter of concern to the police. Referring to the case of Iris Webber, a notorious criminal and lesbian in interwar Sydney, Armfield commented:

> [Lesbianism] is a problem the authorities must face, and it is a difficult one. It will require the co-operation of the wisest and best of our medical specialists, police, clergy, and welfare workers, because it is on the increase. Those who practise it aren't all as open about it as Iris Webber. They are furtive and subtle, and the leaders in the cult are shrewd and persistent in their eagerness to corrupt others ... Sooner or later, and the sooner the better, this menace will have to be faced by the authorities. It is a menace too serious to be ignored just because it is such an ugly and unpleasant issue to drag out into the open.[11]

Members of the Vice Squad apparently shared Armfield's view that lesbianism was a 'cult which, unfortunately, has a much wider vogue than the average citizen suspects.'[12] Such attitudes helped to shape the stance of the police toward lesbianism, and despite the absence of any specific legislation prohibiting sexual acts between women, the police utilised a range of minor, broadly defined offences to target lesbians, thereby rendering certain forms of lesbian practice or identity illegal.[13]

The strongly disapproving attitudes of some members of the police force, combined with the absence of a public discourse on lesbianism and the enforcement of laws against male homosexuality, produced considerable

---

10 These views reflect those of English legislators who rejected a proposal to legislate against female same-sex sexual practices in 1928. See Laura Doan, *Fashioning Sapphism* (New York: Columbia University Press, 2001).
11 Kelly, *Rugged Angel*, pp. 79–80.
12 ibid., p. 80.
13 For discussion of other forms of legal discrimination against lesbians, see Ruth Ford, 'Lady-Friends and Deviationists: Lesbians and the Law in Australia 1920s–1950s', in Diane Kirkby, ed., *Sex, Power and Justice: Historical Perspectives on the Law in Australia, 1788–1990* (Melbourne: Oxford University Press, 1995), pp. 33-49; Ruth Ford, '"Filthy, Obscene and Mad": Engendering "Homophobia" in Australia, 1940s–1960s', in Shirleene Robinson, ed., *Homophobia: An Australian history* (Sydney: Federation Press, 2008), pp. 86–112; and Cranenburgh, 'From Invisible to "Menace"', pp. 48–53, 59.

confusion about the precise state of the law relating to lesbianism. Margaret, who became aware of her own same-sex desires in the late 1950s, recalled having a general sense that lesbianism was prohibited. Having met a young woman at work to whom she was attracted, she was apprehensive about approaching the woman for fear of the consequences:

> Well, I felt that this was a big responsibility for me, seducing this young woman and putting her on this path to disaster or that I'd get into trouble, surely, because it wasn't appropriate to do that – I don't know if it was a criminal offence, but I suppose if somebody found out about it, it'd be pretty serious.[14]

While Margaret was unsure of the exact consequences she might be faced with, the perception that lesbian sexual practice was, in fact, illegal, was relatively widespread before the 1970s and both the police and members of the public – including lesbians themselves – acted accordingly. When 15-year-old Sandra Willson attempted to put her arm around an older female friend in 1950s Sydney, the woman called the police and a female officer warned Sandra: 'You do realise that your behaviour constitutes a criminal offence?' She was told that if she contacted the woman again, she would be brought before the Children's Court.[15] A few years later, her sexual practices brought her into contact with the police again. Now 17 and living with her girlfriend in a small Bondi flat, Sandra wrote to a friend describing her new domestic circumstances. The letter fell into the hands of the friend's mother who, believing Sandra's lesbian relationship to be illegal, contacted the police. That Sunday, Sandra and her girlfriend Barbara were at home in bed when the police arrived at the door. Referring to Sandra's letter, an officer claimed: 'Now you can't try to deny you are a homosexual because the letter states quite plainly that you are. And that you are living with this other girl as "man and wife."'[16] The police searched the flat, apparently commenting on any evidence that the two girls were sharing a bedroom, and Sandra recalled:

> They acted like a law unto themselves and I hated their bastard hides for it. I wanted to rush them to attack them, but their size alone showed this would be folly. But I was also cowed by the feeling that they were right, and I felt such shame. I knew it was a criminal offence to make

---

14   Interview with Margaret Jones, 12 September 2007.
15   Sandra Willson, unpublished memoir, p. 15. I am grateful to the executors of the Willson estate for permission to read and quote from this memoir.
16   ibid., p. 44.

love to anyone of one's own sex. Men over the age of eighteen could actually go to jail for up to three years for it. Not a public performance, but for an act done behind their own bedroom doors, in their own home and lodgings.

It was a criminal act. Against the laws of God and man![17]

The police took Sandra and Barbara down to Central Police Station on Liverpool Street where they were charged with 'being exposed to moral danger'. Sandra, who, as the elder of the pair, was portrayed as the seducer, was sentenced to detention at the Girls Training School in Parramatta, while Barbara was released into the care of her parents.

Child welfare legislation was widely used in early and mid-twentieth century NSW to control socially unacceptable, but rarely criminal, behaviour by teenage girls. Kerry Carrington and Margaret Pereira have argued that 'The blurring of delinquency and neglect led to the expansion of juvenile justice intervention into the lives of young people which allowed the Children's Court the jurisdiction to punish children for non-criminal conduct.'[18] Girls were charged under the NSW Child Welfare Act 1939 as either 'neglected' or 'uncontrollable' and 'exposed to moral danger' for behaviours such as truancy, sexual activity or being the victims of sexual abuse. A broad range of agents, from the police to social workers, education professionals and psychologists, advised on and intervened in cases, basing their determinations as much on family and social background and current medical and psychiatric theory as on the specific details of the relevant offence or charge. Girls could be sentenced to an indeterminate period in a child welfare institution such as Parramatta Girls Training School, sometimes only ending when they turned 18, although girls charged with a criminal offence would usually only remain for between six and nine months. There was no formal system for distinguishing between girls convicted of a criminal offence and others, although a broad attempt was made to keep girls deemed 'corrupt' apart from the rest. Conditions in the home were tough and perceived misdemeanours were punished with solitary confinement or harsh and humiliating tasks such as the scrubbing of floors.[19]

---

17   ibid., p. 44.
18   Kerry Carrington and Margaret Pereira, *Offending Youth: Sex, Crime and Justice* (Sydney: The Federation Press, 2009), p. 28.
19   See Carrington and Pereira, *Offending Youth*; Bonney Djuric, *Abandon All Hope: A History of Parramatta Girls Industrial School* (Perth: Chargan My Book Publisher Pty Ltd, 2011); and http://www.parragirls.org.au/ (accessed 1 February 2012).

For adult women, a range of other laws relating to vagrancy and public decency were utilised by the police to express disapproval of lesbianism, in the absence of specific legislation against female same-sex activity. In the decades after the war, dress codes were employed to contain the activities of butch lesbians in the public sphere, although confusion was again widespread as to the precise state of the law in this regard. Sandra Willson, who regularly dressed in men's clothes on the street in 1950s' Sydney and occasionally wore men's suits to work, made enquiries into the legality of this practice. She was informed by her parole officer that wearing men's clothes was not in itself illegal, but masquerading as a man was: 'There is nothing illegal about it', she was told, 'as long as you make no attempt to portray yourself as a male. You can't, for instance, use a men's urinal but will always have to use the women's convenience.'[20] Laurie, however, recalling her experiences as a butch lesbian in Sydney in the 1960s and 1970s, maintained that laws did regulate women's dress. 'Some law', she said, required that, 'With the butches, in those days, you had to wear, if you dressed butch – three piece suits and that – you had to wear a bit of women's apparel, didn't matter what.'[21] Rae agreed, claiming: 'Back then the laws were quite strange. God help you if you didn't wear a bra, for example, because, if you were picked up by the police, you had to be wearing three pieces of women's apparel. Now I don't wear a bra, if I'd been picked up, I'd have been really in trouble. No, you had to have three pieces of women's apparel on.'[22] Vagrancy laws, which prohibited indecent and disorderly behaviour, had been used in NSW and elsewhere in Australia to target cross-dressing since the nineteenth century, although research has demonstrated that the penalties faced by those who came to the notice of the police could vary widely.[23] However, it is unclear whether any law specifically defined male impersonation in terms of items of apparel and it is interesting that the apparently widespread belief in such legislation is also reflected in US butch lesbian communities of the postwar period. In their study of a lesbian community in Buffalo, New York, in the mid-twentieth century, Elizabeth Kennedy and Madeline Davis note that 'Many narrators mention the legal specification for proper dress, although some said it

---

20   Willson, unpublished memoir, p. 29.
21   Interview with Laurie van Camp by Sandra Mackay, Pride History Group Collection, 18 February 2008.
22   Interview with Rae Morris by Sandra Mackay, Pride History Group Collection, 4 December 2008.
23   Lucy Chesser, *Parting with My Sex: Cross-dressing, Inversion and Sexuality in Australian Cultural Life* (Sydney: Sydney University Press, 2008).

required three pieces of female clothing, [and some] two.'[24] Kennedy and Davis were unable to locate 'a New York State law about what constitutes male or female impersonation, despite the unanimity of narrators on the subject' and, drawing on the work of Nan Hunter, concluded that 'a judge in a particular case made a ruling that two or three pieces of clothing of the "correct" sex negated male or female impersonation and that set a precedent used by law enforcement agencies.'[25]

Laws against insulting or offensive behaviour were also interpreted broadly by police to include demonstrations of affection between women or visible manifestations of a lesbian identity. Addressing a seminar on 'Female Homosexuality' at Sydney University in 1975, Helen Coonan outlined a number of ways in which lesbians were discriminated against in law, and noted that 'lesbian behaviour can be prosecuted and has been prosecuted under the catch all phrase of "offensive behaviour".'[26] In 1978, the feminist and gay press reported that two women had been arrested and charged for hugging on the grass in a Sydney park.[27] Women in lesbian bars were also subject to police harassment. Jan Hillier, a Melbourne butch lesbian, recalled the 'frightening times' she and her friends experienced on a trip to Sydney in the 1960s:

> I remember I once went to Sydney with Hank and Speedy and a few of the butch lesbians. We all got on the train and off we went and we got all dolled up and went to some gay bar in William Street. Well Bumper Farrell raided the place, scooped us all up and put us in the Darlinghurst cells for the weekend. We were only kids, 16 or 17. He locked us up for being drunk and disorderly and left us there for the whole weekend. No charges were ever laid. On the Monday we had to go back to Melbourne to work. I was terrified my mother was going to find out I'd been in jail ... I've never been that fond of Sydney.[28]

Such police tactics continued into the 1970s and, in March 1978, lesbian and gay campaigning group CAMP NSW complained that clientele at the

---

24 Elizabeth Lapovsky Kennedy and Madeline Davis, *Boots of Leather, Slippers of Gold* (New York: Routledge, 1993), p. 180.
25 ibid., p. 411, n. 29.
26 Helen Coonan, 'Discrimination in the Law', in 'Female Homosexuality. Seminar Two: The Conditioning Processes in Society and the Family' (Sydney: CAMP NSW, 1975).
27 *Melbourne Women's Liberation Newsletter*, December 1978, p. 8.
28 'The Bad Old Days', *Lesbians on the Loose* Issue 103, vol. 9, no. 7 (July 1998), p. 20.

lesbian nightclub Ruby Reds had been arrested on charges of using offensive language.[29]

While no legislation explicitly targeted female homosexuality, therefore, the very absence of a public discourse around lesbianism and the law left women in considerable doubt as to which behaviours were legal and which, if any, were not. As a result, many women absorbed a general and ill-defined sense that desire between women – and any outward expression of it – was not only unacceptable but potentially punishable in some way.

Medico-scientific attitudes to lesbianism

Lucy Chesser has argued that 'medical discourses have been crucial in the creation and popularisation of sexual categories. While the degree to which these categories were available to women varied tremendously in the 1960s, they were a necessary prerequisite for the construction of modern lesbian identities.[30] Certainly the medical model of homosexuality had been sufficiently popularised by the mid-century as to prompt a wide range of social commentators, including judicial authorities and the clergy, to refer to homosexuality as an illness, and to regard it as a problem requiring the assistance of medical professionals. However, the extent to which medical discourses and practitioners in mid-twentieth century Australia actively shaped individual women's notions of their same-sex desires is questionable.

Studies of male or female homosexuality were largely overseas in origin in the mid-twentieth century, as research into and discussion of lesbianism by Australian scientists and doctors was virtually non-existent for much of this period. *The Medical Journal of Australia* (hereafter *MJA*) and the *Australian and New Zealand Journal of Psychiatry* contain no reports of Australian research into the issue before the 1970s, suggesting that this was not a subject of active concern to the medical profession in Australia. However, there is evidence that Australian practitioners were aware of overseas debates and literature and many of the key British and American works on homosexuality were referred to in Australian texts or reviewed in medical journals. Australian medico-scientific discourse therefore largely reflected broader international trends in thinking on the subject.

---

29 *CAMP News Bulletin* no. 28, 12 March 1978, p. 1; *Red and Lavender: Newsletter of the Socialist Lesbians and Male Homosexuals*, September 1977.

30 Lucy Chesser, 'Negotiating Subjectivities: The Construction of Lesbian Identities in Melbourne, 1960–1969' (unpublished Honours thesis, Melbourne: University of Melbourne, 1993), p. 18.

A review of *The Invert and his Social Adjustment* by 'Anomoly' in the *MJA* in 1927 commented that 'Medical men know or ought to know that the invert is such through no fault of his own', demonstrating the continued dominance of late nineteenth-century arguments that homosexuality was a congenital condition.[31] In the mid-1940s, this argument was reiterated with the support of recent research into hormones. In a report on Herbert Greenspan and John D Campbell's work in *The American Journal of Psychiatry*, the reviewer notes that: 'Observations, they claim, drawn from androgen-oestrogen urine levels in homosexuals tend to enhance the conviction that homosexuality is constitutional in nature ... They believe that true homosexuality is not an acquired vice but a biological anomaly.'[32] However, in the years after the Second World War, the literature suggests the growing influence of psychoanalytic thinking, with an increasing assertion that homosexuality was an acquired condition resulting from arrested psychosexual development. Only a few years later, in a 1948 report of a British Royal Society of Medicine meeting on homosexuality, the *MJA* noted that a distinction was being drawn between congenital homosexuals, for whom treatment or punishment was ineffective and inadvisable, and 'pseudo-homosexual persons' in whom:

> The persistence into adult life of the homosexual tendencies that are natural and indeed universal during adolescence is symptomatic of a failure of development, an arrest of normal psychological growth at the pre-adolescent stage of homosexuality.[33]

By the 1960s, Robert Reynolds suggests, a clear trend was noticeable away from the earlier understanding of the homosexual as a 'type' of person, toward an emphasis on homosexuality as an acquired form of behaviour: 'the logic of a 1960s medical knowledge', he argues, 'suggested that the homosexual need not exist.'[34] A broad consensus of medical thinking emerged on the key role of parents in 'making' a homosexual, with the *MJA* noting in 1969 that:

> As has been found in studies of male homosexuality, the family background and upbringing of the lesbians [in FE Kenyon's study] was less likely to have been a happy one. The relationships of the lesbian women with both their fathers and their mothers were poorer than

---

31 'Inversion', *The Medical Journal of Australia* (hereafter *MJA*), 10 December 1927, p. 818.
32 'The Homosexual as a Personality Type', *MJA*, 22 December 1945, p. 473.
33 'Homosexuality', *MJA*, 7 February 1948, p. 175.
34 Robert Reynolds, *From Camp to Queer: Remaking the Australian Homosexual* (Melbourne: Melbourne University Press, 2002), p. 16.

those for the control group, and only 56% reported their childhood as having been a generally happy one, as opposed to 92% of the controls.[35]

Emily Wilson suggests that the popularity of such psychoanalytic approaches to homosexuality resulted in part from a desire to promote the psychiatric profession's role in tackling the 'problem' of male homosexuality, as an alternative to legal frameworks.[36] A review of Louis S London and Frank S Caprio's *Sexual Deviations* in 1950 certainly dismissed the imprisonment of homosexuals as 'futile' and claimed that:

> London and Caprio have rendered a service to that branch of medical jurisprudence which embraces sexual deviation. They have shown that no person is born deviated; but that the conduct of adulthood is often trammelled in the past ... [the sexual deviate's] development has been arrested at a childish level ... Only the wider dissemination of this knowledge will prevent the present injustice and ultimately benefit society and the individual.[37]

While legal approaches to homosexuality offered, at best, the temporary solution of containment, an increasingly optimistic medical literature seemed to hold out the promise of a permanent cure.

Much of the literature on homosexuality in Australian journals and other texts focused on male homosexuals, addressing the more pressing social problem apparently posed by homosexual men. Comments on lesbianism were frequently confined to observations on the comparative incidence of homosexuality in men and women. In 1932, Robert V Storer touched briefly upon female homosexuality in his *A Survey of Sexual Life in Adolescence and Marriage*. After outlining the origins of the terms 'lesbian' and 'sapphism' in Greek antiquity, Storer examined the question of how widespread lesbianism might be in the present. At odds with many medical commentators of the period, Storer concluded that 'homosexuality is probably commoner amongst women than men owing possibly to the easier heterosexual gratification in the case of the male.'[38] In drawing these conclusions, he referred – somewhat confusingly – to a recent study of 1000 unmarried college women, which found that 184 had admitted

---

35 'A Study of Lesbianism', *MJA*, 24 May 1969, p. 1095.
36 Emily Wilson, '"Someone Who is Sick and in Need of Help": Medical Attitudes to Homosexuality in Australia, 1960–79', in Robinson, *Homophobia*, pp. 148–171.
37 'Paraphilic Portraits', *MJA*, 25 November 1950, p. 799.
38 Robert V Storer, *A Survey of Sexual Life in Adolescence and Marriage* (Melbourne: Science Publishing Co, 1932), p. 189.

to homosexual experiences, and to an Australian study of 100 adolescent boys, of whom 27 admitted previous homosexual practices.[39] In contrast, Prof Neil McConaghy argued in 1973 that: 'Of course overt homosexual behaviour is much less common in women. When it does occur, it is rare for Lesbian women to be exclusively homosexual.'[40] In a 1949 review of George W Henry's *Sex Variants*, which contained detailed case histories of male and female homosexuals, the *MJA* suggested that the apparently lower incidence of homosexuality in women might be explained by cultural factors which made it easier to conceal homosexual tendencies in women. The editorial noted:

> Surprisingly, quite a number of women have related their experiences in minute detail. It is unusual to obtain an admission from women of homosexual tendencies. In them such trends are concealed by those demonstrations of affection which, however insincere, are common to their sex. Furthermore, they possess the capacity for convincing denial in the face of almost overwhelming evidence.[41]

The editorial went on to describe the characteristics of female homosexuals which had emerged from Henry's case studies, portraying lesbians as 'masculine women' and noting the 'incidence of instability in other members of the family, the frequency of alcoholism in lesbians and their continual fear of infidelity by the partner.'[42] This characterisation of lesbianism reflected earlier interwar portrayals, such as Sydney surgeon Herbert Moran's account of cross-dressed lesbian murderer, Eugenia Falleni. Recounting his first impressions of Falleni, whom he visited in prison, Moran observed:

> The stature was short and the gait slouching. She still seemed to be deliberately exaggerating the stride of a man. The grey eyes were restless and afraid; the face olive-tinted, lined, hairless. Such a head would easily pass for a man's ... She was flat in the bust. The voice was low-pitched and raucous ... Obviously this was a woman with the mental capacity of some lower animal ... She was just a half-wild creature who felt herself apart and different, who had grown cunning and furtive, hiding her secret and satisfying her needs. She must have long since

---

39   He is presumably referring here to Katherine Bement Davis' *Factors in the Sex Life of Twenty-two Hundred Women* (London: Harper and Brothers, 1929).
40   N McConaghy, 'The Doctor and Homosexuality', *MJA*, 13 January 1973, p. 69.
41   'Homosexuality', *MJA*, 19 March 1949, p. 382.
42   ibid.

learned how the common people hated the habit she practised. She must have gone always harassed with fear.[43]

Ruth Ford notes that press reports at the time of Falleni's trial in 1920 represented Falleni in similarly masculine terms, although such portrayals coincided with an understanding of Falleni's cross-dressing as a form of fraud or deception, rather than an indicator of innate sexual inversion. Ford concludes: 'the notion of sexual inversion – though circulating within medical and sexological literature and the press – was far from hegemonic, even in the medical profession. Older moral legal discourses of deception and fraud and the carnival freak tradition blended with medical discourses of sexual inversion and "sex-perversion".'[44] As the 1949 *MJA* review indicates, this emphasis on fraud in relation both to cross-dressing and lesbianism persisted into the 1940s and 1950s.

Treatment patterns for lesbianism were similarly not outlined in any detail in the medical literature; in the absence of comparable legal penalties, psychiatrists and other medical practitioners may not have considered the need for treatment to be as urgent in the case of lesbians as in homosexual men. In a 1969 review of FE Kenyon's British study of lesbianism, the *MJA* observed with surprise that 'despite the few social difficulties associated with lesbianism, one in four of his sample would like to become entirely heterosexual.'[45] Treatment for homosexuality in the early postwar decades appears to have focused on psychotherapy, but by the early 1960s, letters and articles in Australian journals point to a growing interest in behavioural treatments such as aversion therapy. WSG Rowe wrote to the *MJA* in 1962 to report that, although 'the treatment of homosexuality and other sexual perversions by psychotherapy has altogether been somewhat disappointing', he was intending to test overseas claims that 'such sufferers have been successfully reorientated to heterosexuality by conditioning techniques.' 'This is done', he noted:

> By associating homosexuality (by means of photographs, movie film and tape recorders) with unpleasant sensations aroused by a drug, such as Apo morphine, and subsequent positive conditioning of heterosexual

---

43 Herbert M Moran, *Viewless Winds: Being the Recollections and Digressions of an Australian Surgeon* (London: Peter Davies, 1939), pp. 234–235.
44 Ruth Ford, '"The Man-Woman Murderer": Sex Fraud, Sexual Inversion and the Unmentionable "Article" in 1920s Australia', *Gender and History*, vol. 12 no. 1 (2000), p. 176.
45 'A Study of Lesbianism', *MJA*, 24 May 1969, p. 1095.

interests with erotic drive (aided by intramuscular injection of testosterone).[46]

In a full-length article five years later, however, Rowe reported that he had achieved limited success with aversion therapy alone and was now combining it with psychotherapy as part of a longer-term treatment program. Homosexuality, he argued, 'is a symptom of a personality disorder and not considered by me to be an isolated condition in a well-adjusted individual'; psychotherapy was therefore effective in bringing about 'changes in the personality toward emotional maturity and improvement in the handling of interpersonal relationships.'[47]

Where lesbianism was the specific focus of discussion, the medical literature pointed to a greater emphasis on psychotherapeutic approaches, rather than behavioural therapies. Douglas Vann, a consulting psychiatrist in Western Australia, wrote to inform the *MJA* in 1974 that:

> In Canberra between 1958 and 1961 only five homosexuals were referred to me and they were all tribadists [lesbians]. One was bisexual and wished to rid herself of homosexuality; psychotherapy in her case was relatively quickly successful. Her dominant partner only entered psychotherapy in the hope that she would be able to convince her partner of its futility. When it became clear that success was likely, she stopped coming and found another partner. Two others imitating the tribadism of the dominant leaders responded rapidly to reoriental psychotherapy, whilst the fate of the fifth escapes my memory, except that I know she became heterosexual during treatment.[48]

Other case studies reported the use of psychotherapy in treating lesbianism into the mid-1970s, although with limited success.[49] LK Gluckman informed the *Australian and New Zealand Journal of Psychiatry* of the use of psychotherapy in treating a 32-year-old Maori 'chronic lesbian' who had been brought to a doctor by her husband. Diagnosing 'moderate peaks on both the sexual deviation and psychopathic scales', the psychiatrist embarked on a treatment of psychotherapy, with the result that:

---

46 W S G Rowe, 'The Treatment of Homosexuals', *MJA*, 25 August 1962, p. 321.
47 William S Rowe, 'The Treatment of Homosexuality and Associated Perversions by Psychotherapy and Aversion Therapy', *MJA*, 30 September 1967, p. 638.
48 'Homosexuality', *MJA*, 16 March 1974, p. 414.
49 See, for example, Anthony Dinnen and David S Bell, 'Psychotherapy in a Large Open Family Group', *Australian and New Zealand Journal of Psychiatry*, vol. 9, no. 2 (1975), pp. 93–98.

> Within eight weeks she was back with her husband and her emotional feelings for Zeta [her female lover] were minimal. Her lesbian drives were less prominent than they had been since adolescence and she was able to cohabit fairly regularly with her husband, although there was no emotional satisfaction in this for her. Six months later the husband reported the marriage had never been so happy or stable. It is not suggested she is cured.[50]

Such comments suggest that lesbianism may have been perceived by some psychiatrists as a problem only to the extent that it interfered with a woman's ability to fulfil marital and maternal obligations. If, as in this case, the woman was able to 'cohabit' with her husband and he was satisfied that the marriage was 'happy' and 'stable', the patient's own lack of 'emotional satisfaction' was insignificant: a cure was unnecessary.

However, other accounts suggest that a broad range of attitudes towards lesbianism existed amongst the medical profession from the 1950s to the 1970s, and individual practitioners and hospitals employed a variety of treatment programs. Kris described her experience at Parramatta Mental Hospital in the mid-1960s as very traumatic. She had been scheduled at the age of 17, after taking an overdose following a pack rape, and was confined in a locked ward in the hospital for over three months. She was prescribed Librium and was scheduled for shock treatment, which did not take place due to the strenuous objections of her family. However, her release from the hospital was delayed by her psychiatrist's insistence on attempting to 'cure' her lesbianism. She explained:

> Yeah I was supposed to sit and talk to him and ... He was so obsessed with me not being able – being normal, that [the rape] wasn't going to turn me into a lesbian. He told me a lesbian life was not a very nice life. That you know, it was a really hard life and it was not a nice life. I had to convince him, to get out of there, that I was going to you know, have a – live a nice, happily, married life and stuff in the future. My mum was going: 'please tell him because you get out.' I said, 'No, I can't mum. I can't, I can't do that, I can't.' I wanted to but I couldn't, I just couldn't because it's something in me you know.[51]

---

50 LK Gluckman, 'Lesbianism in the Maori: A Series of Three Interconnected Clinical Studies', *Australian and New Zealand Journal of Psychiatry*, vol. 1, no. 2 (1967), p. 100.
51 Interview with Kris Melmouth, 25 August 2011.

Kris's experience was echoed by another lesbian who wrote to lesbian and gay newspaper, *Campaign*, in 1977. She explained:

> I am a 26 year old lesbian who has been in a large Sydney psychiatric hospital for the last 18 months. Because I insist that I won't change my ideas and my mind about being a lesbian, the doctors give me shock treatment, aversion therapy, large doses of tablets and injections. I am desperately unhappy, but I refuse to tell them what they want to hear – that I want to get married and have children, and lead a so-called 'normal life'.
>
> My psychiatrist is middle-aged and every day he wears a blue pin-striped suit and tells me that he is determined to make me change and be a normal girl. Because I hate this so much and have no one to turn to, I have contemplated suicide as the answer to my situation.[52]

Both accounts point to a continued concern amongst the psychiatric profession with attempting to 'cure' lesbianism, often against the wishes of the patient and even in patients whose sexuality was not the cause of their admission to hospital. It is unclear how frequently behavioural treatments such as aversion therapy and shock treatment were used in instances of female homosexuality, but personal testimonies point to their fairly widespread use in the 1960s and 1970s. Less frequently, surgical intervention was also contemplated, sometimes with devastating consequences.[53]

While medical models of homosexuality undoubtedly became increasingly dominant in professional circles in Australia throughout the mid-century, their influence on the attitudes of ordinary women is much less obvious. There is limited evidence of individual women seeking out medical literature as a source of information on same-sex desire, or voluntarily requesting the assistance of a psychiatrist.[54] Censorship of literature on homosexuality made it extremely difficult to obtain access to medical texts discussing homosexuality. Nicole Moore has demonstrated that while Customs banned

---

52 Letter from 'Desperate' to Jane's Column, *Campaign* Ed 27 (December 1977), p. 53. See also Letter from Mrs S.B., Orange, NSW to Jane's Column, *Campaign* Ed. 34 (July 1978), p. 52.
53 One in Seven Collective, dir., *Witches, Faggots, Dykes and Poofters* (1980).
54 Although Naomi Cranenburgh's work suggests that in Victoria at least, psychiatry may have had a more significant impact on some lesbians: Cranenburgh, 'From Invisible to "Menace"'. For a comparison with the UK, see Rebecca Jennings, '"The Most Uninhibited Party They'd Ever Been To": The Postwar Encounter between Psychiatry and the British Lesbian, 1945–71', *Journal of British Studies*, vol. 47, no. 4 (2008), pp. 88–904.

many works on the subject outright, others were considered by the Literature Censorship Board and passed for restricted circulation amongst professional readers only. Sydney-based author Frank Walford's banned 1933 novel, *Twisted Clay*, depicted the difficulties his lesbian protagonist experienced in obtaining medical texts on homosexuality. Comparing this passage with a similar depiction of a lesbian heroine's search for knowledge in Radclyffe Hall's British novel, *The Well of Loneliness*, Moore observes:

> In *The Well*, it is Krafft-Ebing's work, probably *Psychopathia Sexualis*, that Stephen reads, even though Ellis' theories were more sympathetic than Krafft-Ebing's, and there is no Freud nor Jung. Walford's book portrays an Australian context in which those books are much more difficult to obtain, however, even for the wealthy daughter of a successful doctor. She can't read them in the pater-connoisseur's library nor in the public one, but must go out and buy them anonymously and with difficulty.[55]

A number of key sexological texts were passed by censors, including Krafft-Ebing's *Psychopathia Sexualis* in 1937 and Havelock Ellis' *Sex in Relation to Society* in 1945. Several more were passed with restrictions preventing their general circulation, including Albert Moll's *Perversions of the Sex Instinct: A Study of Sexual Inversion Based on Clinical Data and Official Documents*, which was restricted until 1969, and George W Henry's *Sex Variants: A Study of Homosexual Patterns*. As Walford suggested in his novel, despite the difficulties, persistent readers were sometimes successful in accessing this literature. When Sandra Willson was arrested for murder in 1959, press reports noted that a police search of her flat had resulted in the discovery of a number of notebooks recording her relationships with women, together with a copy of Magnus Hirschfeld's *Sexual Anomalies and Perversions*, which had been restricted by the Board in 1946 and was not released for general circulation until 1964.[56] However, Sandra's awareness of and interest in medical constructions of sexuality were unusual – the result of her previous experience as a patient in a mental hospital – and there is very little evidence in personal testimonies of women seeking out or referring to such texts.[57]

From the 1950s onwards, popular sex-education work began to play an important role in disseminating psychiatric ideas regarding lesbianism more widely. Naomi Cranenburgh argues that, while the majority of sex

---

55   Nicole Moore, *The Censor's Library*, Brisbane, University of Queensland Press, 2012.
56   *Daily Telegraph*, Thursday 11 June 1959.
57   See Rebecca Jennings, 'Sandra Willson: A Case Study in Lesbian Identities in 1950s and 1970s Australia', *History Australia*, vol. 10, no. 1 (2013).

education works for girls before and during the Second World War failed to mention lesbianism, a small number contained inexplicit references to intimate relationships between girls. In her 1935 work, *The House Not Made With Hands*, Josephine Bamford warned her readers: 'The girl who says "I have no time for boys" ... is not normal ... the sign of a warped and perverted nature.'[58] However, by the 1950s, such warnings were becoming increasingly explicit. *A Guide to Womanhood* asserted:

> Sometimes a friendship between girls oversteps the bounds of calmness and good judgment. It is unwise and even dangerous ... when their meetings call for overwrought kissing and embraces ... Sometimes there are disturbed girls or women who become too deeply attracted to a member of their own sex in a physical way. This may result in mutual masturbation or other sex contact ... They may create habits which will develop to patterns of homosexual behaviour.[59]

Without discussing psychiatric views in any detail, these works represented female homosexuality as neurotic and a signifier of mental illness, and their broader reach helped to promote a medical model of homosexuality in the postwar decades.

Nevertheless, given the difficulty of obtaining access to medical literature, most women's encounters with current medico-scientific thought on homosexuality would have occurred through face-to-face encounters with medical professionals. Joyce Geake, a young woman born and raised in a middle-class Sydney suburb, took the decision to consult a psychiatrist about her same-sex desires in the 1950s. She reflected in her autobiography:

> After about five years of conflict I decided that the wisest alternative [was] ... to go to London to seek what I hoped to be the best psychiatric help available at the time – at Tavistock Clinic ... I saved hard for two years to meet travelling expenses, and when I left for London, no-one knew, except the skilled and particularly helpful social worker who had supervised my university training, that my main object was to seek psychiatric help ... I had high hopes for my term of therapy at

---

58 E. Josephine Bamford, *The House Not Made with Hands: Talks to Older Girls* [1935] 2nd ed and 5th ed (Kyneton: Armstrong Brothers, 1939 and 1943), p. 32, cited in Cranenburgh, 'From Invisible to "Menace"', p. 22.

59 *A Guide to Womanhood: A Reliable Sex Education Booklet for Young Women 15 Years and Over* (Sydney, Melbourne, Brisbane and Adelaide: Father and Son Welfare Movement of Australia, 1961) p. 27 and 1962 edition, p. 29, cited in Cranenburgh, 'From Invisible to "Menace"', p. 48.

Tavistock Centre, but unfortunately the psychiatrist who saw me was not able to help me, though he was very kind and understanding. After nine months of twice-weekly sessions, I discontinued therapy on his recommendation, feeling at that time more disturbed than when I had started there, probably because of the loss of hope involved. Efforts to change my love object from female to male had proved ineffective, but treatment had been free of charge, so I was no worse off except for a degree of mental stress and disappointment.[60]

Joyce's experience was unusual, however, both in her personal decision to consult a psychiatrist and in her choice of doing so in London. Both reports in the medical literature and personal testimonies suggest that the majority of women who did visit doctors and psychiatrists throughout this period were referred by a third party rather than seeking advice themselves. In the 1950s, Sandra Willson was taken to the doctor by her mother when she read in Sandra's diaries of her feelings for women. Sandra recalled that the 'psychologist ... acknowledged my condition and said I actually did prefer women "because I had a secret love for my mother"', an explanation which Sandra dismissed as 'Rubbish!'[61] Following two encounters with the police for attempting to seduce a married woman and later hitting a fellow schoolgirl, Sandra was referred by the Children's Court to a mental hospital for treatment of her homosexuality. The Court advised that she undergo a course of aversion therapy, but it is unclear whether Sandra actually received this treatment. Many years later she remained unsure of her medical 'diagnosis' or treatment plan and when her psychiatrist, Dr Gilchrist, later told another court that Sandra had been suffering from a 'personality disorder', she was surprised and confused:

> When Dr Gilchrist got up and testified that I had suffered from a 'personality disorder,' even I myself was confused and no longer understood what she was implying. This classification, for all I knew, could have merely been a euphemism for my homosexuality. This classification, however, carried weight. It meant something of some sort, and had substance – whatever it was.[62]

---

60 Joyce Geake, 'Shadows and Substance: Reflections of a Lesbian' (Sydney: unpublished manuscript, 1973). Mitchell Library, MLMSS8701, pp. 29–30.
61 Willson, unpublished memoir, p. 13.
62 ibid., p. 102. See also Melbourne's *Lesbian Newsletter*. August 1977, pp. 4–5 for an account of a lesbian woman's experience of aversion therapy after being referred by her parents to a psychiatrist.

For many women, their sole encounter with a psychiatrist occurred as a result of training for a profession such as teaching or nursing. In this context, the emphasis was less upon treatment than on assessing the suitability of individual women for entry into a profession with the intention of promoting a culture of heterosexuality. Penny Short was interviewed by a psychiatrist at the Medical Examination Centre run by the Department of Health when she was offered a teaching scholarship at Macquarie University in the early 1970s. After some detailed questioning, she informed the psychiatrist that she was homosexual and the psychiatrist replied: 'Well that's o.k., I know some bisexual people and they are rather nice; so that's o.k. by me, but don't let the Department of Health find out or you will be in trouble.' When Penny contributed a poem describing lesbian sex to Macquarie University's student paper *Arena*, however, she was recalled to see another psychiatrist. As a result of this interview, Penny was declared 'medically unfit' and lost her scholarship.[63]

While the views of psychiatrists and medical professionals were clearly regarded as influential by the courts, social welfare workers and other professionals, their impact on the ideas of lesbians themselves was much more limited. In contrast to the UK and US, few Australian women seem to have consulted either medical texts or individual doctors in making sense of their desire for other women.[64] In describing their early reactions to an awareness of same-sex desire, women rarely used the language of sickness, suggesting that the medical model of lesbianism had not been widely disseminated on a popular level. Instead, concepts of lesbianism as 'evil' and 'immoral' persisted, indicating the continued dominance of religious attitudes toward homosexuality.

Christian morality

Although church attendance in Australia was gradually declining in the postwar period, the churches maintained an influential position as voices of

---

[63] 'Victimisation by ed. Dept', *Refractory Girl*, Summer 1974, p. 11.
[64] Jennings, '"The Most Uninhibited Party They'd Ever Been To"'; Lillian Faderman, *Odd Girls and Twilight Lovers: A History of Lesbian Life in Twentieth-Century America* (New York: Penguin, 1992); Vernon A Rosario, ed., *Science and Homosexualities* (New York: Routledge, 1997); Henry Minton, *Departing from Deviance: A History of Homosexual Rights and Emancipatory Science in America* (Chicago, University of Chicago Press, 2002); Ronald Bayer, *Homosexuality and American Psychiatry: The Politics of Diagnosis* (New York: Princeton University Press, 1981); Jennifer Terry, *An American Obsession: Science, Medicine, and Homosexuality in Modern Society* (Chicago: University of Chicago Press, 1999).

authority on matters of morality and sexuality. Christian notions of sexual morality therefore had a significant influence on attitudes toward lesbianism in this period.[65] In his 1966 *Profile of Australia*, Craig McGregor claimed:

> In general the Australian attitude towards religion is one of apathy: most people think of themselves as Christian, but they don't bother to do anything about it. Nevertheless, the influence of the churches is strong within the community and they form a vocal and powerful pressure group at Government level. It is largely due to the churches that hotels and cinemas are closed, sport frowned upon and gambling positively prohibited on Sundays. They are a major source of the puritanism which afflicts Australian life, upholding strict censorship, inveighing against immorality and teenage delinquency, taking part in attacks upon the academic freedom of universities and from time to time attempting to destroy the secular nature of the State education systems.[66]

Education was one of the primary areas in which the churches were able to disseminate teachings on gendered roles and sexuality. The Catholic Church in particular stressed the importance of children being educated in Catholic schools, and enjoyed considerable success in this regard: even in the 1960s, when the Catholic education system began to decline, only 30% of Australian Catholic children were enrolled in state, rather than Catholic, schools. Prior to the 1960s, this meant that the vast majority of Catholic girls were being educated by nuns. Personal recollections of girls' Catholic educations emphasise the importance which was placed on sexual purity.[67] Sex was represented as legitimate only as a means of procreation within marriage and girls were taught that extra-marital sexuality was a mortal sin. While explicit discussion of sexuality was strongly discouraged, girls were offered a choice between two acceptable roles as adult women: nuns or mothers. One woman, who had been a Catholic schoolgirl during the Second World War, recalled:

> I can remember Reverend Mother in my last year saying to a group of us, 'Whatever you do, don't be old maids. If you're not going to be a

---

65 In 1933, for example, 46% of the population in Sydney claimed an Anglican affiliation, but by 1961, this figure had dropped to 40%. See Bruce Kaye, ed., *Anglicanism in Australia: A History* (Melbourne: Melbourne University Press, 2002), p. 120.
66 Craig McGregor, *Profile of Australia* (Melbourne: Penguin, 1968, c.1966), p. 356.
67 Patrick O'Farrell, *The Catholic Church and Community: An Australian History*, 3rd revised edn (Sydney: NSW University Press, 1992), p. 415.

nun' – obviously number one was to be a nun – 'for heaven's sake get married.' I remember going to chapel once, and I used to pray a fair bit (I was pretty good on the praying – mainly for something I wanted) and thinking, 'I hope I won't be like Auntie Jennie, an old maid', and yet feeling that I would be.[68]

The Anglican Church was similarly concerned with sexual morality, attacking rising figures of extra-marital pregnancy and urging stricter censorship of 'indecent' American films.[69] Although fewer Anglican, Presbyterian and Methodist girls were able to attend church schools, Sunday schools and social groups such as the Girls Friendly Society offered an alternative sphere in which to promote Christian morality. In these churches, as in the Catholic Church, female same-sex desire was rarely explicitly condemned. Instead, many women absorbed a sense of prohibition indirectly through broader Christian teachings about sexual morality, as Margaret's story indicates.

In the late 1950s, 30-year-old Margaret Jones experienced a sexual encounter with another woman for the first time, while on an Atlantic crossing. Born in the Sydney suburb of Manly in 1927 to working-class parents, Margaret had been given a strict Catholic upbringing, and her attitudes toward sexual practice had been strongly influenced by Christian morality. She explained:

> I was in fact virginal until I was twenty-one. As a proper devout Catholic should be, because I'd been imbued with this whole sense of the horror of losing one's virginity and coming to one's husband deflowered as it were, and heard all the horrors of pregnancy and so I was determinedly virginal and waiting to keep myself for the chosen man.[70]

In her 20s, Margaret married a Hungarian Catholic, but the marriage was not a success and a few years later she left her marital home and embarked on a trip to Canada, the US and Europe. It was on the final leg of this journey, aboard a ship bound from Florida to Europe, that Margaret encountered, and was seduced by, Brigetta. Margaret found their first kiss 'a bit unsettling, of course. I wasn't given to these things and I was – I wasn't repulsed – I was offended, I think.' Her reaction was shaped by a sense that to kiss another woman 'was an unnatural and dirty and unchristian and improper thing ...

---

68   Cited in Janet McCalman, *Journeyings: The Biography of a Middle-Class Generation 1920–1990* (Melbourne: Melbourne University Press, 1993), p. 182.
69   David Hilliard, *Godliness and Good Order: A History of the Anglican Church in South Australia* (Adelaide: Wakefield Press, 1986), p. 93.
70   Interview with Margaret Jones, 31 August 2007.

inappropriate and bedevilled.' Despite this, Margaret's physical pleasure in the experience prompted her to seek a repeat of it, and she and Brigetta soon embarked on a steamy shipboard romance which lasted until they reached their destination.[71]

Attempting to make sense of the encounter many years later, Margaret recalled both a lack of clarity in her understanding of lesbianism and a clear sense of religious prohibition against same-sex desire. The two women had not discussed the nature or meaning of their affair, but Margaret 'assumed [Brigetta] was one of those lesbians'.[72] It was only later, on her return to Sydney, that Margaret began to reassess her own identity in the light of her experience, and to consider that she, too, might be one of these women:

> But still I realised that I could have been one of these lesbian people because the experience was pleasurable enough to think that that was where I might be. But there were no lesbians in Sydney, as there were none in the world as far as I knew: I'd never seen anything about them or photographs or read anything about them. I suppose if something was written, it was in the most damning terms, you know, they were evil and terrible people and, of course my good Catholic background would tell me that they certainly were evil, that they were not going to marry or procreate or do any of those nice Catholic things.[73]

Margaret's strong sense that desire between women was prohibited by the church, she explained, was shaped both by a silence on the subject and by repeated injunctions that sexuality was only acceptable within marriage, for the purpose of procreation:

> Oh no, they, I don't think they ever used the word [lesbian]. We did talk about single women – women who weren't married – in some sort of pitying terms, that the poor girl couldn't find anyone and she'd never have children, never know the joy of marriage and husbands and little children, but they wouldn't necessarily have been lesbians, they would just have been unlucky they couldn't attract a feller, so I suppose I was amongst that group of the unmarried.[74]

While religious discourses, therefore, together with legal and medical frameworks, were influential in articulating social disapproval of male

---

71 ibid.
72 ibid.
73 Interview with Margaret Jones, 12 September 2007.
74 ibid.

homosexuality, it was their very silence on the subject of female same-sex desire which conveyed the unacceptability of lesbianism. The absence of public discussion of the issue left many women struggling to make sense of their same-sex desires, aware only that there was 'something' fundamentally 'wrong with them'. As a tool of social repression, this pervasive silence was highly effective. Without clear parameters defining exactly what constituted female same-sex desire as a crime, a sickness or a sin, many women policed all aspects of their lives, and kept much of themselves hidden. Ultimately, the promotion of normative female sexuality, rather than the condemnation of 'unacceptable' behaviour, produced a sense of failure and loss for many who lived through this era. As Beverley reflected: 'It's a terribly unfortunate thing that you should be born like this, because you miss out on a great many things ... I don't know [what], I really don't know ... but you do miss out on a lot of things.'[75]

---

75   Interview with Beverley, 22 December 2008.

Chapter 2

CONCEALMENT AND ISOLATION

In the mid-1960s, Deborah, a young architecture student, read a novel which helped to crystallise her vague sense of difference into a recognition of herself as a lesbian. With that awareness came an almost immediate conviction that this identity was something she had to conceal. She recalled:

> At some stage very soon after that, I think I decided that if that was who I am, then I'd just have to, I couldn't let anybody know about it, to begin with, because I even had, even though it's not discussed, you have a sense that it's not something that should be discussed. I don't know where you get that from either. Where do you get that from? … Just the fact that it's not around you … because I can't ever recall having heard anyone say anything negative about gay people, it just never was there in the conversation. And maybe that absence was enough to signal that it was verboten.[1]

Female same-sex desire remained almost entirely absent from cultural discourse in mid-twentieth century Australia and the silence which surrounded the subject inhibited many women from articulating their own experiences, suggesting through an absence of discourse that female homosexuality was not an acceptable topic for discussion.

The decades immediately after the Second World War have long been characterised by historians as years of concealment and repression.[2]

---

1   Interview with Deborah [pseudonym], 13 November 2008.
2   Graham Willett, 'The Darkest Decade: Homophobia in 1950s' Australia', in John Murphy and Judith Smart, eds, *The Forgotten Fifties: Aspects of Australian Society in the*

Influenced by the rhetoric of the gay liberation movement, historiography has represented the 1970s as a defining moment of freedom, in which a previously frightened, closeted lesbian and gay community found confidence and a sense of self-worth through the open and proud articulation of a sexual identity.[3] This triumphal account has meant that both the experience of living in a culture of silence and the sophisticated ways in which individual women forged lives for themselves in this context have been largely neglected by historians. Similarly, the continued impact of a culture of concealment after the 1970s has been erased. This chapter will therefore attempt to complicate this narrative, moving away from a construction of visibility and invisibility as polar opposites, towards a more nuanced understanding of the structures of meaning and practices of being that are inherent in these cultures of silence and expression.

The potential consequences of openly declaring a lesbian identity in the mid-twentieth century, ranging from loss of employment to social ostracism, prompted many women to conceal their desires and sexual identities in this period. For some women, and particularly those in relationships with other women or those with access to lesbian friendship networks, negotiating the culture of concealment involved a complex and creative process of constructing alternative narratives and 'double lives'. For others, the greatest impact of concealment was isolation, and women describe both the pain and loneliness of isolation in this period and the ways in which they used literature, film and subscriptions to overseas lesbian magazines as a means of mitigating that isolation. Consumed by lesbian readers, literary and media representations of same-sex desire in the mid-twentieth century both reinforced and unsettled the definition of lesbianism as an isolated form of existence, while overseas lesbian magazines offered individual women the opportunity to reach out to other lesbians discreetly, becoming members of the discursive communities they created. All, however, enabled isolated lesbians to seek some confirmation that they were not alone, without compromising the discreet identities which facilitated their survival in a hostile society.

1950s (Melbourne: Melbourne University Press, 1997, [a special issue of Australian Historical Studies, vol. 28, no. 109]), pp. 120–132; Garry Wotherspoon, *City of the Plain: History of a Gay Sub-Culture* (Sydney: Hale and Iremonger, 1991); Liz Ross, 'Escaping the Well of Loneliness', in Verity Burgmann and Jenny Lee, eds, *Staining the Wattle: A People's History of Australia Since 1788* (Melbourne: McPhee Gribble, 1988), pp. 100–108.

3   On gay liberation rhetoric, see Robert Reynolds, *From Camp to Queer: Remaking the Australian Homosexual* (Melbourne: Melbourne University Press, 2002).

The imperative to silence

The cultural construction of desire between women as unacceptable led many women to fear exposure as a lesbian to parents and family. Robbie recalled:

> It was, without even knowing it, you knew that it was a taboo thing that you didn't go and approach your parents and discuss your feelings with them because they would have been horrified and probably wouldn't have known anything much anyway. But it was just something you instinctively knew you had to keep to yourself because it wasn't something that was nice and it wasn't something that was normal.[4]

Virginia hoped to protect her parents and her relationship with them by concealing this aspect of her life: 'I was more worried about my parents. Like I didn't want my parents to be hurt or them to think differently of me, that was probably my main motivation.'[5] The fear that it would damage relationships with family or friends led many women to conceal their lesbianism, while other women also feared material consequences such as the loss of employment or housing. Coral, who was a musician based in Sydney with her girlfriend in the 1950s, recalled:

> You just didn't talk about it in those days, did you, outside your circle, you didn't talk about it. You went out of your way to disguise the fact that you were gay, you were a lesbian and you were living with a woman … But I travelled a lot, I travelled a lot with companies and theatrical groups and musicians and I could never tell them, never. Some of them sort of suspected but they didn't say anything. You had to be so careful. Really, I've seen people fired, sacked, from the show because … it was acceptable for a gay man. But the girls, no.[6]

For those in the public service and the armed forces, the risks were more clearly defined. In the context of Cold War fears about homosexuality as a security threat, Decision No. 432 was enacted in 1964, requiring male and female homosexuals with access to confidential data to be dismissed from their jobs.[7] For many women, however, the potential consequences of

---

4   Interview with Robbie Hepner by Lucy Chesser.
5   Interview with Virginia Binning and Ruth Ritchie by Sandra Mackay and Rebecca Jennings, Pride History Group Collection, 7 April 2007.
6   Interview with Coral and Rachel by Lucy Chesser, Australian Lesbian and Gay Archives, 20 April 1993.
7   Naomi Cranenburgh, 'From Invisibile to "Menace": Lesbians in Australia from 1939 to 1965' (Honours thesis, Monash University, October 2010), pp. 48–9.

exposure as a lesbian remained vague and ill-defined, and this uncertainty itself compounded the fear. Helen recalled that, when she first became aware of her same-sex attraction in the 1960s: 'It was a very hard time, because you weren't allowed to talk about it and you couldn't sort of, well you didn't feel that you could reveal it to anyone, you didn't know what might happen if you did. It was very hard.'[8]

Concealment strategies

Faced with a range of apparent and more obscure dangers, most women in mid-twentieth century New South Wales, who became aware of their lesbianism sought to conceal their same-sex desires and relationships from those around them. Reflecting on the options which had been open to her as a young lesbian in postwar NSW, Joyce recalled:

> In late adolescence the situation is fraught with conflict, misgivings and often extreme loneliness, particularly (as was common in my youth) when there was no one to talk to about the empty future which seems to lie ahead. The years from twenty to thirty are for most homosexuals filled with searching for some sort of reconciliation or solution, and gradually one sorts out in one's mind the six alternatives which lie open:-
>
> The first one is to seek psychiatric help – but one realises this is not only expensive, and long-term, but holds no great hope of change, and also requires explanation both to family and employer, since very few psychiatrists are available for long-term therapy outside working hours.
>
> The second one is to turn away from love altogether and try to find satisfaction through work, preferably in creative or altruistic fields where some emotional outlet is possible ...
>
> The next alternative and I think the most usual one, is to lead a double life, so that the richest and most important aspect of your life is forced into a pattern of deceit, furtiveness and role-playing, and always overlaid by guilt, and anxiety, because of the deception.
>
> Another alternative is to marry anyway, and this is also quite a frequent occurrence ...

---

8   Interview with Helen [pseudonym], 23 April 2008.

> Another less frequent solution is to marry a homosexual person of the opposite sex, just for the convenience and social acceptability of the situation ...
>
> In some cities, and in some settings, one has the alternative of being quite honest about the situation as soon as one becomes aware of it, but this, even with today's "new morality" is relatively difficult in most places.[9]

The possibility of 'turn[ing] away from love altogether' was a common initial response to the acknowledgement of same-sex desires, but for many women this option produced considerable tensions. Deborah recalled that, having determined that she could not discuss her lesbianism with her family, the only remaining option appeared to be to shut down all possibility of emotional expression. However, this course of action was not as simple as it first appeared:

> So I just decided I'd have to, I'd be single the rest of my life, you know, I'd stay, be my own person the rest of my life, if that was the way it was ... I couldn't let the family know because of ... all of those sort of things, and if I'm never going to like a bloke like that, well I'll just ... concentrate on my career and do all that. But I kept falling in love all over the place![10]

When this policy failed, 'the most usual' alternative, as Joyce observed, was to lead a double life, and this strategy was adopted by many women in different forms. Leading a double life prompted women to construct multiple accounts of themselves and their actions, either inventing cover stories which appeared to indicate a more conventional existence or emphasising one aspect of their lives while downplaying another. When Beverley was planning to relocate from New Zealand to Sydney in the 1930s to embark on a new life with a potential lover, she constructed an alternative narrative centred on her identity as a career woman, in order to render the relocation acceptable to her family. However, at the last moment, Beverley's relationship fell through and 70 years later she still vividly recalled the distress of feeling compelled to travel to Sydney, despite having nowhere to stay, because she could not tell her family what had

---

9   Joyce Geake, 'Shadows and Substance: Reflections of a Lesbian' (Sydney: unpublished manuscript, 1973). Mitchell Library, MLMSS8701, p. 27.
10   Interview with Deborah [pseudonym], 13 November 2008.

happened. Beverley explained that during a previous visit to her cousins in Sydney:

> This particular woman became very enamoured of me and of course I went home and she said 'Will you come back? I'll look after you.' And so stupid [I] went home and after about 6 weeks I, I worked in General Motors in New Zealand and I got a job here [in Sydney] at General Motors before I would let myself come over here because I wouldn't come over without a job. And anyway, about 5 or 6 days before I was due to leave New Zealand, I had a letter from her, saying that her friend had … this woman had a letter from me in her pocket and her friend, her partner, whatever they're called, found it. I don't know how true this is. And she wrote, 'Don't come over, because it'll cause too much trouble. You are breaking up my life.' I couldn't do anything, I had to come! Imagine those 5 days waiting to come on the ship and come over here. I had nowhere to go … That was a terrible thing to do. Imagine, one week before I came over here, I couldn't say anything at home, I couldn't. She said, 'Tell your parents that you've decided you're not coming.' How could I? I'd already got a job here, I couldn't give them a reason. It wouldn't be possible to give them a reason. They wouldn't know the first thing about it.[11]

Beverley felt that her parents would be unable to understand the nature of her relationship with and feelings for this woman, and, rather than inform them of her lesbianism, she opted to take the risk of building a new life in Sydney on her own.

Margaret similarly sought to protect her parents from the knowledge of her sexuality by appearing to conform to the Catholic ideals of chastity and sexual innocence to which she had been raised. When she began a relationship with another woman in her 30s, she took considerable steps to hide it from her family. For Margaret, therefore, embarking on a relationship with a woman in the 1950s meant embarking on a life of deception and concealment – her memory of this love affair was defined by the imperative of keeping it hidden. Feeling that she was responsible for introducing her younger partner, Jann, to a life of deceit, Margaret explained her sense of guilt:

> Even then I knew it was difficult, because it was such a secret I had to keep, so I knew, and the way we were foxing around and lying and telling everyone different stories, I knew it was a very difficult position

---

11 Interview with Beverley and Georgina, 22 December 2008.

I was placing her in so I told myself that I wasn't going to, that she shouldn't be damaged by me seducing her, encouraging her into this way of life.[12]

Margaret and Jann constructed an elaborate cover story for their life together, presenting themselves as friends and work colleagues while regarding themselves as lovers and partners.

While Beverley and Margaret were concerned primarily with concealing their lesbianism from their families, a number of women described how their parents, particularly their mothers, were complicit in helping them to hide their same-sex attraction from society at large. Paddy and her partner Robbie met as nurses in the 1950s, but ultimately left the profession after being exposed as lesbians and losing their jobs. From there the women became travelling musicians, passing themselves off as sisters with the support of Robbie's parents. Paddy explained:

> We couldn't afford to be open about our lesbianism. We'd already been discriminated against, lost our jobs, and that wasn't through being open – we thought we were being very hush-hush! ... We eventually established our own school of music and had more pupils than we knew what to do with ... The money we earned helped to buy house and land, enabling us to bring Robbie's parents to Australia [from the UK]. Since they had adopted me, and I'd already had my name changed [to Robbie's] by deed-poll, in the public eye we were sisters, a cover-up which put a stop to any questions – except the perennial 'Why aren't you married?' We answered with an equally perennial excuse, 'Oh! In our day, nurses weren't allowed to marry, so we never have!' It annoys me that convention forces you to do these things; you've got to live a lie.[13]

Some families became aware of a woman's lesbianism despite her attempts at concealment. In their study of the lesbian bar community which existed in Buffalo, New York between the 1930s and 1950s, Elizabeth Kennedy and Madeline Davis argue that this was almost inevitable given the nature of family life and the roles of unmarried women in this period. They suggest:

> As in work life, discretion was the rule for family life. However, the goal of keeping employers and fellow workers completely ignorant of one's lesbian identity, and the strategy of absolute separation between

---

12 Interview with Margaret Jones, 12 September 2007.
13 Paddy Byrnes, 'La Vie en rose 1956', in Margaret Bradstock and Louise Wakeling, eds, *Words from the Same Heart* (Sydney: Hale & Iremonger, 1987), pp. 27–28.

work life and social life, were not directly applicable to family life. By definition, family takes an active interest in its members' social life, and expects its members to participate in the same activities. For a lesbian to separate her social life and family life inevitably raised suspicion at the same time that it offered protection. This was particularly true in the 1930s and 1940s when unmarried working-class women were expected to live at home with their families rather than developing independent lives.[14]

Families, they claim, were frequently aware of their daughter's lesbianism but often collaborated with women in hiding it, and avoided raising the issue, even amongst themselves. In Australia too, even women who were not part of the sort of lesbian social scene Kennedy and Davis were describing often found it difficult to conceal their same-sex desires from their families. When Helen formed an attachment to a ward sister during her nursing training in the early 1960s, the pressure of having to conceal her feelings, and the sense that acting on them was 'strictly forbidden', prompted her to attempt suicide. The attempt failed and during her recovery, she was sent to see a psychiatrist and recalled:

> And the psychiatrist said to me 'Why did you do this?' and I told him. And he said 'Well don't you tell anybody else otherwise they'll throw you in the nut factory' – well he didn't say nut factory – 'you'll go into a mental hospital and just keep your mouth shut and don't say another word about it'. And so I did. I never ever said another word about it … 'Just don't talk about it. It's not true, it's not happening, you're not that kind of person and therefore don't say it again.'

Helen's mother had been invited to attend the interview and was consequently also made aware of Helen's feelings. Helen remembered:

> My mother was aware of this and she was really upset because she didn't know what to do. But she was very supportive of me … She just said 'Put it out of your head, [Helen].' I mean she was following what he was saying, I think. She said 'Just don't, don't talk about it'. I mean, I think it was something that flabbergasted her. But realistically she felt it was best, because I think she was really anxious that I finish my qualification. I didn't want to get chucked out of nursing, not at

---

14 Elizabeth Lapovsky Kennedy and Madeline Davis, *Boots of Leather, Slippers of Gold: The History of a Lesbian Community* (New York: Penguin, 1993), p. 57.

third year after being there all that time. And that's what could have happened. I could have been you know, turfed out. So I went, sort of did what they expected of me, and got through nursing.[15]

Although Helen remembered both the psychiatrist's and her mother's advice as well-intentioned, aiming to shield her from the consequences of wider exposure, she ultimately felt compelled to suppress her same-sex desire and conform to broader social expectations of heterosexuality. She began to date boys and some years later, married, before finally constructing a lesbian identity for herself in the 1980s.

Helen's experience was typical of many women in this period, who entered into heterosexual marriages despite being aware of same-sex desires, either in the hope that marriage would 'cure' them of their homosexuality, or simply under pressure to conform. When Elizabeth met her partner, Joy, at a fete organised by the lesbian and gay campaigning group CAMP Inc in the early 1970s, Joy was married with two children. They entered into a relationship and Joy subsequently divorced her husband. Joy's experience of previous heterosexual marriage was sufficiently common that she was able to form a married people's sub-group within CAMP. When Elizabeth and Joy joined the lesbian social group Clover in 1972, Elizabeth recalled 'There seemed to be quite a few married women, not, I didn't meet any that were living with their husbands at the time, they were divorced or separated or things like that but they had been married and there were children around quite a bit.'[16]

Literary representations of same-sex desire

For those women who lived discreet lives or who were unable to locate other lesbians in this period, literature and other cultural representations of same-sex desire played an important role in alleviating their sense of isolation. Novels with lesbian characters or themes enabled women both to find a language for their own desires and to realise that they were not alone. Their significance to women in this period is testified to by the frequency with which lists of lesbian literature appeared in early issues of lesbian and feminist journals. Although identifying and obtaining lesbian-themed literature could be problematic without the assistance of such lists, reading these works offered women the opportunity to engage with a discourse of same-

---

15 Interview with Helen [pseudonym], 23 April 2008.
16 Interview with Elizabeth by Ruth Ford, Australian Lesbian and Gay Archive, 6 May 1992.

sex desire without the risks of exposure inherent in reaching out physically to other lesbians. In an article entitled 'On the Virtues of Remaining in Your Closet!', contributed by 'a gaygirl' to lesbian and gay paper *Campaign* in the 1970s, one discreet lesbian drew on a rich array of cultural sources to reinforce her impassioned plea for the right to conceal her sexuality.[17] The author attached no personal details to the article and observed that she planned to 'post this anonymously from a suburb I don't live in'. Her family, she claimed, was hostile to homosexuality and unaware of her own same-sex desires, as were her friends and work colleagues. Nevertheless, she noted that 'about the time I discovered I was gay, I read everything I could on the subject of homosexuality.' The article demonstrated that, while maintaining a 'closeted' identity in everyday life, she had been able to actively participate in a discursive lesbian and gay community through the medium of the press, the theatre and *Campaign* itself. In assembling her arguments, she referred to a letter to the editor of an Australian newspaper by a gay man; an article in *Time Magazine* entitled 'Gays on the March'; and a performance of Peter Kenna's play *Mates* at the Nimrod Theatre in Sydney. Her consumption of cultural representations of homosexuality had helped to shape her own sense of gay identity and community, and ultimately enabled her to enter into dialogue with that community without conflicting with the need for concealment.

In earlier decades, however, women's need for such literature, and the difficulties of locating it, were correspondingly increased. The cultural imperative to silence desire between women and to conceal it from families and society at large was reinforced for much of the mid-twentieth century by the paucity of literary and media portrayals of the subject. Margaret commented that books were neither accessible nor relevant in her attempt to make sense of her same-sex desires in the late 1950s:

> It didn't occur to me again that there would have been books on such a topic. And let us look at where was public reading in those days. There was only public libraries and there wouldn't be such a book in the library – well, if there was, you'd have had to ask the librarian for it. 'Excuse me, miss, have you got a book on lesbians?'! No, and as we know, I hadn't read, I wasn't a reader, I'd had no education and no interest in reading or understanding of it, so I knew nothing more than just those brief sexual acts.[18]

---

17 Anon, 'On the Virtues of Remaining in Your Closet!' *Campaign no. 18*, p. 9.
18 Interview with Margaret Jones, 12 September 2007.

As Margaret noted, literary representations of desire between women were extremely limited prior to the 1970s and were rendered largely inaccessible by the difficulties of locating them. For working-class women such as Margaret, who had not been raised in a culture of reading, literature did not in any case represent an obvious source of information. Strict censorship laws further restricted access to such works in Australia.

The importing of books and written materials deemed indecent or obscene was banned under the Trade and Customs Act 1901, and thereafter many of the decisions regarding which titles should be banned were taken arbitrarily by individual Customs officials who seized books at the point of entry into Australia. In 1933, the Book Censorship Board (renamed the Literature Censorship Board in 1937 and ultimately disbanded in 1967) was established to consider those books which were deemed marginal or literary.[19] The presence of homosexuality as a theme was accepted as grounds for censorship and Nicole Moore argues that:

> Censors actively targeted the expression of same-sex desire, descriptions of gay, lesbian, bisexual, transsexual, and cross-dressed sexual practice, the elaboration of gay and lesbian identities as identities, agitation against restrictions on the expression of same-sex themes, as well as many other forms of meaning moving beyond a straight, reproductive model for intimacy and sexual life. Until late in the twentieth century, homosexuality was seen as a pornographic and perverted form of obscenity where present in literary or popular novels, avant-garde poetry or films of all kinds, magazines or postcards. From the earliest moments of government censorship in Australia, and increasingly as an explicit priority, the erasure of homosexual meaning from as many public fora and discourses as possible was achieved to a significant degree.[20]

A number of notable lesbian novels were banned, severely limiting the availability of literary representations of female same-sex desire. Radclyffe Hall's controversial British lesbian novel, *The Well of Loneliness*, was banned in 1929, following its obscenity trials in the UK and US. Moore claims that Australian censors attempted to obtain a copy of the novel following its prohibition in England in 1928. However, they were unable to locate one as

---

19   Nicole Moore, 'National Parapraxis: Sex and Forgetting in Australian Censorship History', *Australian Historical Studies*, vol. 36, no. 126 (2005), pp. 296–314.
20   Nicole Moore, *The Censor's Library* (Brisbane: University of Queensland Press, 2012), p.131.

such copies as had been circulating in Australia had apparently been sent to England in the wake of the trial to be sold on the lucrative black market there. In the absence of a review copy, Customs officials banned it sight unseen on the basis of English law. The ban was lifted in Australia some time between 1939 and 1946, unusually prior to the UK release date of 1949. However, the absence of a high-profile obscenity trial like that which occurred in the UK, Moore argues, meant that lesbian identity was not publicly debated in Australia in the same way. She claims:

> The book's sensational prosecution in the UK and equally sensational acquittal of obscenity charges in the US attracted some ongoing press coverage in Australia, but Customs worked hard to remove it from circulation silently and without scandal. It was withdrawn from public access before a copy even could be procured, and banned with no reference to expertise or community standards and no accountability to an uninformed public, while underground copies were elaborately tracked and seized.[21]

The secrecy surrounding *The Well*'s subsequent Australian release further limited its availability in Australia, where many booksellers remained unaware that it was now legally possible to order copies and offer the novel for sale. It was not until the mid-1960s that US lesbian pulp fiction, such as Tereska Torres' *Women's Barracks*, was allowed through Australian Customs and it was a further decade before the first Australian lesbian novel, Kerryn Higgs' *All That False Instruction*, was published.[22]

Despite the difficulties of locating literary representations of female same-sex desire in mid-twentieth century Australia, however, some women clearly managed to do so. By the 1960s a number of international lesbian novels were officially available in Australia, but even a generation earlier, despite strict censorship, women were able to obtain a limited range of lesbian-themed literature. Beverley recalled buying a copy of *The Well of Loneliness* in 'one of the big bookshops in Sydney' immediately after the war while 'C.P.' told British lesbian magazine *Arena Three* about her experience borrowing the novel from a Sydney library in 1950:

> I recall the day, back in 1950, when a friend warmly recommended *The Well of Loneliness* as a book that would interest me. With all the brave

---

21 Moore, *The Censor's Library*, p.134.
22 'Banned in Australia', http://www.austlit.edu.au/specialistDatasets/Banned/bullockMoore.

innocence of 18, I rushed off to the local twopenny lending library (do such establishments still exist?) in a very suburban little backwater of Sydney, Australia, to ask for a copy. At once a copy was brought from the shelves – which couldn't have held more than a few hundred books – and off I went, down the blistering hot asphalt road, heart thumping, to read the entire book in one afternoon, in the garden in a temperature of over 100°F. The book depicted a way of life and thought as alien as life on Mars to me. Even so, I read it with a great sense of relief and, somehow, of recognition. Strange as it seems now, looking back, the woman proprietor of the library, far from giving me a suspicious look when I asked for that title, actually discussed the book sympathetically, telling me it was 'such a sad story'. As I grew older, though, I grew less bold. Ever afterwards, if I went to buy or borrow a homosexual book, I always ordered three or four other books at the same time by way of camouflage![23]

In the 1950s, Georgie came across *The Straggler* by Danish novelist Agnete Holk.[24] *The Straggler* was passed by the Literature Censorship Board in 1954, and board member Kenneth Binns noted: 'this is the first time, to my knowledge, that a novel dealing seriously with the subject of lesbianism has been submitted to the board'.[25] Even when women were able to locate lesbian-themed books in bookshops or newsstands, purchasing such a book often proved a challenge for women accustomed to a life of concealment. Kerryn Higgs recalled the difficulties a friend of hers had experienced in attempting to buy *The Well of Loneliness*:

> I remember a friend telling me the story that she was unable to buy *The Well of Loneliness* even though it had no subtitle [identifying it as lesbian] for she was afraid of what the cashier would think, so she pinched it instead.[26]

Higgs was concerned that her publisher's decision to append the subtitle 'A novel of Lesbian Love' to her own novel, *All That False Instruction*, would create similar obstacles for women who wished to obtain the book discreetly.

---

23 *Arena Three*, vol. 4, no. 9 (September 1967), p. 14.
24 Interview with Beverley [pseudonym] and Georgina, 22 December 2008.
25 NAA A3023 Folder 1954, cited in Moore, *The Censor's Library*.
26 Elizabeth Riley, 'Elizabeth Riley talks with Sue Ross about her book All That False Instruction', *Campaign* (June 1976), p. 12.

The impact of lesbian literature on women who had encountered few, if any, depictions of desire between women varied considerably. Deborah described her discovery of Violette Le Duc's novel *La Batarde* in 1965 as a revelation, it being her first encounter with representations of lesbianism. She reflected:

> I was at university and I went into the bookshop to buy some books for my course, and way down the end in the fiction section, I saw this lurid cover on a book. And it was bright lights, and I couldn't really make it out from that far away, but it attracted me. And I went down and it was called La Batarde ... by a French writer called Violette Le Duc. And I didn't know much, I didn't know this person, I didn't know the book, I didn't know anything, but I was very much into the, you know, this was the French philosopher stage of your life, you know your Sartres and all of that and French. So I just had to buy it, and I bought it. And that was the first time I came across any kind of reference to women loving women. And I think she might even have used the word lesbian, so it was the first time I found that word.[27]

For Deborah, the experience had a profound effect on her understanding of her own sexuality. She recalled: 'So I read the book, and then I thought "Wow! This is me, this explains how I feel."'[28] Other women, however, felt that literary portrayals of lesbianism simply reinforced broader cultural messages about silence and isolation. Laurie complained that the cheap paperback novels she read in the 1960s and early 1970s were 'so depressing, there was never a happy ending. They [the lesbian characters] either got killed, or went straight and saw the errors of their ways and all that sort of shit.'[29] When Robyn told her mother that she was a lesbian in the early 1970s, her mother was concerned about the risk of loneliness and Robyn connected this fear with Radclyffe Hall's novel, *The Well of Loneliness*:

> She said, 'Oh, you'll be lonely when you get old'. And I think it's very interesting because she actually told my two sisters and some of her close friends the next day, so I thought that was good that she'd actually come out and said all of that, because that's an acknowledgement of it. But one of her friends said, 'Oh, we'll send you *The Well of Loneliness*'

---

27   Interview with Deborah [pseudonym], 13 November 2008.
28   Interview with Deborah [pseudonym], 13 November 2008.
29   Interview with Laurie van Camp by Sandra Mackay, Prode History Group Collection, 18 February 2008.

and I thought that is the worst book that anyone could give someone, you'd think you end up suiciding or whatever else. And I think she's always clung to it, and I think that's a general perception that you'll be lonely in your own life, and yet in comparison to my two sisters, I have so many friends it's not funny.[30]

When Kerryn Higgs' semi-autobiographical novel *All That False Instruction* was published in 1975, its reception was an indicator of how much, and how little, had changed. Despite the author having been awarded a publisher's prize to develop the book, when the lesbian content of the novel became known, familial disapproval and threats of legal action forced the publisher (Angus & Robertson) to delay publication and the author to publish under the pseudonym Elizabeth Riley.[31] Reviewers in the Melbourne *Age* and *The Australian* objected to the novel's lesbian theme and its depiction of men. Olaf Ruhen complained that the novel was primarily:

> About the exercises and frustrations of tribadism, with a few hetero experiences thrown in for contrast … That the lady can write well is abundantly apparent in many places, but in others a deliberate predilection for gutter language makes much of the communication repugnant.[32]

John Lapsley found the novel's depiction of lesbianism 'sensitive' but commented that:

> The men [Maureen Craig] meets are, almost without exception, emotionally incompetent and, without exception, sexually incompetent … One is forced to quibble with Elizabeth Riley's presentation of the male of the species.[33]

However, the existence in 1975 of a flourishing feminist and gay press meant that the novel was also received into an appreciative political environment and it was widely reviewed in lesbian and feminist circles. Sue Bellamy, reviewing the novel for feminist journal *Refractory Girl*, described it as an 'exceptional piece of work'. Her engagement with the novel derived to a considerable extent from her identification with the experiences of the lesbian central character and, by extension, the author. She observed:

---

30 Interview with Robyn Plaister, 20 December 2007.
31 Harriet Malinowitz, 'Introduction', in Kerryn Higgs, *All That False Instruction* (Melbourne: Spinifex Press Pty Ltd, 2001), pp. xi–xxiii.
32 Olaf Ruhen, *Melbourne Age*, 21 February 1976, cited in Malinowitz, 'Introduction', p. xxi.
33 John Lapsley, *The Australian*, 1975, cited in Malinowitz, 'Introduction', p. xxi.

Concealment and Isolation

> In framework and theme, in setting and evocation, this book is part of a very familiar tradition to me. I feel part of the story, not only in time and events, but in thought processes and ways of conceiving reality.[34]

For lesbian readers, and particularly those outside of the feminist community addressed by Sue Bellamy, this familiarity could be a source of both comfort and discomfort. While for Bellamy and others, reading from the relative safety of 1975, the sense of shared experience was validating, the setting of the book in the different cultural context of 1960s New South Wales could be unsettling. Escaping a rural working-class upbringing, the novel's heroine, Maureen Craig, wins a scholarship to attend university in Sydney, where she embarks on a succession of relationships with other women. However, social disapproval from home and at college constrains these relationships, prompting the women to conceal their feelings for each other. In a dialogue between Maureen and her first lover, Julia, Higgs explores the impact of concealment and the isolation experienced by lesbians in this period:

> 'Perhaps the best thing would be to stop,' Julia suggested.
>
> 'What? Stop sleeping together?'
>
> 'Stop making love. Just be friends.'
>
> 'That's impossible.'
>
> 'But it makes you so guilty, Maureen.'
>
> 'It also makes me happy.'
>
> 'Sometimes. But it can't go on forever, anyway. It's dangerous. It'll have to end somewhere.'
>
> 'I don't see why.'
>
> 'Because, well, women can't spend their entire lives together.'
>
> 'Why not? I like sharing your life.'
>
> 'Can't you imagine what it'd be like living your whole life in secret? Always afraid it'll leak out?'
>
> 'I'm not going to let other people run my life. Anyway, we could escape.'[35]

---

34 Sue Bellamy, 'Fucking Men is for Saints', *Refractory Girl*, June 1976, p. 32. See also Jean Taylor, *Brazen Hussies: A Herstory of Radical Activism in the Women's Liberation Movement in Victoria, 1970–1979* (Melbourne: Dyke Books Inc, 2009), pp. 372–3.

35 Elizabeth Riley, *All That False Instruction: A Novel of Lesbian Love* (London, Angus and Robertson, 1975), pp. 58–59.

Despite Maureen's fantasies of escape, fear of exposure is ultimately too much for all three of Maureen's lovers, who in turn abandon Maureen in search of social conformity. Her story reflected the experience of many women who desired other women in this period but whose relationships were constrained by the pressures of secrecy.

Cultural representations of lesbianism

From the late 1960s, a steady increase in television programs and films began to explore the issue of same-sex desire. On 15 February 1966, Channel 7 courted controversy by airing a ground-breaking documentary on lesbians, entitled 'Love is Love', as part of their *Seven Days* series.[36] The program, presented by Anne Deveson, offered a sympathetic depiction of lesbians as 'normal' women. Using interviews with individual lesbians, it set out to test the existing stereotypes around female homosexuality, claiming that many lesbians are 'attractive girls, not mannish', that sex is a minor aspect of lesbian intimacy and that good lesbian relationships do not have a dominant partner. Nevertheless, the program reflected and reinforced the broader cultural imperative of silence in a number of ways. While many cultural commentators of the period suggested that given the absence of legal penalties, lesbians faced no social difficulties, Deveson asked her interviewees about the problems of being a lesbian, and was told of the need for secrecy, the loneliness and isolation, the difficulty finding and keeping jobs and the anxiety about the attitudes of family. One woman claimed: 'If you wish to lead a normal social life you must lead a double life. I'm not ashamed in any way, shape or form of the way I am.' Interviewees rarely showed their faces, appearing either in silhouette or with their backs to the camera. The response of lesbian viewers to the program is unclear, but viewer surveys of the program's mainstream audience were sympathetic and recognised the difficulties faced by lesbians as a result of the culture of silence. *Sun* newspaper readers identified it as the pick of the evening's viewing, with Mrs Gwen Thompson commenting:

> The show really made you think ... I have known about lesbianism, of course. I knew these people existed, but the show made you realise they are human beings after all and have feelings the same as everybody

---

36 'Love is Love', *Seven Days* Episode 7 (Canberra: ScreenSound Australia, 2003), originally aired Tuesday 15 February 1966.

else. They have this one quirk ... but who doesn't have some quirk that makes them different.[37]

Mrs Little agreed that the program was thought-provoking, arguing: 'It's right that these type of things be brought out into the open – at least it makes people think about them.'[38]

'Love is Love' was followed by an increasing number of programs and films touching on homosexuality in the late 1960s and early 1970s, many of which reinforced a message that life for a lesbian was a miserable, lonely affair, constrained by lies and concealment. The British lesbian play *The Killing of Sister George*, performed in Sydney in 1966, depicted an unequal and emotionally abusive relationship between an older, masculine lesbian (George) and her younger, feminine lover (Childie). Newspaper reports gave a subdued response, focusing primarily on the quality of acting and downplaying the lesbian content. Roger Covell informed *Sydney Morning Herald* readers that the play 'has some intimations of pathos and an insistent murmur of lesbianism'. Harking back to a lost age of innocence, Covell complained that 'Ten or 20 years ago the play would have been content with funny lines and intimations of pathos and would not have needed or been allowed its lesbianism.'[39] Francis Evers in *The Australian* addressed the issue of lesbianism more explicitly. Reproducing long-standing assumptions about same-sex relationships as between a domineering confirmed lesbian and an impressionable feminine woman, Evers described George as 'a beefy, boozy, lesbian radio actress' who 'shares an apartment with a 35-year-old child-woman friend, "Childie" McNaught'. The exact nature of the two women's relationship was not clarified by Evers, who referred to George as Childie's 'mentor' and 'friend'. His review reiterated the loneliness of lesbian existence, both by representing George as the only lesbian character in the drama and with a number of comments on the isolation of George's 'lonely passions': 'The land of Lesbos', he told *Australian* readers, 'is a solitary battlefield.'[40] Three years later, the film version of *The Killing of Sister George* was released in Australia, enabling the drama to reach broader audiences. One lesbian viewer recalled, through the perspective of her subsequent political awareness:

---

37 *The Sun*, Wednesday 16 February 1966, p. 4.
38 *The Sun*, Wednesday 16 February 1966, p. 4.
39 Roger Covell, 'Fun and Pathos on the Dodgem: The Killing of Sister George', *Sydney Morning Herald*, 27 July 1966, p. 15.
40 Francis Evers, 'Neat Truths and Comic Truisms', *The Australian*, 30 July 1966, p. 11.

In 1969 I saw *The Killing of Sister George*. I was a 'closet' gay girl. The film fascinated and disturbed me. I recognised the marginality of the main characters, but sensed that they were somehow pathetic and bad. I remember feeling very guilty, and hating myself to the point of self-mutilation. When I reviewed the film in my mid-twenties I understood a lot more about 'gay identity' in a straight world, and my appreciation of George's resilience in adversity blocked out any sinister messages. I saw the film again after my introduction to feminism and was acutely aware of the skewed stereotypes of George, Childe [sic], and Mrs Mercy, of the film's underlying misogyny, and the implicit message that heterosex was the healthy way to go.[41]

Laurie also recalled *The Killing of Sister George* with mixed feelings, commenting: 'that was a wonderful movie but it was … I gave up on that for a while. Because my life was depressing enough without having to see yourself sort of portrayed as that.'[42]

John B Murray's film *The Naked Bunyip* (1970), which described itself as 'the first serious study of sex in Australia (in a funny sort of way)', included a section on lesbianism which reinforced a sense of lesbians as marginal figures in Australian society. The film was structured as a comic skit featuring a fictional young market researcher assigned to report on sex, but the majority of the film was composed of interviews with real people describing their sexual experiences. Reflecting on the production of the film, John B Murray recalled:

> While I found it a challenge to find practising and retired prostitutes for The Naked Bunyip, that could not be compared to the difficulty of enlisting the participation of homosexuals. I believe that no homosexual, male or female, had agreed to publicly appear on film or television before that time. The search began in mid 1969 and I pursued the matter during filming in three states with no success, except for one man who agreed to a short interview on the condition that his head and torso would not be shown, and that his voice would be dubbed by another's. For nearly nine months following the end of shooting, up until just prior to the last stage of editing and post-production, I continued the hunt … At the last minute … I found two young active lesbians who were also brave enough to participate, but did not agree to

---

41   Casuarina, 'Refusing to be a Woman: Being Not-woman, Not-man', *Journal of Australian Lesbian Feminist Studies*, vol. 4 (June 1994), p. 62
42   Interview with Laurie van Camp, 18 February 2008.

be named. These ... persons could not be seen as representative of all homosexuals. Their experience was a little more traumatic than that of the majority. Yet it gave them the courage to speak out. I quickly got the crew together, and recorded open and frank accounts of their life as homosexuals in a community that neither accepted them nor evidenced much compassion.[43]

The film's depiction of lesbians as ostracised by society was reinforced by Murray's handling of censorship. Murray had envisaged the film as an attempt to challenge Australians to consider their views on sexuality, and when film censors requested that he delete a number of scenes from the film, he decided to incorporate a statement on censorship into the film itself. Instead of simply cutting the required sections, Murray blacked out the offending scenes, allowing viewers to see which sections of the film had been deemed obscene. Two sequences from the lesbian segment were blacked out, one of which had depicted the two lesbians kissing and the other in which one lesbian interviewee explained that she found sex with men repugnant.[44] The effect was to underline the extent to which female same-sex desire was regarded as marginal and unacceptable in Australian society.

Private networks

Early encounters with lesbian-themed literature and film afforded some women a point of introduction into a language and cultural framework for thinking about same-sex desire, but the passive and solitary nature of reading could also leave women feeling more isolated, with no one to discuss their impressions with. However, by the late 1950s the beginnings of an international homosexual movement offered new opportunities for Australian women to reach out to others and especially to seek discursive lesbian networks overseas without revealing their same-sex desires to family and friends in Australia. Rachel recalled that in the early 1960s: 'I think people were sending off subscriptions to American magazines even in those days' and this is confirmed by letters which appeared in a number of overseas magazines from Australian readers.[45] *The Ladder*, produced by US

---

43 John B Murray, 'The Genesis of The Naked Bunyip', *Senses of Cinema*, Issue 38, February 2006, http://sensesofcinema.com/2006/38/naked_bunyip/
44 'Film Censorship 1970–1971: The Naked Bunyip (1970)', Refused Classification: Film Censorship in Australia, http://www.refused-classification.com/censorship/films/1970-to-1971-naked-bunyip.html, accessed 17 April 2013.
45 Interview with Coral and Rachel, 20 April 1993.

lesbian organisation Daughters of Bilitis from 1956 onwards, clearly had an Australian readership. The magazine's round-up of international news frequently referred to stories in Australian and British newspapers, which were derived from clippings sent in by an Australian reader, and from 1970 onwards letters and magazines were received from Marion Norman of the Melbourne Daughters of Bilitis chapter.

British lesbian magazine *Arena Three* also had at least two contributors from New South Wales and potentially many more subscribers and readers. First published in 1964 by Londoner Esme Langley with the support of three or four other women, *Arena Three* provided a combination of articles, sketches, news items and a letters page for 'homosexual women' readers.[46] In 1964, Kate Hinton contributed two articles, including 'The Homophile Down Under', which offered a sketch of lesbian life in NSW and reported on broader social attitudes to lesbianism in Australia.[47] The following year, G Mackenzie of Sydney wrote a number of times, enclosing donations to assist the magazine in continuing its work. She congratulated the editor: 'You are doing a wonderful service to homosexual women. I hope you can keep it going. I look forward each month to receiving A3 and only wish we had something like it out here.' This, she felt, was an idle hope, and she complained: 'I guess we are never likely to see an ad in our paper like those you put in "New Statesmen" etc. I guess our mob would have pups on the spot.'[48] Her wish was apparently echoed by other Australian subscribers as in July 1968 the editor advised readers that 'two Australian girls have recently written from New South Wales to say that, inspired by the example of A3, they would like to start a publication in the Antipodes, and would like our expert advice.'[49] Perhaps discouraged by the rather disheartening advice offered by the *Arena Three* editor, they did not, however, start an Australian magazine.

For Australian subscribers in the 1950s and 1960s, American and British lesbian magazines offered opportunities to feel part of a lesbian community which were not available to them elsewhere. For some, they were invaluable in

---

46 Rebecca Jennings, *Tomboys and Bachelor Girls: A Lesbian History of Post-war Britain, 1945–71* (Manchester: Manchester University Press, 2007); Alison Oram, 'Little by Little? Arena Three and Lesbian Politics in the 1960s', in Marcus Collins, ed., *The Permissive Society and its Enemies: Sixties British Culture* (London: Rivers Oram, 2007).
47 Kate Hinton, 'The Homophile Down Under – What's Up Down Under', *Arena Three*, vol. 1, no. 10 (October 1964), pp. 6–9; Kate Hinton, 'Looking After Mum', *Arena Three*, vol. 2, no. 3 (March 1965), pp. 3–4.
48 Letter from G Mackenzie, Sydney, 'Mailbag', *Arena Three*, vol. 2, no. 10 (October 1965), p. 13.
49 'Standing Up Down Under', *Arena Three*, vol. 5, no. 7. (July 1968), p. 11.

demonstrating the existence of other lesbians and the range of communities and identities which existed. As M B M of NSW wrote to *Arena Three* in 1966:

> I have just read a 1964 copy of your magazine, 'Arena Three', passed on by a former subscriber. This copy is the first I have read and I hope not the last. It is exceedingly honest and witty and quite a revelation to a back-room girl like me.[50]

Letters often expressed the profound loneliness which women who were not part of a lesbian social network experienced in mid-twentieth century NSW. In 1958 Miss S. from Sidney [sic], Australia wrote to *One* magazine, based in Los Angeles:

> I know your magazine is not a lonely hearts magazine, but it seems my only hope. I am very unhappy. I'm desperate to write to a lady who will write to me. I am 26 and I don't like men.[51]

Seven years later, an Australian reader placed a classified advertisement in *Arena Three* stating, 'Lonely Dutch migrant wants correspondence with lady 25/35 interested in migrating to Australia.'[52] While simply reading such magazines helped to alleviate the isolation engendered by the cultural silence around same-sex desire, some women saw these networks as a potential introduction to more personal and intimate relationships. They also provide occasional insights into existing social networks and their role in transmitting information. In 1970, an Australian reader enquired of *The Ladder*:

> I am twenty and my girlfriend (I'll call her Sadie) is twenty-two. We have been sharing an apartment for a year, going to bars, and all that stuff. Yesterday a friend of Sadie's asked her what I was like in bed. When she said I wore striped pajamas and slept like a log, the friend laughed. Now we think maybe we are missing out on something. Could you fill us in?[53]

In the context of scarce cultural representations of lesbianism, it is possible to read this letter as evidence that overseas magazines provided an invaluable source of information, even to women who were part of a wider lesbian network in Australia. However, it is perhaps more likely that this reader, who was part of a more knowing lesbian subculture centred on public bars,

---

50 Letter from M B M, NSW, 'Overseas Page', *Arena Three*, vol. 3, no. 9 (October 1966), p. 2.
51 'Dear Editor', *One*, vol. 6, no. 3 (March 1958), p. 29.
52 'Classified Advertisements', *Arena Three*, vol. 2, no. 3 (March 1965), loose sheet.
53 'Questions for Cassandra', *The Ladder*, October/November 1970, p. 12.

was poking fun at the discreet representations of lesbianism typical of US and British lesbian magazines in this period, which avoided direct references to sexual activity between women out of a concern not to offend either the censors or a sensitive middle-class readership.

While overseas lesbian magazines offered a lifeline to some women in mid-twentieth century NSW, as with other literary representations of same-sex desire, access was limited by strict censorship laws. Several Australian readers of *One* magazine, which catered to both homosexual men and lesbians in the 1950s and 1960s, complained that their copies had been seized by Customs, while readers of *Arena Three* experienced similar difficulties. Such seizures were apparently sporadic and often dependent on Customs building up a gradual awareness of the content of overseas journals. In September 1966, G Mackenzie of Sydney told *Arena Three*:

> I got Bryan Magee's book, 'One in Twenty', but in a way I think it is a pity that he gives publicity to MRG and Arena Three, because I suppose that will be the next thing to be stopped by Customs out here.
>
> I noticed after the 'Grapevine' came out for sale in Australia giving publicity to DOB and 'The Ladder', it was after that time that Customs started to confiscate my copies of 'The Ladder' – they didn't seem to know of its existence before that. 'The Grapevine' was reviewed by Customs in late 1965, before it was allowed to be sold to the public, and in 1966 they confiscated my January and February 'Ladder' and have got 4 more since then. So the publicity for A3 was no good, as far as I am concerned.[54]

G Mackenzie's comments reflect the ambivalence felt by some lesbian readers in this period toward open discussion of lesbianism and lesbian communities. Although a degree of publicity was necessary to enable women to locate resources such as *Arena Three*, increased discussion carried its own risks. Letters to *Arena Three* and *The Ladder* in the 1950s and 1960s indicate that readers used these magazines in different ways. While some women undoubtedly read them in the privacy of their own home, as a means of seeking input from other lesbians without compromising their discreet way of life, others wished to be a more active member of a discursive community, contributing articles and letters in order to enter a dialogue with other readers. For others still, these magazines offered a potential route to a

---

54   Letter from Australia, *Arena Three*, vol. 3, no. 8 (September 1966), p. 2.

material community of other lesbians, which might be reached either by placing lonely hearts advertisements or by requesting information about lesbian social networks based in bars or private homes.

In 1968, the editors of *Arena Three* put two readers from NSW in contact with another from Melbourne, enabling the women to meet directly with each other.[55] A small number of Australian women also travelled to the US and Britain to participate in the social networks attached to lesbian magazines: in 1969 *Arena Three* thanked Rene V, an Australian woman who had been organising the magazine's London social group, for all her work for the magazine, on the occasion of her return to Australia. The editorial team at that time also included another Australian, Carol Potter.[56] While these women lived for some time in the UK and became embedded in British lesbian social networks, others made contact with overseas lesbian groups while travelling. Margaret described a visit she made to the offices of the Daughters of Bilitis while on a trip to San Francisco in the early 1960s. Margaret was staying with friends on a naval camp, and these circumstances shaped her encounter with the Daughters of Bilitis women:

> [T]hey were in an office building, it was just their office where they published that magazine called *The Ladder*. And it was the third floor or something in an office building on Market Street, so I just thought I'd just go up there and see what was happening. But I was dressed in the manner befitting a visitor from abroad staying with a Lieutenant-Commander and his wife and I got there, introduced myself, I was from Australia and one little dyke said 'Are you really a lesbian?' I can see why she asked that question because I looked like some respectable housewife ... And then they said there were all sorts of events and dances and things and could I, would I go with them, but of course I could not, well unless I'd have to make some silly excuse and where would I say that I was going to my hosts?[57]

Encounters with overseas lesbians could be positive and welcoming, offering openings into the vibrant lesbian subcultures which existed in some cities in the US and elsewhere. On this occasion, Margaret felt unable to incorporate this social scene into the respectable parameters of her visit to a naval camp, but, on her return to Australia she did begin to explore the possibilities of lesbian bar culture in Sydney.

---

55 Letter to *Arena Three*, vol. 5, no. 8 (August 68), p. 13.
56 *Arena Three*, vol. 6, no. 12 (December 69), p. 12.
57 Interview with Margaret Jones, 12 September 2007.

Chapter 3

A ROOM FULL OF WOMEN: LESBIAN BARS AND SOCIAL SPACES IN POSTWAR SYDNEY[1]

In November 1971, youth magazine *Go-Set* informed its readers:

> Camp dances in this city are booming: in terms of week-to-week drawing power, the dances are dwarfing the slightly weak straight-dance scene. As well as the dances, there are also a few camp wine bars ... packed with people.[2]

Since the 1970s, Sydney has developed an international reputation for its vibrant gay nightlife, but as a port city Sydney had already been enjoying a homosexual male scene for much of the previous century. Historians have recorded a range of bars, coffee shops and drag balls frequented by homosexual men since the 1930s and possibly earlier.[3] Little, however, has been noted about the social activities of Sydney lesbians or their place in this scene. This chapter addresses this gap, tracing the history of Sydney's lesbian social scene from the 1940s to the 1970s.

---

1 'A Room Full of Women: Lesbian Bars and Social Spaces in Postwar Sydney' was first published in *Women's History Review*, 21:5 (November 2012), pp. 813–830.
2 The Camp Dance Survey, *Go-Set* (13 November 1971), p. 5.
3 Garry Wotherspoon, *City of the Plain: History of a Gay Sub-Culture* (Sydney: Hale and Iremonger, 1991); Pride History Group, *Camp Nites: Sydney's Emerging Drag Scene in the '60s* (Sydney: The Pride History Group, 2006); Pride History Group, *Camp as a Row of Tents: The Life and Times of Sydney's Camp Social Clubs* (Sydney: The Pride History Group, 2007).

Much of the international literature in the history of lesbian social practices has prioritised commercial spaces such as bars and nightclubs, suggesting that these venues represented the international standard of lesbian socialising in this period. Focusing primarily on large British and American cities, historians have charted the emergence of developed commercial lesbian subcultures after the Second World War.[4] However, the lesbian social scene in Sydney in the immediate postwar decades differs significantly from the subcultural patterns described in these accounts and complicates the accepted picture in a number of interesting ways. Available oral history evidence suggests that lesbians only appeared on Sydney's camp social scene – as the early lesbian and gay bar culture was known – in significant numbers in the early 1960s, when they began frequenting bars and cabaret clubs alongside camp men. Prior to this, much of the evidence points to a unique lesbian scene in Sydney, centred on private networks meeting at house parties and later in social groups. The predominance of private rather than public patterns of socialising in the immediate postwar decades had a lasting impact on the development of lesbian social practices and subcultural identities throughout the period being explored. Individual women's use of both public and private space was shaped in a variety of ways by behavioural norms defined in these private social spheres. Moreover, given that, as Elizabeth Kennedy and Madeline Davis claim, 'community is key to the development of twentieth-century lesbian identity and consciousness', these spatial practices also had a significant impact on notions of lesbian identity in the city.[5] This chapter will trace the range of social spaces available to lesbians in Sydney from the 1940s to the 1970s, examining the ways in

---

4   Elizabeth Lapovsky Kennedy and Madeline D Davies, *Boots of Leather, Slippers of Gold: The History of a Lesbian Community* (New York: Penguin Books, 1994;) Elise Chenier, 'Rethinking Class in Lesbian Bar Culture: Living "The Gay Life" in Toronto, 1955–1965', *Left History*, vol. 9, no. 2 (2004), pp. 85–118; Lillian Faderman, *Odd Girls and Twilight Lovers: A History of Lesbian Life in Twentieth-Century America* (New York: Penguin, 1991); Jill Gardiner, *From the Closet to the Screen: Women at the Gateways Club, 1945–85* (London: Pandora Press, 2003); Rebecca Jennings, *A Lesbian History of Britain: Love and Sex Between Women Since 1500* (Oxford: Greenwood World Publishing, 2007); Rebecca Jennings, *Tomboys and Bachelor Girls: A Lesbian History of Post-war Britain, 1945–71* (Manchester: Manchester University Press, 2007).

5   Kennedy and Davies, *Boots of Leather, Slippers of Gold*, p. 3. On the development of lesbian identity in Australia in the early 20th century, see Lucy Chesser, 'Negotiating Subjectivities: The Construction of Lesbian Identities in Melbourne, 1960–1969' (unpublished Honours thesis, Melbourne: University of Melbourne, 1993); Ford, 'Speculating on Scrapbooks'; Ruth Ford *Contested Desires: Narratives of Passionate Friends, Married Masqueraders and Lesbian Love in Australia, 1918–1945* (PhD thesis, Melbourne: La Trobe University, 2000a).

which these spaces shaped social practices and facilitated the construction of lesbian identities.

Lesbian socialising in the 1940s and 1950s

Evidence of a lesbian commercial bar scene in Sydney prior to the 1960s is scarce and seems to point to a limited lesbian presence within a larger, predominantly male, camp scene. A small number of camp men recall occasional pre-1960 encounters with lesbians on the commercial camp scene. Dennis, who frequented the camp male venue Rainard's Restaurant on King Street in the CBD in the 1950s, believed that the two women owners were lesbians. He recalled:

> Rainards was another place we used to go to, too, and that was run by, looking back now, two gay women. It was down in, appropriately, in the Queens Club, downstairs. And there was a Hungarian countess that was on hard times with a black cat playing the piano.[6]

Another narrator suggested that the attendants to the drag queens at the grand artists' balls of the 1950s were lesbians in drag. Some lesbians also mingled with the bohemian underworld of Kings Cross in the 1950s, socialising in cafes and hotels with artists, camp men and Eastern European migrants. In 1955, the sensationalist tabloid newspaper, the *Truth*, claimed:

> Police told *Truth* this week that dozens of mannishly-dressed lesbian couples can be seen in Darlinghurst Rd., King's Cross, every afternoon and night. They live as married couples – 'husband' and 'wife' and practise their disgusting perversions in secret. Sometimes, however, they break out. Recently there was a fierce brawl in the lounge of a fashionable King's Cross hotel. Two female perverts fought bitterly over the favors of a third woman.[7]

Such descriptions suggest that a small number of 'mannish' or tough lesbians, some of whom were known to the police for minor offences such as brawling, vagrancy and indecent language, enjoyed a presence on the bohemian and camp male scene in the 1950s. However, oral history interviews with women who were attracted to other women in this period demonstrate that many women were not aware of the existence of commercial

---

6   Interview with Dennis Fuller by John Witte, Pride History Group Collection, 15 November 2006.
7   'The Sink of Sydney', *Truth* (25 September 1955), p. 7.

camp venues in the 1940s and 1950s and did not frequent them. Coral recalled:

> I was a musician, came to Sydney in '56 and met only gay men ... there were no, even in Sydney, there were no clubs, no meeting places, we had a couple of gay male friends and we used to go to their house for parties but we'd often be the only women there. It was very underground.[8]

Research into lesbian bars and commercial venues outside Australia has shown that lesbian bar scenes had become established in many American and British cities by the 1940s. John D'Emilio and Allan Berube suggest that the Second World War marked a turning point, after which gay and lesbian bars became established in cities across America, and Elizabeth Lapovsky Kennedy and Madeline Davis have demonstrated the existence of a thriving lesbian bar scene in Buffalo, New York state from the 1940s onwards.[9] In the UK, the most well-known of London's lesbian venues, the Gateways nightclub in Chelsea, was open every evening, attracting hundreds of women a night from the 1950s onwards and forming the base for a tight-knit lesbian community with defined subcultural codes of behaviour and dress.[10] However, these large metropolitan centres may not be representative of a broader international trend – lesbian social practices in smaller cities and non-urban areas undoubtedly differed significantly from this model. While London and New York both had populations in excess of eight million in 1948, Australia's two largest cities, Sydney and Melbourne, recorded populations of 1,484,004 and 1,226,409 respectively (in 1947).[11] Lucy Chesser's work on Melbourne subcultures in the 1960s suggests that these population differences had a significant impact on the nature of lesbian socialising in Australia and that a lesbian commercial scene was only beginning to develop in Melbourne in the late 1960s. She notes:

---

8   Interview with Coral and Rachel by Lucy Chesser, Australian Lesbian and Gay Archives, 20 April 1993.
9   John D'Emilio, 'Gay Politics and Community in San Francisco Since World War II', in Martin Duberman, Martha Vicinus and George Chauncey, Jr., eds, *Hidden From History* (New York: New American Library, 1989), pp. 458–9; John D'Emilio, *Sexual Politics, Sexual Community: The Making of a Homosexual Minority in the United States, 1940–1970* (Chicago: University of Chicago Press, 1983), pp. 22–39; Allan Berube, *Coming Out Under Fire: The History of Gay Men and Women in World War Two* (New York: The Free Press, 1990); Kennedy and Davies, *Boots of Leather, Slippers of Gold*, p. 4.
10 Gardiner, *From the Closet to the Screen*; Jennings, *A Lesbian History of Britain*; Jennings, *Tomboys and Bachelor Girls*.
11 Commonwealth Bureau of Census and Statistics, *Official Yearbook of the Commonwealth of Australia No. 38* (Canberra: Commonwealth Government Printer, 1951), p. 528.

The development of lesbian subcultures in Melbourne appears to differ from their counterparts in some of the larger American cities. The scene in Melbourne was much smaller and consequently the process of creating specifically lesbian space took a lot longer. Whereas cities like San Francisco and New York had a number of lesbian bars by the 1950s, Melbourne had no specifically lesbian venues until the very end of the 1960s.[12]

Prior to this, Chesser claims, the only venues available to lesbians were a coffee shop in the city centre, which operated in various locations in the 1950s and 1960s, and a small number of predominantly male, heterosexual hotels (public houses), in which lesbians were tolerated on Saturday afternoons.[13] This pattern reflected that in Sydney, where a lesbian presence was rarely noted on the camp scene in the 1950s or earlier and women only began to join a mixed camp bar culture in significant numbers in the 1960s.

While the emergence of a commercial scene in the UK and US in the decades after the war in part reflected the growing social acceptability of public drinking for women, postwar Sydney was notable for its restrictive female public drinking culture and this also impacted on the nature of the lesbian scene in the city. Licensing laws in place in New South Wales from the First World War until 1957 enforced six o'clock closing of public bars, and these had a significant impact on gendered conventions of public drinking. Legislation explicitly prohibited women from drinking in public bars, confining them to separate saloon bars or 'ladies' lounges'. As the restricted licensing hours began to have an influence on drinking habits, publicans increasingly adapted the layout of their premises to accommodate the large numbers of men who frequented bars for high-intensity drinking between five and six in the evening. The 'six o'clock swill', as it became known, required long bars and large areas of standing room to enable crowds

---

12   Chesser, *Negotiating Subjectivities*, p. 36. See also Pam Nilan, 'I Was Never a Dress Person': Lesbian Stories from the Newcastle / Hunter Region, in Jim Wafer, Erica Southgate and Lyndall Coan, eds, *Out in the Valley: Hunter Gay and Lesbian Histories*, Newcastle: Newcastle Region Library, 2000, pp. 230-233; Graham Willett, 'Camp Melbourne in the 1960s', in Seamus O'Hanlon and Tanja Luckins, eds, *Go! Melbourne: Melbourne in the Sixties*, Melbourne: Circa, 2005, pp. 188-200. Clive Moore refers to a 'lesbian and gay' bar scene in Brisbane from the 1940s to the 1960s, although his discussion focuses almost exclusively on men and it is difficult to determine to what extent women were part of this scene: Clive Moore, *Sunshine and Rainbows: The Development of Gay and Lesbian Culture in Queensland*, St Lucia: University of Queensland Press, 2001.

13   Chesser, *Negotiating Subjectivities*, p. 36.

of male patrons to fit into the bar and order drinks quickly. In this postwar drinking culture, saloon bars were increasingly sidelined and the practice of drinking in hotels became a highly masculinised pursuit.[14] While lounge or saloon bars continued to accept women patrons in some hotels in the 1940s and 1950s, cultural assumptions about hotels as masculine spaces rendered hotel lounges largely unacceptable for the majority of women and those who did frequent them were regarded as 'rough' and unfeminine. It was not until the reform of licensing laws in 1957 that the prohibition on women drinking in public bars was lifted and hotels began to be designed to accommodate mixed drinking in pub lounges. In the meantime, however, the cultural coding of hotels as masculine spaces had become firmly embedded in social norms and women found themselves unwelcome in bars for decades after the legislative change.[15]

Lesbian socialising in Sydney was therefore primarily located in alternative sites in this period, reflecting broader gendered leisure practices in postwar Australia. Same-sex attracted women forged private friendship networks centred on sports clubs, work in occupations such as the army, and artistic circles based around theatres and musicians, and in this period it was these patterns of socialising which dominated the lesbian social scene in Sydney.[16] Beverley and Georgina, who met in the years after the Second World War, recalled a diverse social life in the 1940s and 1950s. The couple met at a picnic organised by a mutual friend and, after building a network of about eight or nine lesbian friends, socialised at picnics, tennis clubs and each other's houses. The women would also go on holiday together, staying in motels or renting an old shack on the Central Coast. In addition to this circle, they were part of a mixed camp social scene. Georgina recalled that they socialised 'with the boys as well, the boys were all in, we knew a lot of the boys, a lot of them. We used to go to their parties and everything

---

14   Walter Phillips, '"Six O'Clock Swill": The Introduction of Early Closing of Hotel Bars in Australia', *Historical Studies*, vol. 19, no. 75 (October 1980), pp. 250–266; Diane Kirkby, '"Beer, Glorious Beer": Gender Politics and Australian Popular Culture', *The Journal of Popular Culture*, vol. 37, no. 2, (2003), pp. 244–256; Tanja Luckins, 'Pigs, Hogs and Aussie Blokes: The Emergence of the Term "Six O'clock Swill"', *History Australia*, vol. 4, no. 1 (June 2007), pp. 08.1–08.17; Tanja Luckins, '"Time, Gentlemen, Please": The End of Six O'clock Closing and the "Post-Swill" Pub', in O'Hanlon and Luckins, eds, *Go! Melbourne*, pp. 174–187.
15   Protests in public bars where the landlord refused to serve women were a regular feature of women's movement activity in Sydney in the 1970s. See *Sydney Women's Liberation Newsletter* (May 1973), p. 6; (September 1975), p. 2.
16   See Chesser, *Negotiating Subjectivities*, p. 34; Ruth Ford, 'Disciplined, Punished and Resisting Bodies: Lesbian Women and the Australian Armed Services, 1950s–60s', *Lilith: a feminist history journal*, no. 9 (1996), pp. 53–77.

else, because we were always very friendly with the boys.'[17] Other sources also suggest that house parties provided an important and long-standing alternative to the bar scene for lesbians in the immediate postwar period. In his semi-autobiographical novel *At the Cross*, Jon Rose describes a camp party at Potts Point in Sydney's eastern suburbs during the Second World War, at which lesbian painters and actresses mixed with drag queens and camp window-dressers.[18] Large-scale house parties on long weekends such as the Queen's Birthday weekend were an aspect of the male camp scene in the late 1950s and early 1960s and it is clear that some lesbians attended these.[19]

The importance of friendship networks and the difficulties for women in socialising in a public bar scene suggest that house parties and outdoor activities may have been central to the lesbian social scene in Sydney in the immediate postwar decades. This tendency to socialise in small networks of friends, rather than as members of a larger lesbian community, shaped the models of identity developing in Sydney. Small private friendship circles tended not to evolve rigid rules of image and behaviour to which newcomers were expected to conform. Instead, women who socialised with circles of lesbian friends in this period typically described themselves as 'discreet' and conforming to wider societal norms. Margaret, who went out to restaurants with her girlfriend in the late 1950s, described their appearance as 'nice, well-dressed secretaries' and herself as 'like some respectable housewife', while Rae, who worked in the city, recalled that she and her friends socialised in dresses, hats and gloves.[20] Coral also remembered that, in the late 1950s, she and her girlfriend: 'Didn't wear trousers or anything like that, of course, dressed very, very nicely' at the mixed house parties they attended.[21] There was limited interaction between different friendship circles in this period, when it was often extremely difficult to locate other lesbians, and there was therefore little opportunity for the development of a larger, collective lesbian identity or subculture.

---

17 Interview with Beverley [pseudonym] and Georgina, 22 December 2008. See also Lyndall Coan (Compiler), 'Filling Some Gaps: Lesbian History Excerpts from the "Hunter Pride' Exhibition", in Wafer, Southgate and Coan, eds, *Out in the Valley*, p. 205.
18 Jon Rose, *At the Cross* (London: Andre Deutsch, 1961), pp. 16–17.
19 Wotherspoon, *City of the Plain*, pp. 135–6.
20 Interview with Margaret Jones, 12 September 2007; interview with Rae Morris by Sandra Mackay, Pride History Group Collection, 4 December 2008.
21 Interview with Coral and Rachel, 20 April 1993.

The mixed camp scene of the 1960s

The 1960s witnessed the beginning of a gradual shift from this pattern of private, discreet lesbian socialising toward the emergence of a more public lesbian social scene – reflecting broader changes in social attitudes towards gender roles and homosexuality and a growing acceptance of women's participation in the public sphere – but the social framework of private friendship networks continued to define lesbians' use of social space.[22] In addition to informal gatherings at individuals' houses, organised camp social groups began to emerge in the 1960s as a unique feature of Sydney's camp scene, extending private networks into public space. These privately organised, non-profit-making groups served a purely social function for their members and Garry Wotherspoon suggests that they 'tended to emerge out of the networks of friends ... [they] represented, as it were, friendship institutionalised'.[23] Although all the social groups were either mixed or men-only in the 1960s, women were often regarded as valuable members. Indeed Dennis, a co-founder of one of the early groups, commented that it was formed partly in order to provide women with a social space, given the continued difficulties for women of entering pubs.[24]

The first group, the Chameleons, was formed in 1962 by a group of camp men and women, including Sydney businesswoman and bar-owner Dawn O'Donnell and her partner Julia. The group organised dances at the Salvation Army Hall in Glebe and the Masonic Hall on Parramatta Road. The early dances included fairly basic drag performances and, as the group took off, they ran camp-only balls at the Sky Lounge in Liverpool Street.[25] The following year, the Chameleons were joined by a second social group, the Pollynesians, which also catered to both men and women. The Pollys, as it was generally known, organised bi-monthly dances at various halls, serving food at tables and entertaining guests with a fully-rehearsed drag show. Beverley and Georgina went to a number of dances organised by social

---

22 Interview with Virginia Binning and Ruth Ritchie by Sandra Mackay and Rebecca Jennings, Pride History Group Collection, 7 April 2007.
23 Wotherspoon, *City of the Plain*, p. 136. I am not aware of such organisations existing outside Australia, but social groups were formed in a number of Australian cities in this period. On Melbourne lesbian social groups, see Lucy Chesser, 'Australasian Lesbian Movement, "Claudia's Group" and Lynx: "Non-Political" Lesbian Organization in Melbourne, 1969–1980', *Hecate*, vol. 22, no. 1 (1996), pp. 69–91.
24 Interview with Dennis Fuller, 15 November 2006.
25 Interview with Dennis Fuller, 15 November 2006; interview with Ian McLean by Robert Colman, Pride History Group Collection, 10 February 2006. See also Wotherspoon, *City of the Plain*.

groups in this period and recalled one which was held in a big building on Castlereagh Street: 'It was down near the railway and it had dancing and all that sort of thing. But … a couple of times there was a call, "Change partners" because the police had come.' Beverley and Georgina would each find a male partner to dance with and the police would 'just stand at the top of the stairs and have a look.' Georgina remembered these dances as relatively sedate affairs:

> They weren't drunken parties or anything like that. I don't think I ever saw any of them drunk. But we used to have a glass of wine there … We'd buy it. It was awful too, sometimes. They used to make it themselves. Terrible![26]

In addition to the dances, many social groups organised regular outdoor events. The Pollys was famous for its annual sporting event, the Polympics. Karen, who joined Pollys in 1971, described the Polympics in this period as a major camp social event, attracting at least 400 people. She said: 'I think it was a time where everyone got together. And you'd, people would bring their animals, you know the dogs, and it was a social gathering and at the same time it was something to show their competitiveness.'[27] Events ranged from hand-bag tossing and stiletto egg-and-spoon for the drag queens, to more serious competitions such as athletics and long-jump.

The emergence of a lesbian bar scene

In addition to these social groups, lesbians were also beginning to join a much longer-standing gay male bar culture in significant numbers, reflecting a broader social acceptance of women and public drinking in the wake of reforms to the licensing laws in the late 1950s. Male narrators recall seeing lesbians on the commercial scene for the first time in the early 1960s, and lesbian narrators begin to discuss their participation in the bar scene from the 1960s onwards.[28] Lesbians socialised alongside homosexual men and drag queens in venues such as Chez Ivy wine bar in Bondi Junction and the Purple Onion coffee shop on Anzac Parade. Virginia, who first visited Chez Ivy and the Purple Onion in the early 1960s, went out on the scene in a group of male and female camp friends and remembered that: 'It was

---

26 Interview with Beverley [pseudonym] and Georgina, 22 December 2008.
27 Interview with Karen Brown by Ken Davis, Pride History Group Collection, 21 January 2007.
28 Interview with Dennis Fuller, 15 November 2006.

very mixed. I hardly went anywhere where it was just for women. I think the women's thing came later, yeah, the segregation side of it.' She spent these nights out drinking gin and tonic, talking to her friends and dancing the twist, as well as enjoying the drag shows that were put on at the Purple Onion and Les Girls.[29] When Carolyn began to frequent Chez Ivy in the late 1960s she also remembered the clientele as very diverse:

> Chez Ivy's was home to guys, girls, drag, bi, crossdressers and straights – I felt comfortable in this group and I would look forward to hitting 'the Club' each night and weekend ... The cat fights and tantrums were ongoing – this added to the fun of the night and drama. We had parents looking for sons and daughters, bomb threats, vice squad raids, scuffles with ex-lovers – but it was fun![30]

Chez Ivy closed at 10pm, but many revellers continued their night out at coffee shops such as Doddy's on Darlinghurst Road and the Coffee Pot in Kings Cross, or at cabaret clubs such as Les Girls or the Purple Onion.

This picture of the 1960s as a period of transition from a predominantly male to a mixed camp scene is supported by accounts which suggest that lesbians, as newcomers, were not always entirely welcome at Sydney's camp venues in this period. One reason for this attitude may have been the behaviour and image projected by some bar lesbians: a number of interviewees recall Sydney's bar lesbians as being quite 'tough' or 'rough' in this period, in contrast to the more flamboyant drag culture cultivated by camp men. Lesbians were widely regarded as being prone to fighting and causing difficulty in bars with their behaviour. Helen recalled the lesbians in one venue as particularly threatening, commenting:

> You had to be very careful there who you looked at because if you dared to cast your eye over some butch dyke's girlfriend, you could be in big trouble! And they carried knives. These butch dykes wore full drag. Three piece suits and pointy toed shoes and carried things like knives and stuff. So you had to really watch them, they were heavy duty.[31]

---

29 Interview with Virginia Binning and Ruth Ritchie, 7 April 2007.
30 Carolyn Bloye on 29 February 2009, unpublished talk given at launch of Pride History Group, *Out and About: Sydney's lesbian social scene, 1960s–80s* (Sydney: Pride History Group, 2009).
31 Interview with Helen by Ruth Ford, Australian Lesbian and Gay Archive, 14 December 1994.

Kris also described the bar culture in 1960s Sydney as violent, commenting that: 'a lot of the women were thugs and you either had to you know, you had to fight ... So I had to fight a couple of – this one woman I had to fight and then the others left me alone you know, in that scene.'[32] Ivy Richter, proprietor of Chez Ivy and in the later 1960s another venue called Ivy's Birdcage, remembered 'the girls' with a distinct lack of enthusiasm. Although the Birdcage, in the rough working-class suburb of Darlinghurst, was surrounded by illegal gambling dens and brothels, Ivy claimed that the only violence she ever witnessed was caused by her own lesbian clientele, a number of whom had to be barred.[33]

Although the majority of venues were mixed in the 1960s, lesbians increasingly made up most of the clientele at a few bars: the Trolley Car near Sydney University, the Sussex Hotel on Sussex Street in the City and the Park Inn opposite Centennial Park. Dennis worked at the Trolley Car, owned by Dawn O'Donnell, when it opened in 1966 and recalled the venue as a 'long, old terraced house' with a licensed bar downstairs until 10pm and an upstairs room which continued to operate illicitly after official closing time. The venue was popular with lesbians:

> Well, you see, the Trolley Car upstairs had a great girl patronage ... More girls than boys ... They used to go to the Sussex Inn, I think it's called, the Sussex Hotel, they used to stay there til 10 o'clock, then they used to come to us and go upstairs in the Trolley Car.[34]

A significant lesbian clientele also mixed with drag queens at the Park Inn in this period. Karen went to the Park Inn in the late 1960s and recalled that 'The majority that went there were women.'[35] Laurie, who had gone there for the first time in the 1960s with her girlfriend Helen and two new friends, also remembered:

> I walked in there and it was like seventh heaven. It was full of lesbians from wall to carpet to wall you know? And drag queens. I saw my first drag show there and that was it for me ... We went there every Friday night to Saturday night for the next ten, fifteen years I think?[36]

---

32 Interview with Kris Melmouth, 25 August 2011.
33 Interview with Ivy Richter by John Witte, Pride History Group Collection, 22 May 2006.
34 Interview with Dennis Fuller, 15 November 2006.
35 Interview with Karen Brown, 21 January 2007.
36 Interview with Laurie van Camp by Sandra Mackay, Pride History Group Collection, 18 February 2008.

A number of the women who socialised in these venues adopted masculine dress codes and identities. Laurie recalled that all the lesbians at the Park Inn were 'butch and femme. Three piece suits, cufflinks, ties, the whole bit.' Laurie herself was introduced to this butch/femme scene by some lesbian friends, who took her clothes shopping in the men's department of Grace Bros and then to get her hair cut into a 'short back and sides' before escorting her to the bar. Her girlfriend, Helen, retained her feminine dress and appearance, as she was adopting a femme identity. Margaret also described the masculine appearance of the other women clientele when she first discovered a camp venue in the 1960s. She explained:

> So I just went out there one Saturday afternoon, sat down and there were all these scruffy looking women sat around, dressed not very becomingly ... like road workers. Oh pants, well I would wear pants, but really old beat up old gear and short hair cuts and rather rough looking, I thought, and their conversation was too, rather coarse, mixed with expletives.[37]

For some women, adopting a butch appearance meant potentially passing as a man. Colette recalled experiencing some confusion on her first encounter with a butch lesbian in the early 1960s:

> In 1964/65 I said to my sister, 'We have to find some lesbians' ... the only gay place at that time was a place called the 'Hole in the Wall', literally a brick circle had been made in the wall ... it was dark inside. It was in Kings Cross in the vicinity of St Vincent's hospital. It was full of *very* interesting people and after about an hour I noticed this very attractive blond boy, there was just something about him, and he obviously noticed me because he came over and spoke and he turned out to be a woman in full drag so this was terribly exciting for me ... she looked like a boy but she was a girl, this was exactly what I was looking for. So we went home together and it was off with the frock for me and she unstrapped and stripped down to a t-shirt.[38]

Colette's reference to the girl unstrapping suggests that some butch lesbians in this period were binding their breasts in order to adopt a more masculine physique, in addition to wearing male clothes.[39] Some of the lesbians who

---

37 Interview with Margaret Jones, 18 September 2007.
38 Interview with Colette Parr by Digby Duncan, Pride History Group Collection.
39 See also interview with Laurie van Camp, 18 February 2008, who describes strapping down her breasts as part of the performance of a butch identity in this period.

frequented Ivy Richter's venues in the 1960s were similarly capable of passing as young men. Ivy recalled one occasion on which gender ambiguity led to an altercation between one of her lesbian clients and a member of the licensing police. She explained:

> [T]he licensing sergeant came in, he said: 'I believe you've got a lot of nonsense going on here', he said, 'You've got underage people.' I said, 'No, I haven't.' He said: 'What about that young feller there?' I said: 'That young feller there's a girl!' So I brought this girl over to meet Sgt Kinnerburra and she said 'I know him.' She said, 'Anyway, I was down in your lock-up yesterday. Why didn't you look that up?' She gave him a whole mouth full of cheek.[40]

The extent to which femme women were a part of the Sydney scene in this period is more difficult to determine. While a small number of accounts refer to butch/femme partnerships and communities, many focus primarily on butch lesbians, suggesting that butch identities predominated. It is also possible that many femme partners of butch lesbians occupied a more transient position in the lesbian social circles of this period and were therefore less visible. Davis and Kennedy noted that, in the butch/femme community they documented in 1940s and 1950s Buffalo, 'many fems ... became butch, others went straight, and others claimed to be too shy to be interviewed.'[41] A similar picture emerges in Sydney. In her account of a casual encounter with a butch lesbian at the Hole in the Wall in Kings Cross in the 1960s, Colette describes herself as removing her 'frock', suggesting that her own appearance was more feminine than that of her butch partner. Colette herself was a newcomer to the bar on this occasion and implies that she was not part of any coherent lesbian community at the time. Accounts of the Park Inn hotel in this period also suggest that the predominantly butch lesbian clientele mixed with other women as well as drag queens. Laurie, who had gone there for the first time in the 1960s, recalled that women of all classes mixed there and 'there was one table that was reserved permanently for when the prostitutes came in, from Kings Cross, and they were all gay.'[42] The hotel owner, Ken (Kandy) Johnson, claimed that nurses made up a significant group amongst the more butch regulars and remembered one occasion on which he had received a call from the local hospital, attempting to locate one of their nurses, who was needed to assist on an operation. He recounted the caller's description of the nurse in question:

---

40   Interview with Ivy Richter, 22 May 2006.
41   Kennedy and Davies, *Boots of Leather, Slippers of Gold*, p. 18.
42   Interview with Laurie van Camp, 18 February 2008.

> 'This is Bev Sweets, dahls. Listen, you know Amelia? They call her Buzz. She's got real short hair, like a bloke.' [Kandy reflected:] Half the girls had blokes' hair. 'Listen, she's wearing a dark grey man's suit, a deep blue shirt and a black tie.'
>
> I spotted her, drunk as a skunk trying to chat up a pretty young prostitute. 'I see her,' I screamed. 'I'll go get her.'[43]

Kandy's account of this exchange suggests that camp women who identified as butch – wearing men's suits and short hair – may have interacted with more feminine prostitutes in his bar. Whether or not some of the prostitutes had sexual relationships with women, Kandy's account suggests that others may not have immediately identified them as camp, defining them instead primarily as 'prostitutes'. How the women themselves defined their sexual identity, if at all, is even more elusive, in the absence of accounts by femme participants in this scene.

The possibility that femme identities may not have been clearly identified as lesbian identity models is also suggested by Elizabeth's account of roles in her suburban social circle. Unlike the majority of women socialising in private friendship networks in the mid-century, who described their roles and appearance as conforming to mainstream ideals of respectable femininity, Elizabeth recalled her private house party scene in the late 1960s as organised around a restrictive form of gendered role-playing. Moving largely in middle-class circles, outside of the bar scene, she claimed:

> Yes, I think there were roles. And I don't think they were good ones. I think they were ... like Joy used to like me to wear long gowns, and I had long hair, and she liked that and I went along with it. And she wore three piece suits, but tailored ones, I mean they weren't, they were ones she had made specially for herself, and a gold watch fob and you know, all the trappings.[44]

Despite her partner's expectation that she adopt a feminine appearance, however, Elizabeth does not appear to have developed a clearly defined femme identity. Explaining the relationship between their respective roles, Elizabeth was unsure of the term for a feminine partner, commenting:

---

43   Ken (Kandy) Johnson, *Kandy: What a Drag!* (Sydney: Vegas Press, 2009,) p. 93.
44   Interview with Elizabeth by Ruth Ford, Australian Lesbian and Gay Archive, 6 May 1992.

> You were a butch lesbian or you were a, whatever, I don't know what you call it, but anyway, you were one or the other and that's how it worked and I thought that makes sense.⁴⁵

Elizabeth's ambivalence toward her femme identity was also apparently reflected by those around her, as she recalled attracting criticism of her appearance from a woman at a party. The woman commented that Elizabeth shouldn't 'think you can fool us wearing that dress', suggesting that she regarded the adoption of a feminine appearance as an attempt to hide a lesbian identity. This account suggests that feminine lesbians may have been viewed with distrust in some Sydney lesbian circles, and perhaps not regarded as having an important or valued role in the community.

Other accounts, however, suggest that both butch and femme identities were consciously adopted by some women as an indication of membership in a lesbian community. Laurie had been introduced to the butch/femme scene when she moved from Perth to Sydney in the 1960s and she and her girlfriend Helen adopted butch and femme identities respectively. She had been sitting in her local pub with Helen after work one Friday, when two women came in:

> They had dresses on but really short hair and I said to Helen, 'I think they're like us'. And we were playing darts and the juke box and we got to talking to these women and this woman June ... wanted to take us to this place called Kandy's at Paddington, Woollahra, and she said, 'but you can't go like that. We'll have to take you and fix you up.' I didn't know what she was talking about but anyway she took me to Grace Bros and we bought a pair of corduroy pants, checked shirts, desert boots ... [from] the men's section, which was so embarrassing for me, I'd never been in the men's section. And then on the way back, I thought it was over because I had hair down to my bum, and she made me go into a men's barber shop and I had short back and sides ... Helen still stayed the same because it was butch and femme in those days. I was the butch.⁴⁶

After introducing them to butch/femme fashion, June and her girlfriend Karen took Laurie and Helen to their local bar and the new arrivals soon became regulars. Descriptions such as Laurie's are reminiscent of postwar butch/femme lesbians in the US and UK, where the commercial bar scene

---

45   ibid.
46   Interview with Laurie van Camp, 18 February 2008.

fostered a highly nuanced subculture based around butch/femme role-playing, and new entrants to the community were expected to adopt either a butch or femme style and behaviour. This was often a highly conscious process in which new members chose an identity and experienced a rite of passage in which they adapted their image to fit the new identity. For Laurie, the decision to become a butch was taken by her new butch friend, June, on the basis that Laurie was a better pool player than Helen.

Although adopting butch/femme identities enabled individual women to fully participate in lesbian communities, they also identified butch lesbians, in particular, more clearly to the wider community. Her butch image rendered Laurie highly visible as a lesbian and she described herself as 'very out' throughout the 1960s. This identity had significant repercussions for her relationship with mainstream society. She recalled:

> If I was just walking up the street, holding my girlfriend's hand, a carload of guys would go past and yell out 'leso', you know, and all that sort of shit. And um, then they'd pull round the corner and come back, and they'd always pick on the butch one.[47]

Personal narratives such as Laurie's suggest that, while a number of lesbian identity models in the 1960s were characterised by an emphasis on secrecy and discretion, others, such as butch/femme, were highly visible and confrontational. Butch/femme lesbians, like Laurie and Helen, forged their identities in social spaces which they shared with prostitutes, gay men and drag queens and as a result they understood their lesbianism within a broad, cross-gendered community of sexual minorities. Similarly, the shared nature of the camp social scene in the 1960s meant that many more discreet lesbians in this period also defined their identity alongside gay men, in terms of a shared attempt to evade detection by mainstream society.

However, despite the presence of consciously butch women on the commercial lesbian scene in the 1960s, butch/femme did not represent a pervasive subculture in the Sydney camp bar scene in the manner described by historians of US lesbian subcultures. Oral history accounts suggest instead that butch lesbians coexisted with women of more conventional appearance, often sharing the same social spaces. This reflects the situation in Melbourne in the same period, where Lucy Chesser has found that:

> while there were sizeable lesbian social groups which organised around role playing in Melbourne in this period alternative models of lesbian

---

47   ibid.

relationships were often available to women from working class backgrounds ... In addition, butch/femme role playing appears to have decreased in importance as the 1960s progressed.[48]

In Sydney, other lesbians who socialised both within and outside of the bar scene in the 1960s do not recall the early scene as a butch/femme culture and did not themselves adopt either a butch or femme identity. Virginia did not recall a butch/femme scene at Chez Ivy and the Purple Onion in the early 1960s, although she conceded that 'some of them probably were pretty butch', while Carolyn described Chez Ivy's lesbian clientele as a relatively diverse cultural group.[49] The fluidity of lesbian dress and identity on the commercial camp scene in Sydney in the 1960s reflects the predominance of small, private networks in the preceding decades and indicates the absence of a long-standing and developed subculture in the bars of this period.

Moreover, the ways in which women made use of the new public spaces becoming available to them continued to be shaped by private networks and patterns of socialising. Both the bar scene and the camp social groups in the 1960s were relatively secretive and enclosed, making it difficult for outsiders or the authorities to identify them. In the absence of any homosexual press, bars and clubs did not advertise and only a few individuals were lucky enough to stumble across them by accident. The mainstream press could occasionally give a hint but most women were introduced to the camp scene by friends from elsewhere.[50] Virginia first visited camp bars with friends from a North Shore ballroom dancing club she belonged to, and Karen began socialising with lesbians she met at a hockey club in the late 1960s. Carolyn and her girlfriend were first introduced to Chez Ivy by a lesbian couple they met by chance on holiday on the Central Coast.[51] The enclosed nature of the scene in this period also leant a secretive atmosphere to socialising, which some women remembered as exciting. Ruth recalled:

> It was far better than, it's all out in the open now, you felt like you were, had this very special sort of semi-secret society that you were part of and that other people were excluded from.[52]

---

48 Chesser, *Negotiating Subjectivities*, p. 37.
49 Interview with Virginia Binning and Ruth Ritchie, 7 April 2007; interview with Carolyn Bloye by Sandra Mackay, Pride History Group Collection, 9 November 2007.
50 Interview with Margaret Jones, 18 September 2007.
51 Interview with Virginia Binning and Ruth Ritchie, 7 April 2007; interview with Karen Brown, 21 January 2007; interview with Carolyn Bloye, 9 November 2007.
52 Interview with Virginia Binning and Ruth Ritchie, 7 April 2007.

Lucy Chesser argues that the sense of belonging to a secretive lesbian subculture in this period played an important role in affirming women's lesbian identities and giving women a sense of pride in escaping detection.[53]

Friendship circles continued to be important, not only in introducing women to venues, but in the ways in which individual lesbians made use of the spaces available to them. Unlike the pattern of socialising in London's lesbian venues in the 1960s, where each bar or club possessed its own community of regular clientele with specific behavioural codes and identities, venues seem to have played a less important role in shaping identity on the Sydney scene. Women moved more freely from one venue to another, but as groups rather than individuals. Virginia commented:

> [I]t was more getting together with your group and doing something together, whether it be go to one of these clubs or. Like I would never have gone to one of these places by myself, I would never have done that. And it was just, you know, mixing with a crowd, and you'd kind of do things together.[54]

In this sense, the commercial camp scene which emerged for lesbians in the 1960s reflected earlier patterns of socialising in the city. Women continued to structure their social networks around small, private circles of friends and simply extended the location of their social activities as new spaces became available to them. Sydney's lesbian socialising in the 1960s was defined by one's circle of friends, rather than a regular haunt, and as a result women moved easily between the social spaces offered to them.

Clover and the continuance of private social practices in the 1970s

A number of new commercial venues were established in the 1970s, which, as in the 1960s, attracted lesbians as part of a mixed crowd. Dawn O'Donnell and Roger Claude Teyssedre opened Jools, an upmarket nightclub, on Crown Street in 1973. Frequented by a straight and gay clientele, Jools was spread over three floors and regularly hosted guest performers such as Marcia Hines, The Supremes, The Village People and Lana Cantrell.[55] Another major gay nightclub, Capriccios, also opened on Oxford Street in the early 1970s, staging drag shows for a mixed audience. However,

---

53 Chesser, *Negotiating Subjectivities*, p. 41.
54 Interview with Virginia Binning and Ruth Ritchie, 7 April 2007.
55 S D Harvey, *The Ghost of Ludwig Gertsch* (Sydney: Pan Macmillan, 2000).

tensions between the lesbian and male patrons continued to pose difficulties for women in the 1970s and lesbians were made to feel unwelcome in a number of venues. As a result, despite the development of public social spaces for lesbians centred on the expanding commercial bar scene, older private patterns of socialising continued to play an important role in Sydney's lesbian social scene in the 1970s.

A range of social groups still catered for a mixed gay and lesbian membership, including the Pollys club, which continued to organise dances and social events throughout the decade. In the early 1970s, however, it was joined by a women-only group, Clover, which became an institution on the Sydney lesbian scene. Clover was formed in 1972 when Jan McInnies and three friends attempted to go out on the camp bar scene in Oxford Street one night and were forcibly excluded from a venue on the grounds that they were women.[56] The friends decided to form a women-only group of their own, initially called The Clover Single Ladies Recreational Club, and advertised for members in the *Nation Review*. The original advertisement stated: 'Conservative camp ladies don't exist?? We do!! We've got an exclusive club with a membership of four!! Would you like to join and make it more?'[57] Prospective members contacted the group by post and were vetted at an informal interview before being admitted to the club. Early meetings were held in members' homes but by the mid-1970s Clover had established themselves in permanent clubrooms on Victoria Road, Drummoyne, where they had a bar and disco every Friday night. Although some of the group's events were soon attracting over a hundred women, the organisers sought to maintain a friendly, family atmosphere, modelled on Clover's house-party origins, in contrast to the commercial bar scene, which was perceived as public and alienating. Jan McInnies remembered:

> It was just like once you knew a few people you could walk in and everyone was friendly and everyone would say hello. They'd remember you and you weren't just a blob sitting there in the corner having a drink. It wasn't just a bar where you came and went to the bar and bought your drinks you know. People were friendly and if it was your first, people would make sure in the committee. They had to go and talk to you. Introduce you to other people.[58]

---

56   Interview with Jan McInnies and Margaret Cummins by Sandra Mackay and Rebecca Jennings, Pride History Group Collection.
57   Clover Businesswomen's Club, *A History of Clover* (Pride History Group Collection, 1987).
58   Interview with Jan McInnies and Margaret Cummins.

As the group developed, it held dinners in restaurants and organised bushwalking and other excursions, as well as participating in sporting events run by Pollys.

Jan McInnies recalled that in the early years the membership was diverse: 'I was just amazed at all these different women. There were different ages, different backgrounds. It was just fantastic.'[59] However, the group's description of itself as 'Conservative camp ladies', together with the vetting process, inevitably shaped Clover's identity, and it tended to appeal more to slightly older women and those who had previously been married and had children. This image was reinforced by the decision to change the name in the mid-1970s to Clover Businesswomen's Club. Reflecting on the choice of the new name, Jan again sought to define the group against the bar scene, recalling: 'We just wanted to keep it nice ... We didn't want it rough, yeah. We'd been out a few times and seen different, you know. We didn't want it to be that sort of big, butch whatever.'[60] Diana started going to Clover events in the late 1970s after several years going out on the bar scene and confirmed that this strategy was effective on its own terms: 'It had a much more professional clientele and a much higher, if you like, class of people ... I think that was partly age related.'[61] For younger lesbians, this was a less attractive proposition. A number of young women went along to Clover and found it full of 'role-playing' and non-political lesbians.[62] The occasional dances that the group organised, however, had wider appeal and drew in both long-standing club members and younger women.

The impact of political movements in the 1970s

The development of political movements such as feminism and gay liberation in Sydney in the 1970s had a significant impact on the lesbian social scene in the city, opening up a range of new possibilities. Like Clover, many of the new gay and feminist groups which formed in the early 1970s sought to establish alternative social activities to those offered by a commercial bar scene that they regarded as 'sleazy' and exploitative. In 1977 *Ad Hoc*, the newsletter of the Sydney University Active Defence of Homosexuals on Campus group, articulated a common view when it informed its readers:

---

59   ibid.
60   ibid.
61   Interview with Diana [pseudonym] by Rebecca Jennings, 23 April 2008.
62   Interview with Sandra Mackay by Rebecca Jennings, 2 July 2007.

Finally, a gay / feminist pub has been opened near campus. The publican of the Native Rose (cnr. Cleveland and Shepherd sts. Chippendale) has made the facilities of the beer garden (which is very spacious) and the billiards room available to gay / feminist people. This is a very good opportunity to gain a pub which is unlike the gay bar scene, i.e. It has a friendly atmosphere without rip-off prices and with cheap food available.[63]

Other groups organised their own social activities, such as the annual Lesbian Teachers' Tea Party held by the Lesbian Teachers' Group for Sydney and rural New South Wales-based lesbian teachers, and the lesbian film night run by Leichhardt Women's Health Centre in the late 1970s.[64] When the homosexual political organisation CAMP NSW was founded in Balmain in 1970, the group began to organise regular social events for its members. The women's group held weekly coffee nights at the organisation's clubhouse, where existing members could discuss political concerns and new members could drop in and find out more about the group.[65] Other social activities followed, including barbeques and swimming parties at people's houses. These events were often the first entry for some women into a lesbian social scene and provided opportunities to make friends and meet partners in a semi-private environment.[66] Saturday night parties were also common, together with occasional larger fundraising dances held in suburban town halls and other suitable venues.[67] However, tensions within the group over the sexist attitudes of some male members prompted lesbians to gradually withdraw from the organisation during the 1970s and politically inclined lesbians increasingly invested their energy in feminist politics.[68]

The burgeoning feminist culture which developed in the city over the course of the decade prompted a significant shift in Sydney's lesbian scene, from the mixed spaces of the 1960s towards the emergence of a women-only social scene in the 1970s. Spearheaded by women active in Women's Liberation and the Women's Electoral Lobby, this trend nevertheless had

---

63 'Native Rose Hotel', *Ad Hoc*, 1(2) (May/June 1977), n.p.
64 Interview with Robyn Plaister by Rebecca Jennings, 20 December 2007; *Lesbian Film Night* flyer, undated, Mitchell Library. Ephemera. Folder 1970–1979.
65 *CAMP Women's Association Newsletters.* Mitchell Library. Folder 25, Gays Counselling Service of NSW Papers. MSS 5836; See also Sue Wills, 'Inside the CWA – The Other One', *Journal of Australian Lesbian Feminist Studies*, no. 4 (June 1994), pp. 6–22.
66 Interview with Elizabeth, 6 May 1992.
67 Interview with Margaret Jones, 18 September 2007; See also interview with Ian McLean, 10 February 2006.
68 Wills, Inside the CWA.

a major impact not just on those women directly involved in organised feminism, but on many other lesbians outside the movement as well. With the rise of feminist politics came a new approach to social activity, founded on the idea of celebrating womanhood and strengthening bonds between women. Women's dances occurred at town halls across Sydney throughout the 1970s; these were major social events attended by hundreds of women. Often organised as a fundraiser for the political campaign of the moment, they served both a political and a social function for Sydney's lesbians and attracted feminist and non-movement lesbians. Sandra, who went to both lesbian bars and women's dances with her feminist friends in the early 1970s, remembered the dances as a unique and important space for women. She explained:

> And they were totally different to the bars, because [at the dances] we were trying to enact our kind of ideology ... of anti-fashion and not marking femininity at all and the idea that women should not be objectified was very strong ... and also people would always be, everyone would take their tops off and be dancing without any tops on! I shudder to think of it now, but you know that kind of thing, dancing around in big circles, and they'd have women's bands.[69]

Valerie, who did not regard herself as fully integrated into feminist politics, nevertheless had fond memories of the women's dances, recalling: 'They were great fun, because there was lots of loud music and dancing and pot and alcohol and you know, you usually went home with somebody afterwards.'[70] The loud music was provided by the range of women's bands which were beginning to emerge from feminist culture in this period, both in Sydney and across Australia, with names such as Stray Dags, Hen's Teeth and Sheila. Women's bands were extremely popular, both because their lyrics often reflected the beliefs and lesbian-orientation of their listeners, and because their music was founded upon an inclusive, woman-centred ideology.[71]

---

69   Interview with Sandra Mackay, 2 July 2007.
70   Interview with Valerie Odewahn, 20 May 2008.
71   In conscious rejection of the perceived masculine bias of the rock 'n' roll music industry in this period. See Louise Douglas and Elizabeth Fletcher, 'Women in the Music Industry: "The Exhaust Pipe of Your Love is Enough to Keep Me Warm" – Women in Rock 'n' Roll', *Refractory Girl* (December 1979), pp. 44–47; *Programme of Workshops and Sessions at the 6th National Conference for Lesbians and Homosexual Men. Sydney, 30–31 August 1980*. Mitchell Library, Folder 71, Gays Counselling Service of NSW Papers, MSS 5836; Kathy Sport, 'Below the Belt and Bleeding Fingertips: Feminist and Lesbian Music in the Late 1970s', *Australian Feminist Studies*, vol. 22, issue 53 (July 2007), pp. 343–360.

Women's music nights sprang up in hotels across Sydney, attracting large groups of women who came to hear their favourite musicians perform.[72]

The development of a feminist and lesbian and gay political culture in Sydney in the early 1970s also had a significant impact on the commercial bar scene, both providing a larger self-identified lesbian community in search of social space and enabling the exchange of information about specific venues. The increased public discussion of lesbian and gay issues prompted by the new political campaigns resulted in wider media coverage of the camp bar scene and, in November 1971, the youth magazine *Go-Set* published a review of camp venues in the city.[73] As the decade progressed, a growing number of gay and feminist political groups produced newsletters, journals and other print media, and many offered their readers regular information on the commercial bar scene. In April 1978, the *Sydney Advocate* published a 'Sydney Guide', which included a comprehensive list of lesbian and gay bars and clubs in the city, complete with opening times and locations marked on a map.[74]

The trend toward women-only social spaces pioneered by the women's movement was reflected in the public bar scene. At the heart of the lesbian scene was Ruby Red's, a women's bar and nightclub opened by Dawn O'Donnell. Located above a liquor store on Crown Street, this small and slightly seedy venue was a converted steakhouse.[75] Diana, a nurse who was a regular at Ruby's in the 1970s, described the club as 'disco in the early part of the disco era and the changing colours in the dance floor and the strobe lighting and the mirror balls.'[76] The bar catered for women only, with men admitted only as guests of female patrons or to work behind the bar – an earlier attempt to employ female bar staff had been abandoned because 'they were giving out too much free grog.'[77] Ruby's was frequented by women from many different occupational, political and class backgrounds and Dennis, who worked behind the bar with his boyfriend, George, remembered distinct types of lesbians going there: George on the back bar 'had the truck drivers and [Dennis] had the lipsticks' at the front bar. Dennis recalled the 'lipsticks' as 'lovely girls': often models, businesswomen or government employees,

---

72   Interview with Robyn Plaister, 20 December 2007; Interview with Chris Pearce by Rebecca Jennings, 6 November 2007.
73   Doing the Round of Camp Places, *Go-Set* (13 November 1971), p. 6.
74   Sydney Guide, *Sydney Advocate*, 1 (14 April 1978), pp. 15–18.
75   Interview with Dennis Fuller, 15 November 2006; Harvey, *The Ghost of Ludwig Gertsch*, pp. 113–14.
76   Interview with Diana [pseudonym], 23 April 2008.
77   Interview with Dennis Fuller, 15 November 2006.

who tended to avoid the rougher 'truck drivers', positioning themselves in different parts of the bar and visiting at different times.[78] Drinking and dancing were the main activities recalled by women who frequented Ruby's, but the venue offered other possibilities as well. Valerie explained:

> There were always sections in Ruby's. You know, there was the wall if you wanted to be picked up, and if you were down the back it was always a bit rougher, and if you went to the downstairs toilets you could usually get into a fight down there. It sort of catered for all sorts.[79]

As in the 1960s, fights were relatively common in Ruby's and other lesbian venues, where excessive drinking (in addition to the occasional use of recreational drugs including marijuana), could lead to disagreements over girls; Valerie vividly recalled that Ruby's also employed a 'very big woman' as a bouncer.[80]

The decades from the 1940s to the 1970s witnessed a significant transition in Sydney's lesbian scene, from mixed private social networks to a more gender segregated public scene. While the international scholarship has emphasised the importance of a commercial bar scene in defining lesbian socialising in the postwar period, the Sydney scene demonstrates that this model does not necessarily apply to smaller cities or non-urban areas. Local factors such as licensing laws and cultural attitudes to women and public drinking meant that only a small minority of 'mannish' or 'rough' lesbians socialised alongside camp men and other members of the demi-monde in hotel lounges in the 1940s and 1950s, with lesbians only joining the commercial camp scene in Sydney in significant numbers in the 1960s. Instead, for many lesbians in the early postwar decades, private friendship networks developed from sports clubs, occupational or artistic circles defined patterns of socialising at house parties, picnics and on holidays. This mode of socialising in small groups impacted on the development of lesbian identity in the city, prompting many women to conform to conventional notions of feminine appearance and behaviour and limiting the scope for the emergence of distinctive lesbian subcultures and styles. Private friendship networks similarly defined the spatial practices of lesbian socialising in Sydney as late as the 1960s and 1970s, leading to the development of unique organised social groups

---

78   ibid.
79   Interview with Valerie Odewahn, 20 May 2008.
80   ibid.

in the 1960s and also shaping the ways in which women used commercial venues such as bars and nightclubs. This commercial lesbian scene began to expand from the 1960s onwards, with increasing numbers of women joining camp men on the mixed scene as the decade wore on. However, the emergence of political movements in the 1970s – particularly the widespread influence of feminism – again reshaped patterns of socialising, prompting the development of women-only spaces and encouraging increasing gender segregation on the commercial scene.

Chapter 4

LESBIAN POLITICS

The 1960s and early 1970s witnessed a wave of left-wing political activism on a range of social issues from penal reform to Aboriginal land rights and women's rights. In Sydney and across Australia, moratoriums were held against the Vietnam War, attracting large numbers of protestors from political and social radicals to ordinary Australians. Meanwhile, in New York and London, a politics of gay liberation was beginning to be articulated. News of the riots which followed police harassment of lesbians and gay men at the Stonewall Inn in New York in 1969 was brought to Australia by activists such as Dennis Altman, and inspired a group of Sydney lesbians and gay men to consider the political position of homosexuals in Australia. On 10 September 1970, Australia's first explicitly political lesbian and gay organisation, Campaign Against Moral Persecution (CAMP) Inc, was founded in North Sydney by John Ware and Christabel Poll. The group intended to form a body of people who could put the homosexual viewpoint across publicly and help develop the confidence of individual homosexuals. As Christabel Poll explained:

> As far as the wider society is concerned, we should concentrate on providing information, removing prejudice, ignorance and fear, stressing the ordinariness of homosexuality and generally reassuring and disarming those with hostile attitudes. Concerning homosexuals, we think a policy of development of confidence and lessening of feelings of isolation and guilt, where they exist, is vital.[1]

---

1 Christabel Poll, 'Gay Liberation', *The Old Mole* no. 7, Sydney University, 26 October 1970, p. 5.

Their approach to mainstream society placed them within a pre-existing liberal tradition and they found allies in the Humanist Society and the Council for Civil Liberties, who were sympathetic to a political program which sought homosexual law reform and social acceptance. John and Chris recognised that visibility was central to these aims and to this end CAMP held a number of public demonstrations and media appearances, as well as encouraging members to 'come out' and publicly acknowledge their sexuality. The political aims of the group, however, did not sit easily with the pastoral ambition to lessen 'feelings of isolation and guilt' in the homosexual community, and the 1970s witnessed increasing tensions over these issues, which were ultimately resolved by the end of the decade when the group decided to focus its energies on providing a counselling service to lesbians and gay men.[2]

CAMP's emphasis on visibility was shared by a second gay activist group, Sydney Gay Liberation (SGL), which emerged from a CAMP consciousness-raising group in late 1971. Despite their common roots, SGL critiqued CAMP as otherwise 'reformist' and 'conservative' in nature. They advocated a more theoretically informed and angry challenge to society, in contrast to CAMP's more conciliatory stance. As *Gay Lib News* explained in an article on the forthcoming 1973 Gay Pride Week:

> We've got to encourage those who are gay but don't realise it or have repressed their sexuality, to express their gayness with pride, joy and love. We've got to hit hard those who repress us, without apology, till they change, and also liberate themselves in the process. We've got to attack the institutions that oppress us. Confront them, and demand them to explain or justify their oppression.[3]

After initially sharing CAMP's clubrooms in Darling Street, Balmain, SGL moved into their own centre at 67 Glebe Point Road, Glebe in 1972, where they remained an active political presence until 1974. Despite their differences, SGL and CAMP worked together on a number of issues, including confronting leading psychiatrists over the use of aversion therapy to 'cure' homosexuals and challenging the views of the churches on

---

2   For a more detailed discussion of the establishment and aims of CAMP Inc, see Graham Willett, *Living Out Loud: A History of Gay and Lesbian Activism in Australia* (St Leonards NSW: Allen & Unwin, 2000); Robert Reynolds, *From Camp to Queer: Remaking the Australian Homosexual* (Melbourne: Melbourne University Press, 2002); and Denise Thompson, *Flaws in the Social Fabric: Homosexuals in Sydney* (Sydney: Allen and Unwin, 1985).
3   'Gay Pride Week', *Gay Lib News*, no. 10 (July 1973), pp. 1–2.

homosexuality.[4] Sue Wills, who was co-president of CAMP from 1972 to 1974, led the campaign to challenge psychiatric views on homosexuality. An academic and one-time psychology graduate from the University of Sydney, Wills persuaded well-known practitioner of aversion therapy, Neil McConaghy, to grant her an interview explaining his methods and reasoning. The ensuing article, 'Intellectual Poofter Bashers', was published in CAMP's newsletter *Camp Ink* and also distributed to delegates at a conference on 'Psychiatry and Liberation' organised by McConaghy in 1973, which was jointly protested by CAMP and SGL.[5] Although such protests were effective in raising doubts amongst some psychiatrists about the necessity and efficacy of treating homosexuality, Wills later reflected that the true victory was in persuading homosexuals themselves not to accept or participate in treatment:

> We'd started out – or I'd started out – trying to stop McConaghy offering aversion therapy and taking people from the courts. The change happened but it didn't happen like that. What we succeeded in doing was stopping gays seeking his help. They no longer saw any reason. I mean, as it became more acceptable, as people stopped being told … that you're sick, you're deranged, you're a menace. Why? I'm not going to go to aversion therapy. There's nothing wrong with me. So he stopped getting clients and patients, and the courts stopped referring people.[6]

In the early 1970s, the gay movement in Sydney represented for a number of women their first contact with other lesbians outside their relationship or small network of friends. Robyn recalled joining CAMP with her partner, Marg, as the beginning of a new social and political phase in her life:

> We knew no other lesbians. And it wasn't really until we saw a TV programme that came on air, on the ABC. And there were two couples interviewed: there were two guys, Peter De Waal and Peter Bonsall-Boone … who were interviewed about their life together. And then there were two women, Sue Wills and Gaby Antolovich. And … they

---

4   John Lee, 'What the Psychiatrists Said and What We Did', *Gay Lib News*, no. 11 (August 1973), pp. 9–10; Katy O'Rourke, 'Bible Bashers Turn Poofter Bashers', *Gay Lib News*, 28 April 1974.
5   Sue Wills, 'Intellectual Poofta Bashers', *Camp Ink*, vol. 2, no. 11, p. 4–11; John Lee, 'What the Psychiatrists Said and What We Did', *Gay Lib News*, no. 11, August 1973, pp. 9–10.
6   Interview with Sue Wills, 23 October 2009.

talked about CAMP NSW, Campaign Against Moral Persecution NSW, which was in Glebe Point Road, and that's when we decided that we would ring them up and go and join the women's group that was attached to Camp NSW and meet other lesbians ...

Well, I do remember going to the first thing, which was a social thing, and it was in somebody's house in their lounge room, and walking in, and there was probably six to eight couples there and I was totally in shock, really. Sort of like, looking but not looking, you know ... [I was] very nervous, whereas Marg wasn't. I mean, Marg was ten years older than me, so she was a bit more socially aware. I was 23, she was 33. I mean she just started chatting to a few people about what they do and stuff. That started our first group of friends, really, that we interacted with.[7]

CAMP was predominantly middle-class and professional – partly, John Ware suggested, due to the unwillingness of the tabloid newspapers to accept adverts for the group, meaning that publicity was confined to papers with a middle-class readership, such as *The Australian* or *The Bulletin*.[8] Commenting on her first experience of the women in CAMP, Robyn, a teacher, reflected:

There was a variety of women. The ones that Marg started chatting to were, one was a university lecturer and another one was a biochemist and so it was a matter of speaking to people who were interested in their profession. But then there was another one there who I saw who rode a motorbike, she was a geologist, and I thought, 'Oh', because she had all the black leather gear on. I was a bit startled, but apart from riding a motorbike, she was fine! ... I think the grouping was really middle-class and professions.[9]

Margaret, who joined the group in her early 40s, recalled the women members of the group as predominantly younger women, reflecting: 'these were younger women, twenties, twenty-five, might have been daringly closer to thirty but they were all younger ... I was older than anyone I'd ever met, that there was rarely could I find a woman of my exact age.'[10]

---

7   Interview with Robyn Plaister, 20 December 2007; the program referred to was 'This Just Happens to be Me', ABC Chequerboard, 31 October 1972.
8   John Ware, 'Twelve Months Past', *Camp Ink*, September 1971, p. 4.
9   Interview with Robyn Plaister, 20 December 2007.
10 Interview with Margaret Jones, 18 September 2007.

Robyn joined CAMP at a relatively stable moment in the group's appeal to women. Despite the role of a woman in co-founding the group, tensions had quickly emerged over the place of women in CAMP NSW. Some women members felt that the group prioritised political issues which were of primary importance to men, such as law reform, and the apparently sexist attitudes of some men in the organisation caused further tension. Margaret commented:

> I found that the guys were ... misogynist, they were all such queens ... trilling and kissing and hissing and dressing up and adopting female names and nothing ordinary like Mary or Betty, you know there was Fiona, was a popular name, or Elizabeth or exotic names, Theresa. And they treated the women very badly and saw us as being their coffee-makers, to clean up the clubrooms after their drunken parties and they were, which I didn't know then, but they were patronising and of course they were misogynist – they didn't like us, they didn't like women as I no more like men now, but for different reasons, probably their mothers or something, or they didn't like us because they in fact wanted to be women and we were and therefore they didn't like us because we had something they couldn't be.[11]

Margaret's recollections highlight the cultural rift which emerged between (some) homosexual men, whose identities had been shaped in an older, predominantly male, underground camp social scene, in which drag was a popular form of entertainment, and a new generation of politically confident women who were attempting to articulate their concerns in gendered terms. Conflict over the right of women to meet as a separate women's group within CAMP reached a head in late 1971, when women ceased to meet at the organisation's headquarters on Darling Street in Balmain. Early the following year, Margaret Jones, the women's group organiser, contacted US lesbian magazine, *The Ladder*, explaining that the former CAMP women were planning to form a group similar to the US group, Daughters of Bilitis. However, in May 1972, Sue Wills, newly elected co-president of CAMP, persuaded them to rejoin CAMP as the Camp Women's Association (CWA). The group remained active throughout 1972, producing a newssheet for 130 readers, but by June 1973, tensions over the sexism of some male CAMP members had again flared up, and the group disbanded. Although individual women continued to work within CAMP

---

11   Interview with Margaret Jones, 31 August, 12 September, 18 September 2007.

throughout the 1970s, the group's appeal to women declined and its female membership was extremely small.[12]

Sydney Gay Liberation's newsletter reflects a similar story of male sexism and declining participation by women. In September 1972, Mim Loftus complained: 'Gay Lib has been functioning in Sydney for about one year now, and even though a small number of women have been aware of that fact, the women, due to a variety of reasons, have not been drawn to Gay Lib as active participants.'[13] The following year, they agreed to hold a weekly meeting 'to discuss the way individual gay libbers related to each other and to women, in what was an attempt to focus our attention on those nasty sexist habits, preconditions, values etc., we all carry around with us to varying degrees, STILL.' Terry Bell proclaimed the meeting a 'dismal failure' which had 'side-stepped' the issues and called on male SGL members to engage in consciousness-raising as a move towards addressing these issues.[14]

Feminist politics

CAMP and SGL have been regarded by historians such as Garry Wotherspoon and Graham Willett as playing a crucial role in reshaping lesbian and gay experience in the 1970s, but their failure to attract or retain lesbian members meant that they had less impact on lesbian culture and identity than on models of gay male identity.[15] In contrast, by the early 1970s, feminist groups in Sydney were enjoying considerable success, appealing to a broad range of women including many lesbians. Women's liberation had emerged in Sydney in 1969 out of a broader spectrum of left-wing protest at that time, and particularly from opposition to the Vietnam War. Recalling her participation in the very early years of women's liberation, Suzanne Bellamy observed:

> [T]his was a very multi-generational, multi-class – but not nearly enough multi-race – coming together. And for that very early period, there was tremendous struggle. The other key thing that I think is important to say is that this period was not one of unity, that in the lost culture of Women's Liberation, there were, I believe, four core principles. These principles were: (1) sisterhood is powerful; (2) consciousness raising; (3)

---

12   Sue Wills, 'Inside the CWA – The Other One', *Journal of Australian Lesbian Feminist Studies*, no. 4 (June 1994), pp. 6–22.
13   Mim Loftus, *Sydney Gay Liberation Newsletter*, no. 3 (September 1972).
14   'Sexism in Gay Lib', *Gay Lib News*, no. 10 (July 1973).
15   Garry Wotherspoon, *City of the Plain: History of a Gay Sub-Culture* (Sydney: Hale and Iremonger, 1991); Willett, *Living Out Loud*.

the personal is political; and (4) direct action. However, we struggled about them, we didn't always agree on what they meant.[16]

Lyndall Ryan agreed, noting that 'the idea of collective action around women was also very important ... The idea that women were actually the real leaders of a revolutionary movement at that time, was very liberating.' For Ryan, consciousness-raising, or 'using the experiences of women to formulate a political program' was fundamental to women's liberation, and consciousness-raising groups quickly sprang up in women's homes and women's centres across Sydney.[17] Women's Liberation used demonstrations and other forms of direct political action to protest specific issues such as the lack of equal pay for women, the need for contraception and child care (to give women choices outside of the domestic sphere) and the need to protect women from sexual and physical violence, as well as to challenge the broader social attitudes to gender roles which underpinned these issues.[18]

Marilyn Lake notes: 'The combination of the new feminist assumption that sexual pleasure was women's right – one of the last rights to be claimed by feminists in Australia – with the critique of sex roles, provided a conducive environment for the expression and exploration of lesbian desire.'[19] Lesbians were attracted by a political critique of patriarchy and demands for equality in the workforce and elsewhere, as well as by an emerging culture which was shaped and populated by women. Valerie recalled the appeal of

---

16 Suzanne Bellamy, in 'Sexual Politics: The Women's Liberation Movement', in Beverley Symons and Rowan Cahill, eds, *A Turbulent Decade: Social Protest Movements and the Labour Movement, 1965–1975* (Australian Society for the Study of Labour History, 2005), p. 31.

17 Lyndall Ryan, 'Sexual Politics: The Women's Liberation Movement', in *A Turbulent Decade: Social Protest Movements and the Labour Movement, 1965-1975*, p. 36. The practice and benefits of consciousness-raising were frequently discussed in the feminist press, for example, 'Consciousness-raising – What's It All About?', *Sydney Women's Liberation Newsletter*, November 1974, p. 4; 'What is C.R.', *Womanspeak*, vol. 2, no. 2, p. 16.

18 Marilyn Lake, *Getting Equal: The History of Australian Feminism* (Sydney: Allen & Unwin, 1999); Verity Burgmann, *Power and Protest: Movements for Change in Australian Society* (Sydney: Allen & Unwin, 1993); Gisela Kaplan, *The Meagre Harvest: The Australian Women's Movement, 1950s to 1990s* (Sydney: Allen & Unwin, 1996); Beverley Symons and Rowan Cahill, eds, *A Turbulent Decade: Social Protest Movements and the Labour Movement, 1965–1975* (Sydney: Australian Society for the Study of Labour History, 2005); Ann Curthoys, 'The Women's Movement since 1970', in Kay Saunders and Raymond Evans, eds, *Gender Relations in Australia: Domination and Negotiation* (Sydney: Harcourt Brace Jovanovich, 1992), pp. 425–447; Susan Hawthorne, 'A History of the Contemporary Women's Movement', *Journal of Australian Lesbian Feminist Studies*, vol. 2, no. 1 (June 1992), pp. 71–79.

19 Lake, *Getting Equal: The History of Australian Feminism*, pp. 242–3.

women's liberation as a heady mixture of 'hands-on' political activism and womanpower:

> I remember the Women's Day Marches, there was always a bit of a fight or something. Somebody, some bloke would try to drive through the women's banner and they'd usually get their doors kicked in, and somebody would sit on the bonnet. It was just this great women's solidarity sort of thing. They were some of the best things those marches in the early days. There was just so much power there. And I guess, from right from when I was a kid, I hated the injustice that women couldn't, weren't equal with blokes, you know. Just always I hated it. Even though I wanted to be a boy when I was a kid, they were allowed to do things that women weren't allowed to do and they got jobs that … So yeah, I loved that Women's Lib sort of thing and those big groups of women.[20]

Valerie was one of many women who saw in the women's movement an environment in which she could express a sexuality she had already identified and acted upon. For other women, involvement in feminist groups such as Women's Liberation and Women's Electoral Lobby enabled them to explore a previously unacknowledged or unarticulated desire for other women. Diana, a North Shore housewife and mother of four, became active in Women's Electoral Lobby after beginning a degree at Macquarie University. She reflected: 'many of us started off as so-called straight and then became lesbians.'[21] Diana described her gradual identification as a lesbian as a personal and intellectual journey. Experiencing difficulties in her marriage, Diana had become aware that, for the first time, she was attracted to another woman: her son's swimming teacher. In an attempt to distract herself from these feelings, she began a university degree, only to find that:

> Macquarie … was a hotbed! … particularly in the Sociology department, there were lots of academics who were lesbian. And also History, and other areas. And it was, there was a Women's Room. And it was heady stuff. They invited radical lesbian feminists from America up to speak, to address staff and students. And so I started reading all this radical literature. You know, I'd go to the library and I'd just be drawn to it. Forget the Psychology I was doing! It was interesting, but I found all that fascinating.[22]

---

20   Interview with Valerie Odewahn, 20 May 2008.
21   Interview with Diana Goldrick, 9 July 2009.
22   Interview with Diana Goldrick, 9 July 2009.

In this environment, Diana felt able to leave her marriage and explore a newfound desire for other women.

For Sandra, who first identified as a lesbian as a teenager in the early 1970s, feminist analyses of sexuality were integral to her developing construction of a lesbian identity. Although Sandra had had boyfriends while at school, she decided she was a lesbian at the age of 18, when she saw two women kissing at a party. She later went on to have a relationship with one of the women herself. However, Sandra remained isolated from the lesbian community for another few years. It was not until she took herself to Women's Liberation House on Alberta Street in the city, in 1973, that she encountered other lesbians. The experience had a profound effect on her life and shaped the way she began to think about her lesbian sexual identity. Sandra was invited to attend a consciousness-raising group, which focused on issues of sexuality, and also became involved in the establishment of Elsie Women's Refuge and Sydney Rape Crisis Centre. This involvement exposed Sandra to debates about lesbian separatism, and she began to adopt a woman-centred lifestyle and limit her contact with the men in her family. Deciding to focus her energies on other women, Sandra lived in one of the many women-only feminist sharehouses in Sydney and formed friendships and relationships with other women in the movement. Her notions of appropriate sexual practice were shaped by the views expressed in lesbian feminist music and literature, which she and her friends enjoyed. Women's dances, organised as social events and fundraisers for feminist campaigns, provided a further forum for expressing a lesbian feminist sexual ideology. Like Valerie, Sandra's notion of lesbian identity was grounded in an understanding of herself as part of a community of women, and although her feminist commitment taught her the importance of being 'open and confrontational', she understood this confrontation in terms of a challenge to notions of femininity as much as to assumptions of heterosexuality.[23]

Although feminist politics and culture appealed to lesbians from the outset, and lesbians became a strong presence throughout Women's Liberation, lesbianism remained a largely unacknowledged aspect of the movement in the early 1970s. Concerns that accusations of lesbianism would be used to discredit feminism encouraged a culture where women who desired other women were expected to downplay their sexuality and prioritise the goals of heterosexual feminism. Robyn recalled:

> [Feminists] didn't seem to understand a lot of [lesbian] issues and they weren't willing to be involved, partly because the argument at that time

---

23   Interview with Sandra Mackay, 2 July 2007.

was 'that's another area to go to; let's look after women that are subject to domestic violence, or need an abortion, let's look after them first, let's argue with the government or whoever about these issues. Let's not bring in lesbianism because we won't get the money, or we won't get listened to if we bring lesbianism into the issue as well ... Even though those women that were working in those areas and always at the forefront of the women's health movement, the rape crisis movement, the refuge movement, were lesbians. There were heterosexual feminists involved, but a lot of the lesbians were doing a lot of the work, voluntary work.[24]

However, by the mid-1970s, lesbians were becoming a more vocal force in the women's movement across Australia and feminist journals demonstrated an increased level of (sometimes contentious) debate on the issue. In January 1973, members of the Hobart Women's Action Group addressed these concerns in a paper entitled 'Sexism and the Women's Liberation Movement', delivered at the Mt Beauty Women's Liberation Theory conference and subsequently printed in Sydney feminist journal *Refractory Girl*. The paper began with a catalogue of personal experiences undergone by lesbians in the women's movement, from 'being told to keep out of the movement because "some women won't come if lesbians are there, and those women shouldn't be put off because Women's Liberation is for all women"' to 'throwing yourself into the child care / pram, bus, struggle to prove you haven't got any interests of your own.'[25] The authors went on to explore fundamental institutions within the movement, such as consciousness-raising groups and the concept of 'sisterhood', arguing that these were premised on an underlying assumption of heterosexuality which ultimately excluded lesbians. The paper, according to the authors, prompted a 'near-hysterical reception' and set the tone for an ongoing debate about the place of lesbians within the movement.[26] The issue flared up again at the 1975 Sydney Women's Commission and in subsequent debates in *Sydney Women's Liberation Newsletter*. Minutes from the Commission noted that lesbians had been accused of being 'sexist and domineering'. In the following newsletter, seven 'lesbian women' responded:

---

24   Interview with Robyn Plaister, 20 December 2007.
25   'Sexism and the Women's Liberation Movement – or "Why do Straight sisters sometimes cry when they are called lesbians?"', *Refractory Girl* (Summer 1974), p. 31.
26   See Katy Reade, '"Struggling to be Heard": Tensions Between Different Voices in the Australian Women's Liberation Movement in the 1970s and 1980s', in Kate Pritchard Hughes, ed., *Contemporary Australian Feminism* (Melbourne: Longman Cheshire, 1994), pp. 198–222.

> To accuse lesbian women of being sexist is like white people accusing black people of being racist or men accusing women of being sexist. This reaction trivialises the experience of the accused and by placing the accused on the defensive the accuser is not required to examine her / his own attitudes.
>
> Lesbianism is not our personal problem, as at least one speaker at the Women's Commission seemed to think, any more than rape, abortion, child care or sexist men are the personal problems of the women involved. All of these are problems or results of this sexist society.[27]

Sporadic calls to include lesbian demands amongst the feminist platform remained unheeded for much of the decade, with the disregard continuing to be attributed to concerns about discrediting the movement. In May 1976, the Lesbian Feminist Collective complained to *Women's Liberation Newsletter* readers:

> On International Women's Day the demands were –
> Save womens jobs
> Unemployment benefits to all women
> Repeal all abortion laws
> Free 24 hour child care
>
> These demands did not include ending heterosexism or the demand for sexual freedom; despite that the lesbian feminist collective marched, provided singing and a speaker and that a sizeable percentage of the movement were lesbians. The omission of these demands is a sell out to respectability.[28]

Lesbian feminism

In the context of a political culture which was resistant to theoretical discussions of lesbianism, many lesbians began to be drawn to more distinctly lesbian groupings within feminism. In January 1973, a group of Melbourne lesbians formed the Melbourne Gay Women's Group, based at the Gay

---

27 'Lesbian Women Answer to November Newsletter', *Women's Liberation Newsletter*, December 1975, p. 2. See also, Lyn Waddell, 'Sydney Women's Commission ... October '75', *Womanspeak*, vol. 2, no. 1, p. 16; Elaine Alinta, 'Letters', *Womanspeak*, vol. 2, no. 3, p. 4.
28 'Lesbian Feminism', *Women's Liberation Newsletter* (Sydney), May 1976, p. 16.

Liberation Centre. By the middle of that year, they had moved to Women's Liberation House and re-emerged as the Melbourne Radicalesbians.[29] Sydney Radicalesbians was formed in September 1973, when Diane Minnis came from Melbourne Radicalesbians to the lesbian feminist sharehouse on Crystal Street in Petersham.[30] In an interview with members of the *Refractory Girl* collective, women from the Radicalesbian households at Crystal Street and Canterbury Castle described a range of political actions that they were engaged in, from giving talks to university students and producing a newsletter to spray-painting buildings with slogans such as 'Lesbians are Lovely' and producing street theatre. The household also 'zapped' gay bars, attempting to persuade the women there to move from the commercial scene into lesbian political activism. One woman recalled:

> The night we went out to the bar – and this drag queen said that we looked like refugees from a disposal store. (laughter) We took over that place and we talked with a fair few women there. One became a regular for awhile. The main idea of zapping gay bars like that is because they rip off gay people so much with the prices. We thought if we turned a few people there into Radicalesbians, and also lost a bit of custom for that bar … that's the idea.[31]

In December 1973, the group organised a Radical Feminist Lesbian Liberation Conference at Minto.[32] Heavily influenced by US and British radical lesbian feminist texts (such as Robin Morgan's *Sisterhood is Powerful* and *Monster* and the US Radicalesbians' essay 'Woman-identified woman'), the group worked to articulate a distinctive lesbian political agenda and to promote debate about lesbianism within the women's movement.[33] In a 'Report from Sydney Radicalesbians', published in *Sydney Women's Liberation Newsletter*, Sivan-Ki explained:

> Our aims are basically feminist ones. As women, and in particular, as lesbian women, we want to destroy the institutions of male culture which bind us and prevent us from finding and being ourselves. At the

---

29 Chris Sitka, 'A Radicalesbian Herstory', http://users.spin.net.au/~deniset/alesfem/s1sitka.pdf, accessed 5 May 2013.
30 Interview with Diane Minnis, 30 December 2012.
31 'A Radicalesbian Lifestyle', *Refractory Girl* (Summer 1974), p. 14.
32 'Conference', *Sydney Women's Liberation Newsletter* (November 1973), p. 13.
33 Robin Morgan, *Sisterhood Is Powerful: An Anthology of Writings from the Women's Liberation Movement* (New York: Random House, 1970); Melbourne Radical Feminists, eds, *Monster, Poems by Robin Morgan* (c.1970); Radicalesbians, *The Woman-Identified Woman* (Pittsburgh: Know Inc, c.1970).

same time, we want to provide the alternatives to enable us to find and be ourselves and to counteract the male culture.[34]

These aims were to be achieved through a combination of theory and action, and the group held regular theory meetings and action meetings as well as consciousness-raising groups.

By September 1975, the formation of a Lesbian Feminist Collective within Women's Liberation demonstrated a growing sense that a distinctive lesbian politics had emerged alongside the mainstream of the women's movement. A report in the Sydney *Newsletter* explained:

> Lesbian feminist collective ... arose to fill the need of synthesising both lesbian and feminist politics. It works on two fronts. It actively works on making the politics of the collective known outside the group as well as giving support to everyone in the collective.[35]

The report suggested that although individual lesbians remained active within and committed to broader feminist politics, there was a growing disjuncture between lesbian politics and culture and the wider movement. The group functioned for over a year and organised a Lesbian Festival in Minto in January 1977, before folding. The decision to re-form the collective in July 1977 was taken in response to concerns that lesbian feminist culture was exhibiting a 'ghetto' mentality. A plea to lesbian feminists to help relaunch the collective reflected:

> There are probably a variety of other reasons [for the earlier demise of the collective] including the fact that the group did not function as well as it might have as either an entry point to lesbian feminist politics for new people nor as a social contact for isolated women. Both the jargon and the ghetto are hard to penetrate ...
>
> Within the movement, there is nowhere [new lesbian contacts] can be referred, even for regular social contact. Though lesbians are active throughout the movement, working for various important feminist issues, we are neglecting lesbian issues and lesbian sisters.[36]

A key aspect of the 'ghetto' mentality that some women identified in lesbian feminist culture was the influence of separatist politics. A belief

---

34   Sivan-Ki, 'Report from Sydney Radicalesbians', *Sydney Women's Liberation Newsletter* (January 1974), p. 5.
35   'Lesbian Feminism', *Women's Liberation Newsletter* (May 1976), p. 16.
36   'Attention all Lesbian Feminists!', *Sydney Women's Liberation Newsletter* (July 1977), p. 9.

had been growing, since the emergence of Radicalesbian politics in 1973, that women should withdraw their energies from men in order to be able to devote themselves completely to the feminist sisterhood, and develop a women's culture free from the insidious domination of patriarchal values. Commenting on her own experience of lesbian separatist politics, Sandra explained:

> Especially working places like the refuge and the Rape Crisis Centre, you really were seeing what men were doing to women and it wasn't good … I did think that the idea of women withdrawing their labour and energy and sexuality, I suppose, from men, was a good solution at the time to you know, the inequalities of existence … And you know, there was an idea that women needed to have women-only spaces because we'd never had that and we saw it a bit like, if men were supportive of us, and understood feminism, then they would be happy enough to stay out of those women only spaces because they would understand our need for it.[37]

Lesbian feminist communities in Sydney were increasingly located in women-only shared households, where male visitors were unwelcome and individual lesbian feminists were encouraged to break off ties with male friends and family members. A cultural movement flourished from this aspect of lesbian feminist ideology, which encouraged the creation of music, literature, poetry and theatre by women, for women, as well as a dynamic social scene based around women-only dances, restaurants and festivals.[38] A desire to provide women-only spaces which would act as a safe haven from patriarchal culture also led to the foundation of rural communities such as that at Mt Firestone in northern New South Wales.[39]

By the late 1970s, lists of 'lesbian demands' were beginning to appear in some Australian feminist literature. In June 1977, *Sydney Women's Liberation Newsletter* reprinted the following demands from the Melbourne-based *Lesbian Newsletter*:

---

37 Interview with Sandra Mackay, 2 July 2007.
38 Kathy Sport, 'Below the Belt and Bleeding Fingertips: Feminist and Lesbian Music in the Late 1970s', *Australian Feminist Studies*, vol. 22, issue 53 (July 2007), pp. 34–-360; Jai Greenway, *Political Acts. Lesbian Theatre in Sydney* (Sydney, Amazon DTP, 1990).
39 Kerryn, 'Amazon Acres, Mount Firestone', *Sydney Women's Liberation Newsletter* (January 1974), p. 5; 'Amazon Acres', *Sydney Women's Liberation Newsletter* (March 1975), p. 10; Judith Ion, 'Degrees of Separation: Lesbian Separatist Communities in Northern New South Wales, 1974–95', in Jill Julius Matthews, ed., *Sex in Public* (St. Leonards: Allen and Unwin, 1997), pp. 97–113.

End Heterosexism: We demand an end to the expectation that every person will only seek out the other sex for all emotional, sexual and economic partnerships.

Lesbian Mothers: We demand the right to bring up children whilst openly living a lesbian lifestyle.

Lesbians at Work: We demand an end to discrimination against lesbians in the workforce. We should be free to be open at work without fears of intimidation, rejection or dismissal.

Lesbian Sexuality: We demand that accurate information on lesbian sexuality be freely available to all women. We demand an end to treatment of lesbians as sexual deviants.

We demand the right to live openly as lesbians.[40]

These demands reflected some of the key areas of concern to lesbian feminists. Radical lesbian feminists advocated working to break down sexual roles, which they regarded as the fundamental building blocks of patriarchal society. In practice this meant rejecting conventional notions of appropriate feminine dress and appearance and many lesbian feminists wore overalls and rejected make-up and the removal of body-hair. In relationships and in shared houses, lesbian feminists strove for equal divisions of labour in contrast to the prescribed gender roles believed to underpin heterosexual marital relations.[41]

Lesbians' rights – as mothers and in the workforce – had been a focus of campaigning by lesbians in the women's movement and the gay movement for a number of years. As public awareness of lesbianism increased and a growing number of women openly identifed as lesbians in the 1970s, a number of divorce cases led to custody disputes centred on the right of lesbian mothers to parent their children.[42] In the context of these debates, and a significant number of lesbian mothers losing custody of their children, lesbian mothers' rights became a key lesbian political issue. Robyn Plaister was active in the campaign and found it to be an issue which drew support from lesbian and gay activists as well as feminists. She recalled:

---

40 'Lesbian Demand', *Sydney Women's Liberation Newsletter* (June 1977), p. 8.
41 Rebecca Jennings, 'Womin Loving Womin: Lesbian Feminist Theories of Intimacy', in Graham Willett and Yorick Smaal, eds, *Intimacy, Violence and Activism: Gay and Lesbian Perspectives on Australasian History and Society* (Melbourne: Monash University Publishing, 2013), pp. 133–146.
42 Rebecca Jennings, 'Lesbian Mothers and Child Custody: Australian Debates in the 1970s', *Gender and History* vol. 24, Issue 2 (August 2012), pp. 502–517.

And then I started the lesbian mothers group, I think in '76 and that was for various reasons. It was partly, because of my interest in what was happening with a lot of the cases, that I wanted to politick heavily on the discrimination that was occurring around the issue of lesbians, because it seemed to me that in cases that were coming up in higher courts, that the kids would be given to the parent who wasn't gay. And it seemed, where the lesbian mother got custody of her children, it would only be because the male was say, an alcoholic, or violent. And where the mother got hold of the children too, if she was a lesbian, there were conditions attached i.e. that the lover didn't live in the same house, or there was no expression of affection between the two of them. So these were the sort of cases that were coming through. So that I was looking partly from that political context. I was also looking to develop a group which would allow lesbian mothers and their children to come together to meet each other, to be a support group. And also for the children of lesbian mothers to meet each other and work out how they deal with it in their world, in terms of being discriminated against by other kids in schools and things like that. I also was looking towards the partners, who did not have children, coming together to be supportive of one another and how they relate to lesbian mothers and their children, although that area of support seemed to happen less. It became more a support group for lesbian mothers, but it worked effectively for quite a few years.[43]

The need to conceal one's sexuality to avoid loss of employment was another central concern for lesbians and gay men from the early years of lesbian and gay activism, both as a form of discrimination and as an issue which prevented many women from 'coming out'. In 1974, lesbian and gay activists mobilised in support of Penny Short, the Macquarie University student who had lost her Teachers' College scholarship after publishing a lesbian love poem in the student newspaper, *Arena*. She had declared that she was in a lesbian relationship during the standard medical examination which occurred at the start of the course, but she had been advised that it would not be reported; however, after the publication of the poem, she was recalled for a further medical examination and declared medically unfit. Large political meetings and rallies were held at Macquarie University and the University of Sydney and over 1000 staff and students demanded the reinstatement of Penny Short's scholarship. The issue received support

---

43   Interview with Robyn Plaister, 20 December 2007.

from the Labor Shadow Minister for Education and left-wing groups such as the Builders Labourers' Federation. Although the scholarship was not reinstated, the protests prompted the NSW Teachers' Federation to issue a statement condemning the termination of a scholarship on the grounds of homosexuality.[44] Penny Short's case indicated the ongoing risks faced by lesbians who chose to be open about their sexuality. This issue was the focus of considerable debate in both the lesbian and gay and women's movement throughout the decade, when political imperatives of visibility conflicted with personal pressures to maintain discretion.

The development of a political culture of openness

By the early 1970s, the question of whether or not to discuss feelings of same-sex desire with family, acquaintances and society at large had become a contentious political issue. Influenced by the success of American and British gay liberation campaigns, early Australian lesbian and gay political organisations such as the Campaign Against Moral Persecution NSW and Sydney Gay Liberation, as well as lesbians within the women's movement, argued that the public expression of same-sex desire was a crucial basis for ending social discrimination against lesbians and gay men. In October 1971, Keith Clinton argued in *Camp Ink*:

> The fundamental stand taken by Camp Inc is that homosexuality is not the dirty little secret which society has always tried to make it. Homosexuals have got nothing to hide or be ashamed of ... Camp Inc started out by saying – Here is the minority! Take a look at us. Listen to us. Come and help us if you like.
>
> This, after all, is the only useful way to go about changing the situation of the homosexual in our society. If homosexuals want to be treated like people, they have got to be seen to be people. Misunderstandings, rumours and slanders flourish when people are ignorant. The best way to get understanding, lay the rumours and kill the slanders is to stand up to them, openly.[45]

His views reflected one of the key values of CAMP Inc, whose central aim, Denise Thompson states, 'was to reach out beyond the confines of a

---

44 Sue Wills, 'Sexual Politics: Gay and Lesbian Rights', in *A Turbulent Decade: Social Protest Movements and the Labour Movement, 1965–1975*, p. 42; 'Victimisation by ed. dept.', *Refractory Girl* (Summer 1974), p. 11.
45 Keith Clinton, *Camp Ink* (October 1971).

homosexual support group, by educating the "thinking public", and challenging the received opinion that homosexuals were "mad/bad/sick" by admitting one's homosexuality openly and publicly and without shame, and demonstrating to people of goodwill that homosexuals were "ordinary folk just like you and me".[46] This emphasis on challenging public opinions of homosexuality led to a partial reframing of media representations of female same-sex desire in the 1970s.[47] When a group of Melbourne lesbians formed Australia's first lesbian organisation, a chapter of the US group Daughters of Bilitis, in 1969, founding members appeared on television shows *The Bailey File* and *This Day Tonight* to publicise the organisation, beginning a pattern of individual lesbians and gay men appearing openly as homosexuals in sympathetic sections of the media.[48] The following year, Sydney lesbian and gay activists appeared in newspapers and on television and radio to discuss the launch of CAMP Inc. On 19 September 1970, Christabel Poll and John Ware, the founding members of CAMP, featured in a full-page article in *The Australian* newspaper. In contrast to media representations of homosexuals in the 1960s, the pair gave their full names and appeared in a photograph with faces to camera, launching a strategic challenge to the culture of concealment.[49]

Women in CAMP and other groups sought to challenge social attitudes to homosexuality in the 1970s through a variety of expressions of sexuality. In 1971, Mim and Sue contributed an article to *Camp Ink* describing their experience of holding hands in public and their motivations for doing so. They explained:

> I feel people have to come to recognise the existence of lesbianism. Some people are actually so unaware of the nature of sensuality and love that they don't feel love can exist outside the limits of the protestantethic [sic] the sooner these people see with their own eyes that it exists the sooner it will be accepted, the more people start seeing homosexuality the more likely they are going to start getting educated (I hope) ... Holding hands in public is a step towards educating the public, towards

---

46   Denise Thompson, *Flaws in the Social Fabric: Homosexuals and Society in Sydney* (Sydney: George Allen & Unwin, 1985), p. 9.
47   In 1974, the comedy drama series *The Box* featured a bisexual character, Vicki Stafford. See Michael Hurley, *A Guide to Gay and Lesbian Writing in Australia* (Sydney: Allen & Unwin, 1996), p. 37.
48   Interview with Francesca Curtis and Phyllis Papps by Gary Jaynes, Graham Willett and Liz Ross, ALGA, 10 January 2008. *The Bailey File* was a Channel 9 program aired late on Sunday nights.
49   Willett, *Living Out Loud*, p. 33–4.

having lesbianism recognised as something that exists. After people realise that it exists, perhaps next generation, they will accept it.

Public reactions to their handholding varied, they noted, from the young men who called out names to the 'secretary-type' girls who whispered and pointed and the 'vast majority' of people who 'look away and look embarrassed'.[50] Most, however, could be disarmed by a simple acknowledgement that yes, they were lesbians. Chris recalled similar reactions when she used her physical appearance to convey her lesbian feminist identity:

> We wore big braces and men's shirts, and I had short hair and yeah, I didn't wear a bra. And I was very much associated with feminism and the whole kind of rejecting that idea that you had to dress as a woman and have these kind of constraints on the way you were ... I mean people thought you looked not that nice. They weren't that happy with being confronted by it. But that's kind of in a way, not why you did it, but that was part and parcel of doing it in a way.[51]

Other women made public announcements about their sexuality, either appearing on television or the radio to discuss their identity as lesbians, or contributing lesbian-themed poetry or articles to the press.[52]

While CAMP initially stressed the importance of 'coming out' as a strategy in changing broader social views about homosexuality, the value of openness in promoting individual health and well-being was also increasingly noted. In an article entitled, 'Living Without Men', published in *Camp Ink* in May 1972, Susan Williamson argued:

> So there has developed a conspiracy of silence and lies with regard to Lesbians. The church calls her a sinner, the law makes her a criminal, and psychiatry tells her she is sick.
>
> Because a Lesbian is raised like everyone else, she will have deep-seated anti-homosexual prejudices. This will be her first obstacle as she struggles to achieve her identity. There is often a period of denial, when she tries desperately to convince herself that she is not 'like them'.
>
> This is one of the worst things this society does to gay people. It breeds guilt, self-hatred, lack of confidence.

---

50   Mim and Sue, 'On holding hands', *Camp Ink* (Dec 71 / Jan 72), p. 10.
51   Interview with Chris Pearce, 6 November 2007.
52   Interview with Sue Wills, 23 October 2009.

This is the significance of the emphasis on gay pride in the gay liberation movement. It is changing the 'coming out' process from an agonizing, terrifying, individual experience, into a beautiful, self-affirmative, social process.[53]

These arguments resonated strongly with some women who were involved in lesbian and gay or feminist politics in the 1970s, or became aware of their ideas. Sue, who went on to become one of the first co-presidents of CAMP NSW, recalled: 'Once I became politically active, I had to come out.'[54] For many such women the process of informing immediate family and friends of their same-sex desires represented a defining moment in their lives, which they recalled in considerable detail. Robyn described coming out to her family as a difficult but inevitable process, when she left her marriage to begin a relationship with another woman:

> That of course was very difficult. I probably had quite a few drinks before – I was at my girlfriend from school's place … and I had to travel, I don't know how I travelled, to my mother's place and tell her and of course she gave me a few more whiskeys. And so yes, I was very drunk by the time I left there, but yeah, I basically had to say, 'Mum, I'm leaving the marriage and I'm a lesbian' and all of that at the same time, so it was very, very difficult.[55]

Sandra also recalled being motivated to tell her mother that she was a lesbian by her strong investment in lesbian feminist values.

> I talked pretty quickly to my mother about it and I didn't talk to my father. I left it to her to say or not say to him what she liked. And I, I mean I'd had a very good and happy family life but I, I just went there, to her home, and I said, 'I've got to tell you something about myself that you don't know, that everyone else knows. I'm a lesbian'. And she was pretty shocked, because … I might have been 19 or something like that, you know, and I hadn't probably left home that long … so it was a big shock. And she said something like, 'Oh!' She was shocked obviously. She said, 'I knew I should have got your teeth fixed!' And it was just like one of those silly things that can be a bit of a joke later … Because what had happened was not long before that … Mum had realised that

---

53   Susan Williamson, 'Living Without Men', *Camp Ink* (May 1972), p. 10, reprinted and condensed from *Womankind*, vol. 1, no. 4.
54   Interview with Sue Wills, 23 October 2009.
55   Interview with Robyn Plaister, 20 December 2007.

> [someone I was sharing a house with] was a lesbian … [and] she said it was, that idea that someone turns you into a lesbian, you know. I wasn't in a sexual relationship with [that woman] at all and I just said 'Oh listen, I don't need to listen to this shit' and I walked out and I was sort of pretty devastated but also I was so full of the whole kind of notion of what you had to do, that if … that's what it meant [then …], but she came back, she came to the house the next day and was pretty accepting.[56]

Like Robyn, Sandra described coming out to her mother as a major crisis point in their relationship, but one which was fortunately resolved through mutual understanding. Nevertheless, Sandra recalled both her sense of the wider political importance of what she was doing and her belief that if coming out had resulted in a breakdown in her relationship with her mother, then that would have been a sacrifice, however painful, which needed to be made.

Influenced by the ideology and sexual identities promoted by lesbian and gay political movements in the 1970s, historiography of the postwar period has tended to characterise the 1970s as a moment of liberation, a key turning point when women passed from lives of concealment to a new climate of openness and self-expression. In his analysis of the way in which this narrative was constructed, Robert Reynolds notes that these new subjectivities were dependent on an opposition 'between being "out" and "in"'. He argues:

> A brief summary of the language CAMP activists used in describing the opposing positions of 'out' and 'in' reveals how evocative this polarity was in creating the new homosexual. Life in the closet was marked by 'hypocrisy' and 'secrecy'. The 'secret homosexual' was 'unhappy' and 'immature', forced to navigate a life of peril that was both 'agonizing' and 'terrifying'. By contrast, to come out was to come into a life that was 'beautiful' and 'self affirmative.' Coming out enabled the individual to claim a place among 'the adjusted' and 'the healthy' instead of the neurotic and maladjusted. In direct opposition to the 'trapped' existence of the 'secret' homosexual's 'double life', the 'open' homosexual was 'real' and 'free.'[57]

---

56 Interview with Sandra Mackay, 2 July 2007.
57 Robert Reynolds, *From Camp to Queer: Remaking the Australian Homosexual* (Melbourne: Melbourne University Press, 2002), p. 55.

While some women, like Robyn and Sandra, made a strong political commitment to coming out as a result of this ideology, the distinction between 'out' and 'in' was much less clearly defined for many others. For women in particular, the influence of feminist ideas and activism in opening up new opportunities and freedoms was often more significant in reshaping their experience than the ideology of 'coming out'. Oral histories describe very real tensions in the 1970s and beyond around the philosophy of openness as a form of liberation, and many lesbians in this period remained ambivalent about the practice of 'coming out'. Valerie, who moved to Sydney in the early 1970s from rural NSW and joined a wider lesbian social scene for the first time, was left bemused by the new ideas she came into contact with there. She recalled feeling under some pressure during this period to 'come out' to her family and society at large, but her awareness of the experiences of lesbian friends left her unconvinced:

> It's interesting because people always talked about telling their families and coming out to their families and stuff and mostly they were traumatic, very traumatic stories. One girlfriend I had, she decided she was going to tell her parents and you know, figured out this story and how she was going to approach it. When she went home one weekend to Bathurst, she told her mother and her mother said 'Oh that's nice dear, so am I!' And so the thing was totally reversed. Then she had to deal with her mother being a lesbian, being married, but also having this lover in another country town that she was having a relationship with. Wow! I mean how unexpected was that. But mostly there were stories of people being chucked out or fathers or mothers not talking to them. So I didn't want to go through that. I didn't want to push it because I didn't know how Mum and Dad would react.[58]

As a result, Valerie never discussed her same-sex desires or relationships with her parents, opting instead to 'make up stories about boyfriends and that sort of thing'. Similarly, she avoided mention of her sexuality at work, through a fear 'of being rejected or rebuffed or something like that'.[59]

Laurie was also bemused by the new language of openness, which characterised the gay bar scene as a ghetto inhabited by closeted and frightened individuals. As a butch lesbian who had socialised on that scene since the early 1960s, Laurie regarded herself as anything but 'closeted': her

---

58   Interview with Valerie Odewahn, 20 May 2008.
59   ibid.

visibility as a lesbian had led to her being physically assaulted on the streets and harassed by police. Consequently she resented attempts by lesbian feminists to change her attitudes, explaining: 'It wasn't that we didn't like them, it was just that we were out and totally out and I think they were trying to teach us something.'[60] Although Laurie later became involved to some degree in the women's movement, she did not embrace the notion of coming out advocated by lesbian feminists. She recalled:

> But it was funny, when I did get involved with that and the politics and that, it was just I thought creating more trouble than it was worth. In the sense that they were just making it harder for themselves and we were getting on with our lives and we'd made our way to that far. What we were doing was pretty brave, I mean we got bashed up and stuff like that.[61]

Much of the conflict between members of the older bar scene and the new political cultures was expressed through dress, being centred on differing understandings of how to articulate a lesbian identity and challenge assumptions about heterosexuality and femininity. Laurie recalled that lesbian feminists critiqued her butch identity, explaining, 'I was supposed not to wear suits and that wasn't cool and it wasn't part of what the feminist movement was about': a position she regarded as hypocritical, given that 'they looked butcher than I did with their overalls and stuff on.'[62]

While these conflicts initially emerged between lesbian political activists and women who defined themselves around a social scene, tensions soon appeared within the political groups themselves. In their accounts of the early years of CAMP Inc and Sydney Gay Liberation, Denise Thompson, Robert Reynolds and Graham Willett all noted the divide which began to emerge between those members who actively embraced 'coming out' as a fundamental aspect of a new lesbian and gay identity and those who felt marginalised by this view and unable or unwilling to implement it in their own lives. The very real risks of loss of employment or career faced by some women in occupations such as teaching, social work or the public service meant that those who otherwise supported the new lesbian and gay politics felt excluded from this newly emerging community. One disgruntled 'gay girl' wrote to gay magazine *Campaign* in the 1970s:

---

60   Interview with Laurie van Camp by Sandra Mackay, Pride History Group Collection, 18 February 2008.
61   ibid.
62   ibid.

> I'm sick of being pushed, pulverized, pestered and pressured by other gays (male and female) to come out of the closet. I'm told I'm living in the Dark Ages, a disgrace to Gay Lib., Women's Lib., Radicalesbianism, Feminism etc. What utter rot!
>
> Generally, closet gays are ... people who want to get on with the ordinary business of living and loving, of holding down steady jobs and maintaining stable love affairs. Many are prominent in community matters, and greatly loved and respected by their square family and friends. Why should they upset all this, since it all contributes to their feelings of self-respect and self-worth, feelings which many overt gays lack almost entirely, I've noticed, because of constant knocks, eye-brow-raising and criticism.[63]

Asserting a right to choose a closet gay identity, 'gay girl' turned gay liberation rhetoric on its head, maintaining that 'feelings of self-respect and self-worth' were the product of discretion rather than overt expression.

Moreover, while the political culture of openness was widely discussed in activist circles from the early 1970s onwards, these ideas did not have an immediate wider impact. Restrictions on advertising in certain sections of the Australian media meant that women often remained unaware of the existence of the lesbian and gay organisations which were emerging in this period. One member of CAMP NSW recalled the difficulties they experienced in informing the wider community about the establishment of their telephone counselling service in 1973, as 'in those days we couldn't get an entry in the telephone directory that mentioned the words 'homosexual' or 'gay' or 'camp.'[64] As a result, women often went through quite circuitous routes to locate lesbian groups. Margaret felt that she had been very lucky to find out about CAMP Inc through a friend of a woman she was having an affair with. She explained:

> Through my connections with this woman I was sleeping with, I met the famous Jo Beaumont who was involved with CAMP Inc, and came to it through that way, rather than other people. Since there was no advertising and nobody knew about it and nobody was in fact a lesbian or a homosexual in those days, I don't know, the people who did find it, how they managed to find it, but I got in through the front door, so to speak.[65]

---

63 'Of Remaining in our Closet: A Viewpoint from a gay girl', *Campaign*.
64 Alison Pressley, *Living in the 70s* (Sydney: Random House, 2002), p. 196
65 Interview with Margaret Jones, 18 September 2007.

For women who were not already part of a lesbian network, locating such groups was even more difficult. Elizabeth described how her former partner had had to make international enquiries before discovering the existence of CAMP:

> No it's interesting what she had to do, she was married with two young children, didn't know anything about the gay scene in Sydney and what she did was write to New York that, the Sisters [sic] of Bilitis, she had to write all the way to New York to find out and they wrote back and said 'Look, dear, no, you've got somewhere there' and they put her onto Gay Inc [sic] in Balmain in Sydney. But that's the route she took. She went into the Post Office in Sydney, got the American phonebook, no she went to the damned Consulate, got the phone book of New York, looked and found it. Now that's what she, that's the effort she had to go to.[66]

Accessing lesbian and gay organisations was often the first of many hurdles for lesbians in the 1970s. Throughout that decade and beyond, lesbian and gay groups continued to be contacted by women whose lives were shaped by secrecy and isolation. In 1977, a young lesbian from southern NSW wrote to CAMP, describing her situation:

> I will be 20 in October. I am employed as an apprentice jeweller first year will be completed as of March the first. I live with my parents and have a happy family life.
>
> No one knows that I'm camp. A best friend in Adelaide thinks I'm bisexual. I told her that because if I told her the truth I'd lose her for sure.
>
> It took her long enough to accept bisexuality also a male friend of mine in Melbourne thinks I'm bisexual.
>
> These 2 people are my dearest friends who I can confide in but I can't go as far as telling them the real truth. I know probably Camp Lib wants to bring everything out to the open and have people accept us.
>
> In my case if anyone who knows me found out I wouldn't have anything. I'm trusting you with my life so I hope you write back and we continue writing.[67]

---

66 Interview with Elizabeth by Ruth Ford, Australian Lesbian and Gay Archive, 6 May 1992.
67 Letter to CAMP NSW, received 20/4/77, Folder 73, Gay Counselling Service of NSW Papers, Mitchell Library, MSS 5836.

Unable to confide in the people around her, CAMP represented to her both a lifeline and a possibility of friendship. She told her correspondent:

> I hope you can help me out and don't think that my problems are silly. I feel so much better knowing I have you to write to. I was so happy when I got your address. My life was a more happy place. Please write back and tell me about yourself … I'll be waiting everyday for a reply. Please don't let me down, I'm depending on you. Your [sic] my last hope for help.[68]

The impact of lesbian and gay and feminist activism was not felt uniformly across NSW or even across Sydney. For women who were actively involved in lesbian or feminist politics, these movements offered radically new ways of thinking about their lesbian identity, community and culture. Some women actively embraced a culture of openness and organised their day-to-day lives and social and family networks around their political commitment. Others, however, engaged only partially with the ideology of 'coming out' or else rejected it entirely. Despite the early excitement of CAMP and the lesbian and gay movement, it was feminist politics which had the greatest impact on women, offering women-only spaces as well as a gendered critique of society. However, as letters such as the one above indicate, the new political movements of the 1970s also represented to many women their first opportunity to reach out to wider social networks of lesbians – and potentially to locate a partner.

---

68   ibid.

Chapter 5

CULTURES OF INTIMACY

In 1966, Channel 7 entitled its ground-breaking documentary on female homosexuality in Australia, 'Love is Love'. After a scene depicting two women dancing together to the sound of the Righteous Brothers' hit song, 'I need your love', presenter Anne Deveson began, 'Love is love, whether it's between a man and a woman, a man and another man or between two women. If the feeling's genuine, then it's all love.'[1] However, the remainder of the 30-minute program, which featured interviews with self-identified lesbians juxtaposed with summaries of the views of leading psychiatrists and other commentators, seemed rather to undermine this claim for the universal qualities of love. In contrast to the cultural dominance of heterosexual married relationships, the women interviewed by Deveson depicted love between women as elusive, hidden and sometimes almost asexual. For women who desired other women in this period, social attitudes toward lesbianism shaped both their experiences of love and their public and private practices of intimacy, rendering love between two women very different from the socially sanctioned kind between a man and a woman.

Oral histories reinforce the impression that the silence surrounding lesbianism in the mid-twentieth century impacted on and shaped intimacy between women significantly in this period. Locating partners was often very difficult, as many women were isolated from lesbian networks and were cautious in reaching out to women whose sexual identity was undeclared.

---

1 'Love is Love: Lesbians', *Seven Days* (Canberra: ScreenSound Australia, 2003 [originally aired by ATN 7, 15 February 1966])

One woman told Anne Deveson that life as a lesbian was lonely because of the difficulty in finding other lesbians: 'You can fall madly for a woman who is as square as an old butter box', she explained. Another, responding to Deveson's question as to whether lesbians have a future, said that she felt she personally didn't have one as she was unable to find a life partner.[2] Letters to overseas lesbian magazines or Australian homosexual organisations also pointed to the desperation of women who had dreamed of a lesbian relationship for years but been unable to make those fantasies a reality. For many, their first concern on making contact with a wider lesbian social network was the hope of finding a female partner. One such letter from a young New South Wales lesbian to CAMP in 1977 represented both a request for friendship and advice from the gay man she was addressing and an expectation that he might provide an opening to a wider lesbian network. She explained, 'I'd like to write to someone in NSW female about the same age who could understand my problem and write to me. If you know of such a girl tell her my situation and all about me and ask her to write to me.' Although ostensibly seeking friendship by correspondence with another lesbian, her letter went on to reveal a deeper hope for something more. She clarified: 'I'm fairly butch so please get someone who isn't otherwise we may clash ... In your search for a female friend for me to write to, please consider blondes.'[3]

Intimacy and identity

The absence of an explicit cultural discourse of female homosexuality for much of the mid-twentieth century opened up a space in which it was possible for women to imagine and engage in emotionally and sexually intimate relationships with other women without claiming a sexual identity around their same-sex desires. Many of these women participated in relationships with other women for a short period before entering into heterosexual marriages, or pursued same-sex relationships clandestinely while married; others understood their sexuality in more fluid terms without seeking to categorise their sexual identity. The voices of these women are often obscured in oral history projects, which tend to represent the experiences of those women who self-identify as lesbian at the time of interview; nevertheless, their presence can be traced between the lines of the stories told by the

---

2   ibid.
3   Letter to CAMP NSW, received 20/4/77, Folder 73, Gay Counselling Service of NSW Papers, Mitchell Library, MSS 5836.

women they entered into relationships with. Sandra Willson's account of her search for a 'wife' in 1950s Sydney refers to two young women, Barbara and Norma, who apparently entered into intimate relationships with her, without claiming or being assigned a homosexual identity. Barbara and Sandra were both in their late teens when they began an affair with each other, but Sandra believed herself to be more knowledgeable about the possibilities of same-sex desire than Barbara. Although Barbara initiated physical contact by taking Sandra's hand as they sat with friends in the dark listening to music, when Sandra later kissed Barbara, she felt that Barbara was surprised by the eroticism of the kiss. Sandra described what happened after she asked Barbara for a kiss:

> She eased herself out from the cramped position beside the bed and stood by the dressing table. I moved toward her. She raised her face slightly to meet mine as I bent to kiss her lips. It was my first real kiss.
>
> My hands moved around her body to hold her close; to hang onto her, lest I fell. There was something pounding away within my head. My body grew light and was floating. All feeling became highly charged on 'full.' This was more than a kiss between friends. This had become a lover's kiss, and she was sharing it with me. As our lips parted, I gazed into her eyes. They were alive with a new light. A puzzled light, but one of which she was fully conscious. It had just dawned on her.[4]

Sandra's subsequent portrayal of her relationship with Barbara cast Barbara as a pliable but reticent figure 'who would thank me for the chocolates I bought each pay day, and would murmur 'No' when I wanted to make love just once too often' but 'went her way, thinking her own thoughts into which I had no insight'.[5] It is difficult to trace Barbara's own desires and subjectivity between the lines of Sandra Willson's account, but her participation in relatively frequent sexual intimacy points to her same-sex desires, while her actions in moving from the hostel where they met to a private flat with Sandra would seem to indicate that she placed some significance on their relationship. Nevertheless, when their relationship was terminated some weeks later by a police raid and the two young women being charged with 'being exposed to moral danger', it was Sandra Willson who was identified

---

4   Sandra Willson, unpublished memoir, p. 27. The author is grateful to Rev Peter Strong, beneficiary of Sandra Willson's estate, for a copy of this memoir, which is in the author's possession.
5   Sandra Willson, unpublished memoir, p. 29.

as a lesbian by the police and Children's Court and detained in a reform school, while Barbara was regarded as a passive object of seduction and released into the care of her parents. When Sandra Willson contacted her again a year or two later, Barbara was engaged to be married and, although willing to be friends with Sandra, rejected her suggestion of returning to their former intimacy.

Sandra's account of her second relationship, with Norma, followed a similar pattern. The two young women met while training to be psychiatric nurses and began a sexual affair while living in nearby rooms in nurses' quarters. The relationship developed gradually and the two women had become accustomed to spending evenings together in Norma's room before Sandra again proposed a kiss:

> [T]hat evening, when it was time to say goodnight, I asked if I could kiss her. She said 'If you like', but I was scared and something held me back. A few nights later, I visited Norma again. She mostly read when I was with her for we didn't talk much. I would read sometimes, or take in my portable and listen to the radio. Eventually it became late, and I left her to change into my pyjamas while she did the same. Then I returned to her and this time I had my courage with me. I bent over her after tucking her in and kissed her on the lips. She did not respond. So I kissed her again passionately. And again, til she responded with passion like my own. Then I undid the buttons of her coat and kissed her breast. Her body arched beneath mine, her hands pulling me close to her. She took me with vigour and passion like she has never done since.[6]

Sandra's account of this first sexual encounter again portrays her partner as both unknowing and desiring, but offers little insight into Norma's feelings about the experience. That this was not an isolated incident, but the beginning of an ongoing relationship which continued in secret over many months, would seem to indicate Norma's commitment to Sandra. However, when the relationship became public knowledge (amid other revelations about Sandra's background as a psychiatric patient), Sandra was asked to resign and Norma was put under increasing pressure by senior nursing staff to end the relationship, which she did. As in Sandra's previous relationship with Barbara, Sandra was apparently interpreted by others as the primary instigator of the relationship with Norma, and Norma was allowed to remain in her post. However, there were significant repercussions

---

6   Sandra Willson, unpublished memoir, p. 46.

for Norma. The termination of the relationship prompted Sandra to have a mental breakdown, during which she shot and killed a taxi driver, a case which occupied the front pages of the Sydney papers for several weeks. Despite the notoriety surrounding Sandra and the murder, Sandra recalled Norma coming to sit behind her during her hearing in the Coroner's Court, and subsequently visiting her at Parramatta Mental Hospital, where she was held for a period prior to her trial. Sandra claimed:

> One certain memory was that Norma had been officially allowed to visit me. We sat, with a supervising nurse, in the top dormitory. I was extremely glad to see her, and was so grateful to her for the visit – but I couldn't express any of it through a sense of intimidation with the supervision and another sense of 'it's far too late.' Norma told me about the problems at Rydalmere, how the staff treated her with horror and suspicion, never with any understanding. She was behind in her classes as well and so wouldn't pass her first year examinations at the end of the year. But there was nothing I could do for her; all my own energy was concentrated on staying alive in this place. So we just paid the obligatory courtesies and I remained embarrassingly bombed out on my medication.[7]

Although Sandra's account gives no indication of Norma's motivations, her actions in supporting Sandra publicly through this period suggest a significant commitment to the relationship. Her association with Sandra, who had become notorious in the hospital where they worked as both a lesbian and a murderer, clearly had negative consequences for Norma, but we have no further details about Norma's experiences. After the meeting described above, Norma was not given permission to visit or correspond with Sandra again, and the couple lost contact.

Margaret also represented herself as a seducer in describing the beginning of her relationship with Jann in the same period. Having enjoyed her first sexual encounter with another woman during a shipboard romance, she returned to Sydney unsure of how to find another woman lover in the context of complete cultural silence surrounding same-sex desire. She explained:

> There was this young woman, who was a receptionist there at the firm [where I worked]. Her name was Jann. And she was very fetching, a red-haired woman, a young woman, she was twenty and I guess I was about ten years older and she appealed to me. So I thought, then

---

7   Sandra Willson, unpublished memoir, p. 72.

how would I go about seducing her, that would be the word, or dating, dating would be the start of it. And she had a … boyfriend too. And she had mummy and daddy of course, lived out in the suburbs … And I was living in the inner city, then, in Eurong Street, in this little bedsitter and I … got pretty friendly with her and the boyfriend and I met her parents. And I was anxious to take it further, and I did … So we then had this affair.[8]

Reflecting on the risks involved in 'seducing' a woman who had not given any indication of same-sex attraction, Margaret observed:

Well of course she could have dismissed me and it would have been very awkward to be still working with her. But she didn't. So, I can't imagine if she, at such a young age and such an innocent young girl would have known what a lesbian was herself, maybe I pitched her such a good tale that she thought she'd try it, I don't, I don't know how I managed that one.[9]

Margaret describes how Jann left home to move in with her, and the couple subsequently went travelling together. However, after a relationship lasting several years, Jann met an American man with whom she fell in love and ultimately married. Margaret's account of this painful episode offers some insight into Jann's understanding of their relationship: 'I felt that I was losing my woman, that she was in love with another, male or not, it was another person. But she claimed that was not the case, that she loved me too.'[10] Even at this crisis in their relationship, Jann had apparently declared her love for Margaret, and Margaret's portrayal of the relationship throughout suggested a loving and emotionally intimate partnership between two committed participants. Margaret suggests that the relationship ended not because of any loss of desire on the part of either woman, but as a result of the advantages of financial security, social position and travel offered to Jann in a marriage to a US serviceman, in contrast to the secrecy and insecurity inherent in a same-sex relationship.

Locating lesbian intimacy

For those women who were in relationships in this period, the pressure to conceal same-sex desire from family and the outside world shaped the ways

---

8   Interview with Margaret Jones, 12 September 2007.
9   ibid.
10   Interview with Margaret Jones, 18 September 2007.

in which they structured their relationships. Afraid of losing their jobs or being rejected by family, women in lesbian relationships frequently presented themselves as single women, attending social or family functions alone or in the company of a male friend. Female partners were portrayed as close friends or companions and the significance of the emotional ties between the women was downplayed. In this context, lesbian relationships were vulnerable to external pressure, with women responding to family pressure or wider social disapproval by leaving female partners and seeking social conformity in heterosexual marriage.

Margaret described the care that she and Jann took in the 1950s to provide an acceptable account of their lives for their parents and families. She recalled: 'We went out a lot, but just as two girlfriends, you know, the older woman I suppose and her young friend, her young office friend, her young colleague from work.'[11] To support their presentation of themselves as friends and colleagues, Margaret and Jann also invented stories of romantic encounters with young men. Jann allowed her family to believe that she was still courting a young man she had been involved with before she met Margaret, while Margaret herself 'imagined all sorts of blokes that I was going out with and what fun I was having with all these fellers and the dates and the exciting things that we were doing.'[12] When the women decided to move in together, a complex narrative was constructed to enable them to do so without the knowledge of their families. Margaret recalled:

> So then [Jann] decided that she would leave her family home and live independently in Sydney and that took a bit of doing. Slowly, you know, saying to the parents, 'It's so far to travel' and, you know, women then were leaving their parents and having, getting flats or rooms and moving into the city, so it was quite a common enough thing that she should want to do that. So then she got an apartment in Elizabeth Bay, ostensibly she got it, but we got it, but I still lived ostensibly in my apartment ... I didn't want it to be seen that I and Jann were living together so I lived in [my apartment in] Eurong Street, for all appearances of course. I was there [in Elizabeth Bay] all the time but I'd come back to Eurong Street and when I was talking to anyone I'd talk about home, meaning Eurong Street and 'the flat', and 'me', and 'it' and not 'us'.[13]

---

11 Interview with Margaret Jones, 12 September 2007.
12 ibid.
13 ibid.

For many women, establishing a home together was fraught with difficulties. Young, unmarried women were often expected to live in the family home in the mid-twentieth century and the need to conceal a lesbian relationship from unknowing or hostile parents meant that there was little space for expressions of intimacy. A young lesbian from southern New South Wales outlined the potential hurdles in a letter to CAMP in 1977:

> I love my parents and family and I wouldn't shift from them until I was 21. So if I ever got involved with anyone they would have to understand this. My wage is fairly small which doesn't enable me to live away from home. Here I don't pay board. What they don't know won't hurt them ... I come from a European family, that's what makes getting around hard. My sister's 21 in July and goes almost everywhere with me.[14]

While concealing a same-sex relationship from family could pose practical problems, openness was often not an attractive alternative. Carolyn, who lived with her parents and younger brother in Petersham in the 1960s, recalled the relationship difficulties she experienced after her parents found out about her sexuality. When her mother read her diary and discovered that she had been having a sexual affair with a female schoolfriend, Carolyn's girlfriend was barred from the house and Carolyn herself was subjected to physical abuse from her father. That relationship ended when the other girl moved away, but a subsequent relationship was also affected by her difficult domestic situation. Carolyn explained: 'Through my friends in the theatre I'd met another woman by this stage and I had formulated a relationship with her and that was pretty difficult, it meant that we went out all the time to meet and I didn't bring her home.'[15] Other women described romantic or sexual assignations in isolated public places such as beaches or parks, where they were able to meet away from the prying eyes of family or acquaintances.[16] Lack of privacy was also a problem for married women in lesbian relationships. One Newcastle woman recalled the difficulties of maintaining a relationship with her female lover in the 1950s:

> It was difficult back then, because at the time I was married and had two children, a boy eight and a girl, eleven ... We didn't know of any other women in Newcastle at the time. You just had to be secretive about it

---

14 Letter to CAMP NSW, received 20/4/77, Folder 73, Gay Counselling Service of NSW Papers, Mitchell Library, MSS 5836.
15 Interview with Carolyn Bloye by Sandra Mackay, Pride History Group Collection, 9 November 2007.
16 Sandra Willson, unpublished memoir, p. 54.

all ... It was so hard. Mary was single and worked in a local factory, so we were only able to meet during lunch breaks and occasionally on weekends and after Sunday mass. I was terrible lonely when Mary left a year later.[17]

For those women who were able to set up home together, there were further obstacles to overcome. Mortgages were not freely given to unmarried women in this period so women who wanted to buy a house together often had to conduct complex negotiations or accept a higher rate of interest. Margaret described her attempt to obtain a mortgage with her woman partner in the early 1970s as a demeaning and difficult process:

> I worked for solicitors ... and through this one particular solicitor I worked with, he of course had connections with the bank manager where he did his own firm's banking and made a recommendation for the bank manager to receive me kindly for the loan for the purpose of purchasing a house. And this bank manager ... said, 'oh what is the purpose of this purchase then, the two of you, is it security in your advancing years'? Again, patronising shit, like, two old girls, two old spinster girls, buy a house and get a cat and a dog and grow old together and have security when they became really old and wouldn't have to go into an old nursing home. But whatever, he gave us the money. At the worst possible rate, not what two real people would be given, at you know the home loan rate, his was what's called a fully drawn advance loan, the terms don't matter but now I see in hindsight it was not a loan intended for a long-term purchase of a home for a married couple. It wasn't an investment loan and we were buying it for investment, he knew it was for our personal residence, but it was just typical of attitudes at the time. But we were lucky to get it, because at that time women could not get bank loans, and often you had to have a male guarantor, your father or your brother or somebody.[18]

Within the home, many couples took care to maintain the appearance of two single women sharing a house, carefully controlling access to the home and ensuring that a bed was always made up in a second bedroom to support

---

17   Lyndall Coan, 'Filling Some Gaps: Lesbian History Excerpts from the "Hunter Pride" Exhibition', in Jim Wafer, Erica Southgate and Lyndall Coan, eds, *Out in the Valley: Hunter Gay and Lesbian Histories* (Newcastle: Newcastle Region Library, 2000), p. 205.
18   Interview with Margaret Jones, 18 September 2007.

the fiction. Margaret described the precautions she and her partner took when they bought their house together:

> And we set up a house, married couple. But at no time were we a married couple ... For Maureen's family, there were two bedrooms but the front bedroom was not used as a bedroom, it was always an office or a study, but we put the folding couch which opened out into a double bed, in that front room and that was ostensibly [her] bedroom, so when any of those relatives would come, we'd scurry and open down the couch and put sheets and blankets and pillows on it and it looked like a bed.[19]

Oral histories suggest that this was a relatively common practice, to the extent that women took careful note of bedroom arrangements when trying to establish whether or not new acquaintances were in a same-sex relationship. Chris recalled using this technique in the 1970s to interpret the exact nature of the relationship between two nursing friends of hers:

> When I was doing my nursing, I had met two women who were also doing mental retardation nursing but with kids, and they had taken a kid home and they were working with that kid, so I'd met them and they were a couple ... And they lived out at Dulwich Hill, which was kind of like the middle of nowhere. And I had visited them and noted that really the spare bedroom was really spare and that the double bedroom was *the* bedroom.[20]

Expressing love and desire

The silence surrounding lesbian relationships which prompted women to take these measures also impacted on levels of communication within the relationship itself. Women whose sexual identities were constructed in silence often lacked a language in which to discuss their emotions, even with their lovers, and certain aspects of their relationship remained unacknowledged. Margaret's account of her first (shipboard) affair with another woman in the 1950s points both to the complexities of finding space for the expression of same-sex desire and the difficulties of openly acknowledging it between themselves. The two women were staying in separate shared cabins and Margaret recalled:

---

19   Interview with Margaret Jones, 18 September 2007.
20   Interview with Chris Pearce, 6 November 2007.

> Well she knew times when her cabin persons had their meal sitting. You know, they had to have their meal between quarter to seven and quarter past eight or something, so we scrambled into her cabin and then scrambled into mine for the breakfast session or, you know, fumbled around on the deck, in the deckchairs ... But obviously the sexual excitement and satisfaction was there, but since I was such an innocent, Brigetta was the instigator of these little activities. Oh, yes, no, she had [done this sort of thing before]. Well clearly, if she'd managed the seduction so brilliantly and cleverly. I didn't question her on it, I assumed she was one of those lesbians, which I certainly wasn't, but she was.[21]

Fears about discovery could inhibit women's self-expression, so that even in private women felt unable to fully articulate their emotion or desire. Sandra Willson described her sexual encounters at home with two female friends in the 1950s as tense occasions:

> But the lie resulted in my being as stiff as a poker during their visits. I knew the hour each was due to arrive at my door, I knew the purpose of the knock on the door, but my greeting would be so rigidly formal. An invitation to a cup of tea, then an invitation to join me in bed. I was always ready for a rejection of the offer. No touching beforehand, no caressing, not even a kiss until we were undressed and hidden in the bed itself. There, out of sight of the world, I could relax and say the things I should have said earlier as between friends. I was fearful to show just how anxious I was to touch and kiss, lest others deem me a sex maniac of sorts. I was fearful to show any emotion at all. But as emotion was constantly raging through me, my attempts at repression were most painful. And incomplete. So I remained a tense, stiff, hurting individual who could bring no pleasure to others.[22]

Psychiatrists and cultural commentators had cast female homosexuals as promiscuous and sexually aggressive for much of the twentieth century, and these ideas impacted on some women's attitudes toward their own sexuality. Sandra Willson believed her fear that she might be regarded as a 'sex maniac' prevented her from expressing desire and affection for her female partners. Margaret, in attempting to describe the presumed lesbian sexuality of Brigetta, the woman she had a shipboard affair with, referred to

---

21 Interview with Margaret Jones, 31 August 2007.
22 Sandra Willson, unpublished memoir, p. 57.

her as 'Oversexed'.[23] The reluctance to be viewed in this way prompted some women to downplay the significance of sexual intimacy in their relationships or to avoid acknowledging it, even to each other. An interviewee in the Channel 7 documentary 'Love is Love' was careful to distance herself from the sexual aspect of lesbian relationships. In response to Deveson's suggestion that one factor in the social hostility towards lesbians might be that some people were 'put off' by the idea of two women being together physically, the interviewee claimed that although she had been in a relationship with another girl for over three years, the 'physical side has hardly anything to it at all'.[24] Nevertheless, cultural references to lesbian promiscuity continued into the 1970s. John B Murray's film *The Naked Bunyip*, released in 1970, included a depiction of a lesbian relationship which drew upon long-standing cultural models of a dominant, promiscuous partner and passive, feminine partner. The butch interviewee, talking while naked in bed with her partner, concluded the piece with the observation:

> If it's just a girl that you see when you're out somewhere and you fancy her, well I suppose it's the same as a man, if he sees somebody he fancies, he takes her.[25]

Representations of lesbians as over-sexed were often linked to suggestions that lesbians were prone to jealousy and that relationships between women were short-lived. Recalling a conversation with a friend of hers in the 1950s, Sandra commented:

> [Denny] knew there was need for caution but she had kept her activities confined to those who she knew 'were,' whilst I had gone outside the field and chosen a partner of the heterosexual variety. She had learned to accept the impermanence of these relationships whilst I, by nature, had sought permanence and security. At her flat, sharing with another female, she made a pretense of dating a boy while she went out with a female. At work, she ignored the women whilst throwing red herrings about boys, and so kept everybody guessing.[26]

Australian readers of overseas lesbian magazines found these concerns reflected in articles and submissions from other readers. In 1959, US lesbian

---

23   Interview with Margaret Jones, 31 August 2007.
24   'Love is Love: Lesbians', *Seven Days* (Canberra: ScreenSound Australia, 2003 [originally aired by ATN 7, 15 February 1966])
25   John B Murray, Director, *The Naked Bunyip*, 1970.
26   Sandra Willson, unpublished memoir, p. 57.

magazine *The Ladder* published the findings of a questionnaire on the longevity of homosexual relationships which had been circulated amongst members, and devoted three pages to discussing the data. After a detailed statistical analysis of the figures gathered, the author of the report concluded: 'The present statistics do appear to show, at any rate, that lasting homosexual relationships, though not universal in the group, are not only possible but by no means rare.'[27] The longevity of lesbian relationships continued to be a point of concern into the 1960s and 1970s, however, and in 1964, K H from New South Wales contributed an article entitled 'What Makes it Last?' to British lesbian magazine *Arena Three*. Observing that 'because there are relationships between women which have lasted literally until death, and others which are still flourishing after many decades, it's worth looking for clues', K H went on to argue that 'mutual tolerance, kindness, and absence of jealousy' were most important in sustaining a relationship, 'with near-parity on the intellectual side a close second.' K H was careful to stress that lesbians were not alone in facing the breakdown of relationships, noting: 'Hundreds of thousands of relationships of all kinds go bust every year for hundreds of thousands of reasons. As many, or more, endure for a lifetime. And in this – the question of success or failure, you and I aren't "different from the rest" at all.' Nevertheless, she suggested, lesbian relationships were 'perhaps, more vulnerable to disruptive pressures' as they lacked 'the security of acceptance, and established usage.'[28]

Social taboos around same-sex desire meant that lesbian relationships were vulnerable to a range of external pressures. Sandra Willson described two relationships she had with women in the 1950s that ended as a result of external intervention: one as a teenager, when she and her lover were brought before the Children's Court and questioned about their affair, and the second when her relationship with a fellow trainee nurse broke down after pressure from senior nurses.[29] Kerry also recounted the negative impact of external intervention on her relationships with other women in the 1960s. Kerry's first affair with a woman was with an actress she had met in a theatre group in her late teens, but the relationship came to an abrupt end as a result of her mother's intervention:

---

27 'DOB Questionnaire Reveals Some Facts About Lesbians', *The Ladder*, vol. 3, no. 12 (September 1959), p. 23.
28 K H (New South Wales), 'What Makes it Last?', *Arena Three* vol. 1, no. 4 (March 1964), p. 3.
29 Sandra Willson, unpublished memoir.

But she must have rung one day at home and Mum answered the phone. And I'd mentioned this woman to Mum and she mentioned it at work, where she was working – she was also working at the North Shore Hospital. And this woman [at the hospital]'s husband was a TV director, and the actress was in a very popular TV show at the time. So this woman told Mum that the actress was a lesbian. When she rang, unbeknown to me, my mother told her that she wouldn't have a job if she rang again, that Mum would make sure she lost her job. And Mum would've, she would've gone hell-bent on that. So that was that. I never heard from her again. And it was only many, many years later that I bumped into her and found out that was why.[30]

A later relationship was also terminated at Kerry's mother's instigation, and prompted Kerry to be more circumspect in future in involving her mother in her personal affairs:

I had met a woman that I wanted to be with and I moved into a room to start with and then she found a flat [and] I moved into the flat. But my mother was just over the top. Mum kept asking all the time when I was living with her and I would have been about 24 I suppose, and I said, 'Yes, I was a lesbian' and she was okay about it that night but then the following day all hell broke loose. Anyway, when I went to live with this woman, my mother then threatened me with her suicide for 6 months. In the end I left that woman because I said to her, 'Well if Mum tops herself, we're stuffed anyway. I couldn't really cope with that.' That was a shame. I left her and lived on my own for the next five years. But I could never then share any aspect of my personal life with my mother and I think that was terrible, because she missed out on so much.[31]

While Kerry and Sandra Willson recounted the impact of direct intervention on their relationships, many more women found that their relationships suffered as a result of the need for concealment and the broader social expectation that women should marry. Cathy Weaver, author of an autobiographical article about lesbians in the personal relationships magazine *Forum*, recounted a tragic story she had heard from an older lesbian:

---

30 Interview with Kerry Blackwell, 9 July 2009.
31 Interview with Kerry Blackwell, 9 July 2009.

One woman in particular told a very sad story. In the early '50s, she established a happy, stable relationship with another woman. Five years later her partner announced she was going to marry a man she hardly knew because her family were pressuring her to marry, and were becoming suspicious about her relationship with her flatmate ... As a result of the separation, the woman in our group was shattered, feeling somehow that if her own girlfriend could not accept their love, that there must be some truth in the ideas of [the] time about lesbianism. She went to a hotel one night with the intention of getting drunk and forgetting her loneliness. She met with a man with whom she slept. Shortly afterwards she discovered she was pregnant. Once again, social pressures decreed the course of her life. *Nice* girls get married in that situation and so she complied.[32]

The loss of a female partner to marriage was a common theme in personal accounts from lesbians in this period, when the social pressure to conform to accepted feminine roles as wives and mothers prompted many women to marry. Margaret described the heartbreak and loneliness she experienced in the early 1960s when her partner of several years left her for a man. The two women had struggled throughout their relationship to conceal their love and commitment to each other from family and society and had adopted a number of strategies to deflect suspicion. One of these was to reinforce stories of boyfriends by going on casual dates with men. After travelling together in the US, Margaret and Jann returned to Sydney and began attending evening cocktail parties at the Hotel Australia, organised by the American–Australian Friendship Society for US troops on leave from Vietnam. Local women were offered free food and drink in exchange for socialising with the men, and would sometimes be invited out on subsequent dates by individual men. Margaret and Jann usually rejected these offers, but on one occasion agreed to go to the cinema with two men from the Navy:

And then, now I think, I think, I'm sure, he asked Jann out and she went. And I thought, well that was good cover, going out with a bloke and that looks good. And she did that a few times. And I don't suppose I thought anything too much about that, really, just a bit of company with this guy ... So he went off back to Vietnam and then apparently he wrote some letters and then Jann wrote some letters and I said hello on the bottom of the letters. And then he announced

---

32   Cathy Weaver, 'Role Your Own', *Forum* 5:7 (July 1977), pp. 12–13.

he was coming back to Sydney on leave again … And then Jann was going out with him. And we had a discussion about that. I'd thought that it was just a nice little pretense and he was good company and nothing much was happening, but I had to realise that at least they were kissing, because, I suppose he'd, for his part, he wouldn't be spending his time with a woman that wasn't even kissing him. But I thought, oh that'll go away and he'd only be here for six days and it looks good. And then she took to spending the night in the apartment with him so we had further discussions, none of which were angry in nature, but puzzled on my part and on hers too, since, since she still loved her Margaret, but then he went away again, off. So we settled back again to being us and he was long gone, but kept writing letters and ringing up and we thought that was the end of that one. But then he came back again … But then it was full-on, she just spent all her time with him.[33]

The Naval officer asked Jann to marry him and, after a trial visit to the US, she did. For Margaret, the development of Jann's relationship with this man was confusing and painful. She explained:

[T]here was never any quarrel really, or great anger on my part, it just seemed to me that that was how the whole thing would have to end up. We couldn't live together or be who we were because of all the restrictions and anxiety and lies and I had said … to myself that I wasn't going to hurt her by luring her into this lifestyle and seducing her as a young woman and dragging her around the world with me and alienating the family and forcing her to lie and that I would 'let her go', to use that word which makes me sound generous, but it wasn't, that I wouldn't impede her, or beg her to stay or offer to marry her instead, which *he* did, damn me.[34]

For Margaret, the social attitudes prevailing in Australia at the time, which idealised heterosexual marriage as the ultimate goal for women, prevented her from competing with Jann's male lover. Despite being assured of Jann's love for her, Margaret felt obliged to accept, without protest, Jann's choice of a way of life which would give her social and family acceptance. However, the repercussions for Margaret were devastating:

---

33   Interview with Margaret Jones, 12 September 2007.
34   Interview with Margaret Jones, 12 September 2007.

So she settled into this big life in the States and they lived on the naval base at first, but in a big house on the naval base. And there was I in Sydney feeling really very bad because this had happened and she'd really gone and I was alone and she was there and I was very sad and lost and depressed and angry and lots of other things. But we were writing all these happy letters because I didn't want her to know I was feeling as bad as I was, so I was writing these happy letters, 'How are you?', 'What fun it must be'. And not telling her how bad I was feeling.[35]

For women like Margaret, who knew no other lesbians outside of their own couple, the breakdown of a relationship could be doubly distressing. Faced with the loss of her beloved partner, Margaret had no one to discuss her feelings with, and was unable to acknowledge the pain caused by the breakdown of a relationship whose existence had been necessarily kept secret from all her family and friends.

Relationship models

The culture of concealment surrounding lesbian relationships prior to the 1970s also impacted on the ways in which couples envisaged their roles within relationships. In the absence of cultural references to lesbian relationships, or real-life lesbian role models to follow, women in same-sex relationships drew upon a range of different models of intimate partnerships in structuring their interactions with each other. In the 1930s and 1940s, earlier notions of same-sex relationships as passionate friendships often shaped the ways that women approached their relationships. Romantic or passionate friendships have been identified by historians as a recognisable pattern in which women, frequently from middle or upper-class backgrounds, structured their emotional lives around a passionate commitment to another woman. Women in such relationships would frequently live together and provide emotional support which enabled them to build successful careers or otherwise live as independent women. Although women in these partnerships would be regarded by society as single women, the emotional importance of their bond with each other could be accepted by family and friends. Any sexual component of such relationships typically remained unacknowledged, with the result that historiographical debates have questioned to what extent these partnerships can be understood within modern concepts of lesbianism.[36]

---

35 Interview with Margaret Jones, 12 September 2007.
36 Carroll Smith-Rosenberg, 'The Female World of Love and Friendship', in Carol Smith-Rosenberg, ed., *Disorderly Conduct: Visions of Gender in Victorian America* (New

A common pattern amongst independent women in the late nineteenth century, romantic friendship models continued to have some currency in the first half of the twentieth century.

Historian and biographer Sylvia Martin represents the relationship between Ida Leeson and Florence Birch in these terms. A Sydney librarian, who was to become the first female Mitchell Librarian in 1932, Ida had a nearly 50-year-long relationship with New Zealand-born Florence, which only ended with Florence's death in 1957. Although Florence worked in New Zealand between 1912 and 1922, she holidayed with Ida in Australia each year and, on her return to Australia, set up home with Ida in Sydney. Their relationship enjoyed social acceptance as an undefined 'friendship' and Martin notes that: 'Everyone I spoke to [about Ida Leeson] knew about Florence's existence; some had met her. They said Ida talked about her constantly, they knew the two women had lived together for years, but nobody knew the origin of their relationship.'[37] Ida and Florence were apparently integrated into each other's families and Martin describes their visits to Ida's brother's house, when 'Ida … used to enjoy playing cricket with her nephews, while Florence sat in the lounge room talking to their mother, May.'[38] It is difficult to interpret the framework in which Ida and Florence's families may have understood their relationship, but an anecdote recounted to Sylvia Martin suggests some awareness of the possibility of same-sex desire:

> There is a Leeson family story that is told, with some amusement, about the time one of Ida's brothers walked into the living room at the house in Leichhardt (where Ida lived with her mother until 1915) and was stopped in his tracks by an unusual sight – Florence, so the story goes, was seated in an armchair while Ida knelt at her feet holding her hands.[39]

It is in the unexpected echo of a proposal scene that the humour of this anecdote lies, suggesting that there was room in the family's understanding

---

York: Knopf, 1985), pp. 53–76; Lillian Faderman, *Scotch Verdict: Pirie and Woods v. Dame Cumming Gordon* (New York: William Morrow, 1983); Sylvia Martin, '"These Walls of Flesh": The Problem of the Body in the Romantic Friendship/ Lesbianism Debate', *Historical Reflections/Réfléxions Historiques*, vol. 20, no. 2 (Summer 1994), pp. 243–265; Sylvia Martin, 'Rethinking Passionate Friendships: the Writing of Mary Fullerton', *Women's History Review*, vol. 2, no. 3 (1993), pp. 395–406.
37 Sylvia Martin, *Ida Leeson: A Life* (Sydney: Allen & Unwin, 2006), p. 68.
38 ibid., p. 77.
39 ibid., p. 71.

of Ida and Florence's relationship for a thread of romance. Ida and Florence's own perceptions of their relationship are more difficult to pinpoint, however, as their personal papers were destroyed by Ida Leeson's family on her death. Nevertheless, Martin gives some indication of the centrality of the relationship in Ida's life when she cites an encounter between Ida and her colleague Nancy Phelan. Nancy was due to embark on a trip overseas the day after Florence's funeral and was surprised to find Ida amongst the group of friends and colleagues who had come to farewell her on her journey. Nancy recalled:

> [Ida] looked absolutely frightful. She was sort of a pale yellow. And she brought champagne and cats' tongues (you know those biscuits), which she loved ... Just a gesture. And I said, 'How are you, Ida?' And she said, 'Bleeding inside'.[40]

Reflecting on the dangers of applying contemporary terms such as 'lesbian' to same-sex relationships in the past, Sylvia Martin comments that 'This was, by any reckoning, a devoted friendship. It cannot be written off as a convenient arrangement where two single women shared a house as a way of saving money and avoiding loneliness.'[41] The question of sexuality in such a relationship is difficult to pinpoint. Martin suggests that 'It is quite possible that Ida loved Florence without ever finding it necessary to categorise her feelings as sexual or otherwise.'[42] Nevertheless, she concludes, 'From the context of their lives ... Ida and Florence lived in what we would call today a long-term lesbian relationship.'[43]

By the 1950s, the prioritisation of marriage as the dominant social model for intimate heterosexual relationships was beginning to have an impact on same-sex relationships. As Lisa Featherstone has noted: '[S]exuality was at the centre of postwar social, political and economic reconstruction: the family, reproduction and heterosexuality were essential to constructions of individual, community and national ideals.'[44] Postwar prosperity, combined with 'conservative understandings of family life', rendered the dream of a 'wife at home in the suburbs, following her duties as hostess, mother and consumer' increasingly attainable for middle and working-class Australians.

---

40 Nancy Phelan, interview with Sylvia Martin, cited in Martin, *Ida Leeson*, p. 192.
41 Martin, *Ida Leeson*, p. 192.
42 ibid., p. 194.
43 ibid., p. 196.
44 Lisa Featherstone, *Let's Talk About Sex: Histories of Sexuality in Australia from Federation to the Pill* (Newcastle upon Tyne: Cambridge Scholars Publishing, 2011), p. 231.

Therefore, although employment rates for women were slowly increasing in the 1950s and 1960s, highly gendered divisions of labour remained the norm in most marriages. The ubiquity of this model in the postwar decades prompted some women to attempt to fit their relationships with women into their understanding of how a heterosexual marital relationship might be organised. Sandra Willson referred to the women she conducted same-sex relationships with in the 1950s as her 'wives', suggesting that she regarded these relationships as similar to marriages. In 1956, she began an affair with Barbara, a young woman she had met at the Salvation Army hostel where they both lived, and the couple found a flat together in Bondi. In a letter to a friend describing the relationship, Sandra referred to herself and Barbara as 'man and wife'. Reflecting on this affair in her memoir, Sandra recalled that she had tried to impose a relationship model derived from her parents' marriage on her own relationship with Barbara. In retrospect, Sandra did not regard this as a success, reflecting that in copying the gendered roles performed by her parents, she had transferred the difficulties inherent in her parents' marriage to her own youthful affair:

> We found a flat for rent at Bondi Beach, took it and moved in, despite the high cost. And my relationship with Barbara ran straight into difficulties. I was living out the role of husband with Barbara as wife, without having previously had a good role model of a husband-wife team to copy … I also thought all real love involved sex and that sex-love made us husband and wife, tying us irrevocably together. My body's reactions to being with Barbara made this very easy for me to believe. I thus got into every role-playing game in any book. I expected Barbara to prepare the breakfast porridge and was surprisingly impatient when she burnt it. When I took over the preparation myself, I wondered how she would react. She, however, was not caught up in the game. I was behaving as if the action, the atmosphere, the appearance of a thing led to its actuality. I was acting as if the illusion would become the reality, given time. And I wondered what had gone wrong, not realising then that it was me.[45]

Sandra's account echoes the growing anxiety in the 1950s around the place of sexuality in marital relationships, which has been noted by historians such as Frank Bongiorno:

---

45 Sandra Willson, unpublished memoir, p. 43.

Couples, and especially women, were increasingly likely to recognise sexual fulfilment as a means of deepening the love between a husband and wife. Many ... had read sexology or sex manuals, and ... [t]heir expectations of what sex could deliver had been accordingly raised.[46]

Sandra Willson's account reflects a similar emerging belief that satisfying sex was both an essential component of an intimate relationship and a vehicle for binding couples together. This assumption that satisfying sexual intimacy was the defining feature of marriage-type relationships was echoed in John B Murray's film *The Naked Bunyip* in 1970. The butch lesbian interviewee, who had been depicted in the film returning home to a feminine counterpart, commented:

> A lesbian relationship is very much the same as a relationship between a man and woman but it's much more lasting. With a man and a woman, when they eventually break up or separate, they become more or less enemies, but with two girls, they usually stay very good friends, usually for the rest of their lives and are very close, as Deborah and myself are now. We used to live together as man and wife, but now we're just very good friends.[47]

The juxtaposition of this commentary with the visual simulation of a woman arriving home to be greeted by another woman with a can of beer, implied that it was sex alone which defined a relationship: sharing a home and expressing affection and concern for each other were not sufficient to make a couple 'man and wife'.

For women like Sandra Willson, who formed same-sex relationships in isolation from broader lesbian networks, the marital relationships of their parents or heterosexual peers provided an influential model for their own partnerships. For the small number of women developing lesbian identities in the context of the camp bar culture or discreet lesbian subcultures in the 1950s and 1960s, however, butch/femme roles offered an alternative model for structuring intimate relations between women. Drawing on the work of US lesbian historians Joan Nestle and Judy Grahn, Pam Nilan argues that despite the critique of butch/femme as an imitation of heterosexuality articulated by lesbian feminists in the 1970s: 'butch and femme roles were never imitations of heterosexuality but unique in themselves. For example,

---

46   Frank Bongiorno, *The Sex Lives of Australians: A History* (Melbourne: Black Inc, 2012), p. 201.
47   John B Murray, Director, *The Naked Bunyip*, 1970.

butch lesbian behaviour and appearance does not take its cue from heterosexual men but from established codes of sexual attractiveness in the lesbian sub-culture itself. That is, butch lesbian style is not a copy of men, but a copy of the way butch lesbians look and act.'[48] In her analysis of oral history interviews with older lesbians in the Hunter Valley region of New South Wales, Nilan suggested that 'Butch and femme roles were important behavioural norms in 1960s and 1970s bar culture for gay men and lesbians, both in Newcastle and elsewhere.'[49] For women who were part of these communities, accepted behavioural norms shaped both their interaction with friends and potential lovers in the public bar scene and the ways in which they structured domestic relationships and expressed intimacy with partners at home. Marion Paull described her own experience of Australian butch roles in the 1960s in these terms:

> So you had to be big and strong. So you had to take responsibility. So you had to be the breadwinner. So you wouldn't be caught dead in a dress (except for the purposes of earning a living, of course, although some butches refused to work unless in trousers) or in the kitchen ... Being butch, being a passing dyke or whatever label you put on it now, was at that time not a political statement or a stand taken; it was just what I did. There were all sorts of rules about how to behave, but these seemed to apply to public behaviour and were the sorts of things I did naturally, like opening doors for her, carrying the heavy stuff, paying the bills. Other things done at home didn't seem to matter much – boring things of everyday life like ironing and housework.[50]

Marion felt that butch/femme roles were particularly important in defining public interactions, commenting that: 'We put on a public façade and invented the rest. In my opinion, there wasn't much butch-femme role-playing within relationships, but those of us who were serious about making our relationships work put in the same kind of effort any couple puts in to make sure that both parties get what they want out of it.'[51] Nevertheless,

---

48 Pam Nilan, '"I Was Never a Dress Person": Lesbian Stories from the Newcastle / Hunter Region', in *Out in the Valley*, p. 224. See also Joan Nestle, 'Butch/Fem Relationships: Sexual Courage in the 1950s', *Heresies*: Sex Issues 12 (1981), pp. 21–24; Judy Grahn, *Another Mother Tongue: Gay Words, Gay Worlds* (Boston: Beacon Press, 1984).
49 Nilan, '"I Was Never a Dress Person"', p. 223.
50 Marion Paull, 'A Letter from Australia', in Joan Nestle, ed., *The Persistent Desire: A Femme-Butch Reader* (Boston: Alyson Publications, Inc), p. 175.
51 Paull, 'A Letter from Australia', p. 178.

Marion recalled that butch lesbians were expected to take on responsibility for paying the bills, while femmes cooked and took charge of much of the domestic work. Other women referred to some established conventions which structured intimate relations between women in the butch/femme community. Laurie, who was a butch lesbian in Sydney in the 1960s, recalled: 'It was frowned upon, the butch getting with another butch, going by society's rules, our society.'[52] Fleur, who had her first lesbian relationship with the 'local dyke, as they called her' in Cessnock in the 1960s, also assumed a pairing between butch and femme when she explained, 'That was like with Ruth, I mean she was a butch dyke. At that time I was feminine, you know, dressed feminine and everything like that.'[53] Although Fleur did not maintain a stable 'femme' identity throughout her life, often wearing butch clothes at other times, her account suggests that it was important for her to present herself in a feminine way for the duration of this relationship with a 'butch' lesbian. Butch/femme codes of behaviour were, however, relatively fluid across time and location, so that for other women this convention does not appear to have been important. When Sandra recalled meeting the first pair of lesbians she had ever seen, at a house party in Lambton, Newcastle, in the 1960s, she described two butch lesbians in a relationship with each other:

> I walked in there, and they were two lesbians, and I nearly died. 'Cause that's the first time that I'd ever seen it, and you could've knocked me over with a feather. They were really butch! They were unbelievably butch! You know what I mean? And they were draped all over each other.[54]

Other women suggested that butch/femme shaped the sexual aspect of women's relationships, dictating the ways in which women were expected to express love and desire to their partners. Marion recalled:

> I don't know about taboos in private, because there was one big taboo and that was that you never told what you had done in bed with someone else. I think I would have liked to have known what other dykes did around sex, because I do remember that it was not all right for a butch to be touched sexually and it is only recently that I've been able to be touched and I sometimes feel awkward about that. Do not assume that

---

52   Interview with Laurie van Camp, 18 February 2008.
53   Nilan, "'I Was Never a Dress Person'", p. 223.
54   ibid., p. 222.

this has meant that my sex life has ever been anything but amazing and wonderful!⁵⁵

Elizabeth, who was a femme in Sydney in the 1960s, described the corresponding femme role as a passive one, although her memories of this period were less positive. She commented: 'Looking back now I reckon I was sexually abused in this regard, that I wasn't allowed to take any action in the sex playing at all.'⁵⁶ As Marion reflected, however, taboos surrounding the discussion of private sexual practice meant that it was often difficult to determine whether behavioural expectations were common across communities or confined to individual relationships. Undoubtedly individual women and couples interpreted butch/femme conventions in particular ways to suit their own circumstances and desires.

Lesbian feminist theories of intimacy

With the emergence of the women's and lesbian and gay movements in Australia in the 1970s, accepted practices of intimacy came under increasing scrutiny. Feminist and gay literature, magazines and newsletters were filled with passionate critiques of the nuclear family as a heteropatriarchal institution which crippled its individual members, oppressed women and promoted compulsory heterosexuality. In the social – and for many, socialist – revolution which was to come, new relational models would emerge to challenge and replace the nuclear family. At consciousness-raising groups and conferences, women began to work out new patterns for intimate relationships, rejecting the monogamous, committed couple as a model. Lesbian feminists were at the forefront of these new ideas, arguing that intimate relations between women offered exciting opportunities to break free from old oppressive structures and to remodel relationships in ways which promoted women's personal growth and directed their energies towards other women.

Many articles in the feminist and lesbian and gay press in the 1970s explicitly critiqued the nuclear family, and the marriage-relationship at its heart, as oppressive institutions.⁵⁷ The nuclear family was anathema to the feminist project in a number of key ways, dividing women from each

---

55 Paull, 'A Letter from Australia', p. 176.
56 Interview with Elizabeth by Ruth Ford, Australian Lesbian and Gay Archive, 6 May 1992.
57 See, for example, Clare, 'Why I Would Like to Destroy the Nuclear Family', *Vashti's Voice*, no. 10 (Autumn 1975), p. 8.

other, forcing women to exist in isolation in a small family unit and limiting women's choices as active members of society. Many of these arguments were framed in anti-capitalist terms, critiquing the nuclear family as a unit of consumption. As Sydney Radicalesbian Pam Stein argued in *Sydney Gay Liberation Newsletter*:

> We believe that the retention of the marriage institution and the nuclear family is the retention of sex roles and the capitalist society which relies on the family as the consumers. The woman in a marriage and a nuclear family is the chief consumer …
>
> The family unit should not be seen as the only economically and socially acceptable unit of society. Central to the liberation of women is the provision of alternatives to the present pattern of child-bearing and housekeeping, which results in women bearing the entire responsibility for the socialization of children and housework while men are forced to be 'bread winners'. Such alternatives would go far towards eliminating the untenable situation where the 'choice' for most women other than unpaid housewives hardly exists.
>
> Marriage is putting love on a commercial basis and gives men the legal sanctions to fucking a woman.[58]

For Stein and others, the nuclear family also represented the first and primary environment for conveying socially approved gender roles. Drawing both on feminist and gay liberation critiques of the family, lesbian and gay activist group CAMP NSW outlined this objection in its submission to the Royal Commission on Human Relationships in 1975. CAMP argued:

> The fundamental way in which nuclear families perform their function as socializing agents is by conditioning their members into adopting certain sex roles. This means that certain roles are assigned to people according to their gender, regardless of their individual personality. These roles serve to uphold the power structure of this patriarchal society by striving to ensure that men take on roles of power and women those of weakness.[59]

---

58 Pam Stein, 'Women's Oppression', *Sydney Gay Liberation Newsletter*, vol. 1, no. 6 (December 1972), pp. 7–8.
59 CAMP NSW, 'Homosexuals and Human Relationships', submission to the Royal Commission on Human Relationships, September 1975, p. 11.

For homosexuals, CAMP continued, the socialising role of the nuclear family had particularly insidious effects, in that it produced and fostered an expectation that all its members would be heterosexual, get married and establish nuclear families. Homosexuals raised in a nuclear family experienced problems developing an awareness of their sexuality and had great difficulty in sharing their sexual orientation with the family.[60]

The gendered roles at the heart of the nuclear family drew considerable critical attention from feminists who argued that power inequalities were inherent in heterosexual relationships. A number of US lesbian feminist theorists in the 1970s therefore presented sexual intimacy between women as a positive feminist choice, and these ideas were widely quoted by Australian lesbian feminists.[61] In 1979, Ludo McFingus echoed this view in the *Sydney Women's Liberation Newsletter*, claiming:

> Lesbian relationships simply cannot duplicate the power relations between men and women. A man has social power invested in him which a woman can parody, but as a woman that power over another woman remains out of her reach.[62]

Intimacy between women, she suggested, was inevitably a relationship based on equality, as it arose between two members of the same oppressed class.

While theoretically a recognition of gendered power imbalances in heterosexual relationships seemed to imply equality and tender consideration in relationships between women, many women found that equality was not, in practice, intrinsic to lesbian relationships. Oral history interviews reflect a sense of uneasy and hard-fought commitment to equality in relationships between women. While many women clearly strove for equality in their sexual and domestic interactions, the complexities of achieving this ideal in practice soon became apparent. Assumptions about equality and mutual understanding in lesbian relationships also impacted on women's expectations of sexual intimacy. Although the finer details of sexual practice received less attention in lesbian feminist circles in this period, a number of women referred to a general emphasis on ideal sex as equal, tender and non-penetrative. For some radical lesbian feminists, the difficulties of achieving equality in relationships were the result of inherent problems in the concept

---

60 ibid., p. 12
61 Charlotte Bunch, 'Lesbians in Revolt', in Nancy Myron and Charlotte Bunch, eds, *Lesbianism and the Women's Movement* (Baltimore: Diana Press, 1975), p. 30.
62 Ludo McFingas, 'The Dust Storms of the Old Paranoia', *Sydney Women's Liberation Newsletter*, Feb/March 1979, p. 8.

of monogamous couple relationships. The personal goals of autonomy and self-reliance were regarded by many women as central tenets of feminism, and couple relationships were viewed as a threat to this aim. 'Couples' encouraged their members to be inward-looking, forging dependent bonds with each other rather than functioning as independent beings or interacting with others.[63] They excluded single women and took precious time and energy away from group endeavours such as political activism. In the context of the supportive sisterhood lesbian feminists aspired to create, monogamous couple relationships could seem restrictive and unnecessary. As Christine O'Sullivan told *Scarlet Woman* in 1977, 'Lesbian relations, like all sexual relations under capitalism, are formed out of fear of isolation.'[64]

The most common practical solution to the problems of monogamous couple relationships was non-monogamy and many women recalled non-monogamy as a central aspect of lesbian feminist sexual practice in the 1970s. In a review of US feminist Kate Millett's book *Flying*, Kathie set out the thinking behind the non-monogamy approach for the benefit of *Vashti's Voice* readers. Millett's theory, Kathie explained, 'involves the breaking down of possessiveness in sexuality, which she sees as the core of patriarchy. If relationships can be free and open, with no strings of ownership attached, then will come the breaking down of the restrictions on sexuality which not only deny women the right to choose what to do with their bodies, but prevent women (and men) from becoming whole people.'[65] Kathie expressed a number of reservations about non-monogamy, and oral history interviews suggest that, while the practice of non-monogamy was widespread in lesbian feminist circles, many women shared Kathie's misgivings. Sandra, who had 'a lot of relationships or sexual encounters' while living in a lesbian feminist collective house in Sydney in the early and mid-1970s, at the same time as having a longer term lover, recalled that she and her lover 'had a lot of issues with ... jealousy'. She recalled that 'there was a kind of fair bit of pressure, self, self-imposed, to try and break down those sort of ideas [about monogamy] and so on. And it was not easy.'[66] Chris also recalled a degree of pressure to conform to a non-monogamous culture. She herself had one serious relationship but was also having 'something' with somebody else. She recalled 'in those days, in that time, that was something that you kind of,

---

63 Jenny and Sue, 'On Primary Relationships', paper delivered at Sorrento Radicalesbian Conference, 6–8 July 1973.
64 Christine O'Sullivan, 'Revolutionary Love', *Scarlet Woman*, no. 5 (March 1977), p. 18.
65 Kathie, '"Flying" and "Fear of Flying"', *Vashti's Voice* no. 11 (Winter 1975), p. 6.
66 Interview with Sandra Mackay, 2 July 2007.

not were supposed to do, but it sort of was described as being okay in terms of ... challenging the patriarchy and all that kind of stuff ... Even though ... everybody was miserable.'[67] Although there was little discussion of these concerns in feminist journals in the 1970s, the difficulties of negotiating non-monogamous relationships were clearly discussed in some circles at the time. In her write-up of the Radical Feminist Lesbian Liberation Conference held at Minto in December 1973, Laurie Bebbington noted:

> During the second discussion 'Monogamy' came in for its usual beating. However, it is becoming increasingly obvious that the 'smash monogamy' rhetoric does not stand the test of experience and that the traditional patriarchal alternative of 'promiscuity' (a nasty word!) has been too easily accepted.[68]

While the attempt to break down the social institution of the monogamous couple was recalled by many women as the most significant of the lesbian feminist ideas about lesbian intimacy, few spoke positively about its impact on their relationships. The practice of non-monogamy was frequently referred to as a source of jealousy and pain, and the experience left a number of women uncertain and disillusioned about how to practise same-sex intimacy in the future. Communication between women lovers, both about their expectations of the couple relationship and about their intentions with regard to other potential lovers, was regarded by many as the ideal solution to these conflicts. This marked a clear shift from patterns of intimacy in earlier decades, when communication within and about lesbian relationships was fraught with difficulty. Constrained by negative social attitudes about same-sex desire, many women sought to conceal their relationships with other women, passing them off as friendships or creating the appearance of heterosexual courtship. The absence of a language in which to articulate love and desire between women impacted on women's expressions of intimacy in private and left women with few role-models for structuring their relationships with other women.

---

67 Interview with Chris Pearce, 6 November 2007.
68 Laurie Bebbington, 'Minto Lesbian Conference', *Refractory Girl* (Summer 1974), p. 6.

AFTERWORD

Shifting cultures of lesbian intimacy reflect the changes and continuities evident in many aspects of lesbian life in New South Wales between 1930 and 1978. For much of the mid-century, the silence surrounding female samesex desire had a profound effect on lesbians, isolating them from potential friends and lovers, prompting them to conceal their desires or relationships from those around them and obstructing women's attempts to make sense of their own feelings and construct sexual identities. Some women were able to resist the taboo in specific ways by forging private friendship networks or by participating in the bar scene, by adopting butch identities or by explicitly declaring their desires for women to family, friends and others. Most, however, were forced to adopt a life of concealment. The development of political activism around lesbian and gay and women's rights in the early 1970s has been presented as a turning point, marking a transformation from the culture of silence to one of visibility and self-affirmation. However, such cultural change only occurred very slowly. For those women whose identities and daily lives were shaped by involvement in feminist or lesbian politics, a profoundly different way of life, revolving around women's communities in which lesbianism was openly acknowledged and even valued, was possible. However, for the majority of lesbians, who socialised in the bar scene or in private networks; who lived discreet lives in the suburbs or the country; who were isolated from other lesbians, living with parents or in heterosexual marriages; or who were simply unable or unwilling to identify themselves as lesbian or find other women, the impact of the culture of silence continued throughout the 1970s.

The year 1978, in which this book ends, marked the beginning of another potential shift in cultural and political life for Sydney's lesbians. Early in 1978 a group of lesbian and gay activists responded to a call from the San Francisco Gay Freedom Day Committee for an international day of action to mark the ninth anniversary of the Stonewall Riots. The Gay Solidarity

Group was formed, with the aim of organising an International Gay Solidarity Day and campaigning for an end to police harassment and other forms of discrimination against homosexuals in Australia. A series of events was planned for 24 June: a morning march, a public meeting, and an evening street party or mardi gras. Over a thousand people turned up to the evening event, which commenced at 10pm on Oxford Street in Sydney. Many of the marchers came in costumes or party dress, singing and dancing their way down the street accompanied by music played from a sound system on the back of a truck.[1] Chris recalled:

> We had heard ... that there was a party on and we were gonna go for, that there was a bit of fancy dress, we were going to walk through the streets ... You know we were very used to having demonstrations and stuff like that, celebrations – that went on quite a bit. So I had a particularly nice double-breasted, pin-striped suit that I had put on and we went off to there. I had a couple of joints in my pocket, you know we were a bit stoned, we were dancing up and down Oxford St.[2]

Organisers had hoped that the party spirit of the event, along with its unusual location on Oxford Street, in the heart of the gay subculture, would encourage lesbians and gay men who frequented the bars to participate. Robyn explained:

> We'd decided, because of what had happened, with the raids that had been done on the gay bars over there, that it was necessary to make people aware of them and have some solidarity. And there was a big thing about, how do we get the bar people involved, because a lot of them we found wanted to be apolitical, didn't want to have anything to do with us, and so we thought we needed to go to them and we needed to make it a bit more of a fun event. And rather than march during the day, to march in the evening ... We went along Oxford Street, because we knew that we could probably attract some of the people out of the bars, if it seemed like fun ... And as we went along we chanted 'Out of the bars and into the streets' ... And of course we were making a fair

---

[1] The events of the first Sydney Mardi Gras have been widely discussed. See, for example, Graham Willett, *Living Out Loud: A History of Gay and Lesbian Activism in Australia* (St Leonards NSW: Allen & Unwin, 2000); Graham Carbery, *A History of the Sydney Gay and Lesbian Mardi Gras* (Melbourne: The Australian Lesbian and Gay Archives Inc, 1995); Pride History Group, *It was a Riot! Sydney's First Gay and Lesbian Mardi Gras* (Sydney: The Pride History Group, 1998).
[2] Interview with Chris Pearce by Rebecca Jennings, 6 November 2007.

bit of noise, and it was quite different to have it on Oxford Street. They certainly hadn't had that sort of thing before. So people did come down out of the bars to watch.[3]

One of the spectators was lesbian bar-owner Dawn O'Donnell, who was 'drinking and sitting out on the awning of the first Tool Shed at 42 Oxford Street ... as they passed.' She recalled commenting to her partner, 'Well this lot is not going to amount to much.'[4] Others also recalled men and women from the bars joining the crowd on the street. As the marchers reached Hyde Park, however, the mood shifted. The police, who had been attempting to move the marchers quickly down Oxford Street, now took the offensive and seized the sound system from the truck. In the confusion, people headed down towards the old heart of the camp subculture in Kings Cross. There, at the El Alamein fountain, with crowds of marchers hemmed in on all sides, the police started making arrests.[5] Robyn remembered the scene as violent and frightening:

> And [the police] came in and they declared it an illegal march and ... they asked us to disperse, that's right. Well we started dispersing, by going back up Darlinghurst Street, but there were too many of us to fit onto the crowded pavements already, from people that were just there anyhow, but who were also looking at this march. And so they started picking on people. The first ones that came were ordinary police in uniforms and then we realised there were plain clothes police and these were from Darlinghurst cop station, which was well known in that era to be totally corrupt and very violent and I was the first one that was grabbed actually – it gets me every time, sorry – anyway, they grabbed me, but there was about three or four women that had grabbed me on one side and I had the cops pulling the other way. I certainly knew it the next day with sore muscles. And there was a paddy wagon there and they were going to throw me into the paddy wagon, but what happened was that I was on the ground, lying on my back, and there was these cops looking down at me and this cop leaned over me and said 'Piss off quickly into the crowd', which I thought was really weird. They let

---

3 Interview with Robyn Plaister by Rebecca Jennings, 20 December 2007.
4 Dawn O'Donnell, 'Dawn at the Awning', Richard Wherrett, ed., *Mardi Gras! True Stories: From Lock Up to Frock Up* (Melbourne: Viking, 1999), p. 33.
5 Organisers had obtained a permit for the evening event but there was some confusion as to where the marchers were permitted to go once they reached the end of Oxford Street.

go of my arms, the women still had hold of me. Meanwhile there were guys trying to rip the police off from behind. And the women sort of dragged me out from underneath.[6]

Although Robyn managed to evade the police, others were arrested and were taken to Darlinghurst Police Station. An angry crowd followed them and further arrests were made. Amongst them was Chris, who spent a tense and uncomfortable night in the cells:

> I was arrested at Darlinghurst Gaol. And so we were all there, everybody's sitting around, everybody's yelling. The cops were there as well, outside Darlinghurst Gaol. And they're still pulling people in. And somebody grabbed a friend of mine and I went after them to get them and then I was grabbed and booted in, and thrown in. And so I had a couple of joints in my pocket – I had to flush them down the toilet! We were all of us in one room and we could hear kind of yelling and screaming and stuff from somewhere, don't know where that was. And I gave a false name because I was on the dole and there was some idea, 'Oh, I'm going to get my dole taken away from me', so I thought, I'll just give a false name, so I made up one. And then from there we were taken to the City Watch House. We were kind of the last ones out, I think. And, you know, I just had a big kind of [bump] on my head, don't know how I got that.[7]

In total, 30 men and 23 women were arrested that night, including many who were badly beaten in the streets and in the cells, and the police action sparked a wave of protests on an unprecedented scale in Sydney. Further arrests were made on 26 June outside the court hearings and at a protest march on 15 July. A campaign was launched to 'Drop the Charges' against those arrested – planning meetings attracted attendances in excess of one hundred people.[8] The charges were ultimately dropped, some dismissed by the courts in October 1978 and others dropped by the police in December 1979. However, the consequences, even for those not arrested, were still significant. The *Sydney Morning Herald* published a complete list of names and occupations of those arrested on 24 June in its paper the following day, while other papers carried photographs of the event. Robyn, who

---

6 Interview with Robyn Plaister by Rebecca Jennings, 20 December 2007.
7 Interview with Chris Pearce by Rebecca Jennings, 6 November 2007.
8 Willett, *Living Out Loud*, p. 139.

was working as a teacher at a Rose Bay private school at the time, faced difficulties at work as a result:

> The trouble was that I had been caught on camera, on the night of the march, and I was splashed across I think the second page of the Telegraph, or whatever, being pulled by cops on one hand and women on the other ... [and] the deputy principal seemed to have got onto it and told the principal and I was hauled in by the principal that afternoon – I think it was in the Monday paper after the Saturday. And she gave me the third degree ... and I knew that if I said I was a lesbian that I would be out of a job, basically, and I thought about what my mother would think, I thought about the car I was paying off, that sort of thing goes through your mind and I thought, 'I need the job', I mean I wish I hadn't. And so I evaded answering her directly and I said I was there as a feminist supporting the march ... and things like that. But she really wanted an answer for the parents who would obviously complain and I don't know if one of them had complained or not. But I think it was sufficient that she didn't fire me on the spot, which was quite amazing, and I was trying to think of who I would get chained up at the front gate to the school in another demonstration, because I could see myself going through all of that. And I didn't have to, I don't think I had the fortitude at that time, having been through the Mardi Gras, to face yet another [confrontation].[9]

For some of those who took part, 24 June 1978 marked a turning point. Kate Rowe recalled: '1978 changed my whole life. I remember the whole march. I was just wild, ecstatic and screaming up and down the street: Up the Lezzos! I did get arrested for saying that.'[10] Activists involved regarded the first Mardi Gras as a moment of radicalisation and Craig Johnston argued that it marked the beginning of a concept of gay community:

> It told me that gay liberation politics had to orient itself to the bar scene. Not because of the parade itself, which took the character of a New Left demo, but because of the presence of bar queens ... Gay radicals had to create ourselves as subcultural denizens, for the movement to grow.[11]

---

9 Interview with Robyn Plaister by Rebecca Jennings, 20 December 2007.
10 Kate Rowe, cited in Pride History Group, *It was a Riot!*
11 Craig Johnston, cited in Pride History Group, *It was a Riot!*

The crossovers between lesbian political activism and the bar scene had been relatively limited in the 1970s, but the events of 24 June have been seen as marking a shift towards closer connections between the two. Graham Willett argues that it was this coming together of a broad spectrum of lesbian and gay interests in Sydney which defined the first Mardi Gras as a key moment:

> What made the Mardi Gras arrests and the subsequent campaign important was not simply the size of the reaction, but the diversity of those who participated in the protests and organising. The Left – gay and straight – was prominent in the campaign, of course. This was the kind of militant resistance to oppression that Leftists lived for. But fully half of those arrested on 24 June were women (which casts further doubt on the belief that they had withdrawn from the movement in recent years), and the campaign also seemed to draw in the kind of people who in the past had been impervious to the demands of the movement – the bargoers.[12]

The Mardi Gras and subsequent rallies of 1978 demonstrated the extent to which women were actively involved in collective lesbian and gay politics, even in the late 1970s. In an account of his participation in the evening event, David McDiarmid reflected:

> It was dykes who were at the forefront of the riot. They came from a strong tradition of feminism and street politics and street confrontations with cops, so they were the ones who took the risks initially. The queens in the initial riot were hiding under cars ... throwing their hands up in the air, going 'This is a nightmare' ... The women had the strength.[13]

While David focused on the central role played by lesbians in the events of 24 June, the overwhelming response to those events also reflected a sense of solidarity between lesbians and heterosexual women in the women's movement, which a historical emphasis on conflicts around sexuality has tended to obscure. In July 1978, *Sydney Women's Liberation Newsletter* reported on a special meeting that had been held at Women's House 'to discuss what the Women's Movement would [do] about the recent arrests

---

12   Willett, *Living Out Loud*, p. 142.
13   David McDiarmid, cited in Kirsten Tilgals (Powerhouse Museum) ed., *Absolutely Mardi Gras: Costume and Design of the Sydney Gay and Lesbian Mardi Gras* (Sydney, Powerhouse Publishing and Doubleday, 1997), p. 6.

on Gay Solidarity Day.'[14] It was noted that 'At such short notice it was great that 100 women crammed into the upstairs room at Women's House'. The meeting agreed that women from a range of women's groups, including Working Women's Charter and the Women's Electoral Lobby, would march with lesbians at the next gay rights march. 'Banners were planned, to reflect the idea of lesbianism as a feminist issue.' The report of the meeting demonstrated both the enthusiastic support offered by the movement as a whole to lesbian feminists on the occasion of the Gay Solidarity Day arrests, and a commitment to make the most of the opportunity the events presented to discuss 'the politics of lesbian-feminism as an issue in the women's movement.'

The momentum which emerged from anger at police actions on the night of 24 June continued throughout 1978 and into the following year. On 24 June 1979, a second parade was planned, and Mardi Gras gradually evolved into the central event of Sydney's lesbian and gay calendar, an event which epitomises the notion of lesbians and gay men as constituting a diverse but united community. However, the subsequent history of Mardi Gras undermines this vision, indicating the ways in which the initial sense of unity experienced in 1978 dissipated and fractures appeared, particularly along gendered lines. One lesbian participant recalled:

> For the next two years there was a sort of conflict. As lesbian feminists, feminist lesbians, we wanted to keep the political side of the gay movement going. And a lot of the gay boys wanted to keep the party side of it going. It was very much centred around gay male sexuality. After that first Gay and Lesbian Mardi Gras it got more and more boysie and there was a big split. Mardi Gras for many years became just a male event. There was a lot of animosity between gay men and lesbians. We felt we'd been taken over.[15]

The decision in 1980 to move the parade to the summer crystallised many of these tensions, with those from the political left, and in particular lesbian feminists, arguing that the decision reflected a depoliticising of the event in favour of popular or commercial interests. Many lesbians withdrew from participation in Mardi Gras and it was not until the late 1980s that these conflicts began to be resolved. By then, the impact of HIV/AIDS

---

14 'Special Meeting at Women's House', *Sydney Women's Liberation Newsletter*, July 1978, p. 5.
15 Alison Pressley, *Living in the 70s* (Sydney: Random House, 2002), p. 201.

on Sydney's gay community had transformed the politics of sexuality in NSW and prompted a renewed sense of solidarity in the lesbian and gay community. This was reflected in the 1988 decision to rename the 'Gay Mardi Gras' the 'Sydney Lesbian and Gay Mardi Gras'. That year also saw the participation of Sydney lesbian motorbike group Dykes on Bikes for the first time, beginning a new phase in the lesbian history of the event. Now a major part of the event, leading the parade, Dykes on Bikes represents the visibility of an alternative lesbian identity in community engagement and representation: women who are not necessarily involved in political activism around their sexuality, but nevertheless wish to declare their desires for other women in the context of a community of women and of lesbians and gay men.

BIBLIOGRAPHY

Interviews

Beverley [pseudonym] and Georgina. Interview by Rebecca Jennings, 22 December 2008.
Binning, Virginia and Ruth Ritchie. Interview by Sandra Mackay and Rebecca Jennings. Pride History Group Collection, 7 April 2007.
Blackwell, Kerry. Interview by Rebecca Jennings, 9 July 2009.
Bloye, Carolyn. Interview by Sandra Mackay. Pride History Group Collection, 9 November 2007.
Brown, Karen. Interview by Ken Davis. Pride History Group Collection, 21 January 2007.
van Camp, Laurie. Interview by Sandra Mackay. Pride History Group Collection, 18 February 2008.
Coral and Rachel. Interview by Lucy Chesser. Australian Lesbian and Gay Archives, 20 April 1993.
Curtis, Francesca and Phyllis Papps. Interview by Gary Jaynes, Graham Willett and Liz Ross. Australian Lesbian and Gay Archive, 10 January 2008.
Deborah [pseudonym]. Interview by Rebecca Jennings. 13 November 2008.
Diana [pseudonym]. Interview by Rebecca Jennings. 23 April 2008.
Elizabeth. Interview by Ruth Ford. Australian Lesbian and Gay Archive, 6 May 1992.
Fuller, Dennis. Interview by John Witte. Pride History Group Collection, 15 November 2006.
Goldrick, Diana. Interview by Rebecca Jennings. 9 July 2009.
Greenaway, Kerry. Interview by Rebecca Jennings. 3 May 2008.
Helen. Interview by Ruth Ford. Australian Lesbian and Gay Archive, 14 December 1994.
Helen [pseudonym]. Interview by Rebecca Jennings. 23 April 2008.
Hepner, Robbie. Interview by Lucy Chesser. Australian Lesbian and Gay Archive.
Lee, G J. Interview by Rebecca Jennings. 31 July 2008.
Jones, Margaret. Interview by Rebecca Jennings. 31 August 2007, 12 September 2007 and 18 September 2007.
Mackay, Sandra. Interview by Rebecca Jennings. 2 July 2007.
McInnies, Jan and Margaret Cummins. Interview by Sandra Mackay and Rebecca Jennings. Pride History Group Collection.
McLean, Ian. Interview by Robert Colman. Pride History Group Collection, 10 February 2006.
Melmouth, Kris. Interview by Rebecca Jennings. 25 August 2011.

Minnis, Diane. Interview by Rebecca Jennings. 30 December 2012.
Morris, Rae. Interview by Sandra Mackay. Pride History Group Collection, 4 December 2008.
Neil, Jennifer. Interview by Rebecca Jennings. 14 September 2009.
Odewahn, Valerie. Interview by Rebecca Jennings. 20 May 2008.
Parr, Colette. Interview by Digby Duncan. Pride History Group Collection.
Pearce, Chris. Interview by Rebecca Jennings. 6 November 2007.
Plaister, Robyn. Interview by Rebecca Jennings. 20 December 2007.
Richter, Ivy. Interview by John Witte. Pride History Group Collection, 22 May 2006.
Wills, Sue. Interview by Rebecca Jennings. 23 October 2009.

Books

Aldrich, Robert, ed. *Gay Perspectives II. More Essays in Australian Gay Culture*. Sydney: Department of Economic History, The University of Sydney, 1994.
Aldrich, Robert and Garry Wotherspoon, eds. *Gay Perspectives: Essays in Australian Gay Culture*. Sydney: Department of Economic History, The University of Sydney, 1992.
Aldrich, Robert and Garry Wotherspoon, eds. *Gay and Lesbian Perspectives IV: Studies in Australian Culture*. Sydney: Department of Economic History and the Centre for Lesbian and Gay Research, The University of Sydney, 1998.
Allen, Judith. *Sex and Secrets: Crimes Involving Australian Women Since 1880*. Melbourne: Oxford University Press, 1990.
Berube, Allan. *Coming Out Under Fire: The History of Gay Men and Women in World War Two*. New York: The Free Press, 1990.
Bongiorno, Frank. *The Sex Lives of Australians: A History*. Melbourne: Black Inc, 2012.
Bradstock, Margaret and Louise Wakeling, eds. *Words from the Same Heart*. Sydney: Hale & Iremonger, 1987.
Burgmann, Verity. *Power and Protest: Movements for Change in Australian Society*. Sydney: Allen & Unwin, 1993.
Butler, Judith. *Bodies That Matter: On the Discursive Limits of 'Sex'*. London: Routledge, 1993.
Carbery, Graham. *A History of the Sydney Gay and Lesbian Mardi Gras*. Melbourne: The Australian Lesbian and Gay Archives Inc, 1995.
Carrington, Kerry and Margaret Pereira. *Offending Youth: Sex, Crime and Justice*. Sydney: The Federation Press, 2009.
Chesser, Lucy. *Parting With My Sex: Cross-dressing, Inversion and Sexuality in Australian Cultural Life*. Sydney: Sydney University Press, 2008.
Cobb, Dita and Barbara Moore. *Dita: The Very Private Life of a Very Public Person*. Sydney: Windermere Press, 1996.
Curthoys, Ann. *For and Against Feminism: A Personal Journey into Feminist Theory and History*. Sydney: Allen & Unwin, 1988.
Dawson, Graham. *Soldier Heroes: British Adventure, Empire and the Imagining of Masculinities*. London: Routledge, 1994.
D'Emilio, John. *Sexual Politics. Sexual Community: The Making of a Homosexual Minority in the United States, 1940–1970*. Chicago: University of Chicago Press, 1983.
Dixson, Miriam. *The Real Matilda: Women and Identity in Australia 1788 to the Present*. Ringwood, Victoria: Penguin, 1984.
Djuric, Bonney. *Abandon All Hope: A History of Parramatta Girls Industrial School*. Perth: Chargan My Book Publisher Pty Ltd, 2011.
Doan, Laura. *Fashioning Sapphism*. New York: Columbia University Press, 2001.

Faderman, Lillian. *Scotch Verdict: Pirie and Woods v. Dame Cumming Gordon*. New York: William Morrow, 1983.

Faderman, Lillian. *Odd Girls and Twilight Lovers: A History of Lesbian Life in Twentieth-Century America*. New York: Penguin, 1991.

Falkiner, Suzanne. *Eugenia: A Man*. Sydney: Pan Books, 1988.

Featherstone, Lisa. *Let's Talk About Sex: Histories of Sexuality in Australia from Federation to the Pill*. Newcastle upon Tyne: Cambridge Scholars Publishing, 2011.

Ford, Ruth, Lyned Isaac and Rebecca Jones. 'Forbidden Love, Bold Passion: Lesbian Stories 1900–1990s'. *Exhibition Catalogue*. History Inverted, Melbourne, 1996.

Foucault, Michel. *The History of Sexuality, Volume 1: An Introduction*. Translated by R Hurley. New York: Vintage, 1978.

Gardiner, Jill. *From the Closet to the Screen: Women at the Gateways Club, 1945–85*. London: Pandora Press, 2003.

Grahn, Judy. *Another Mother Tongue: Gay Words, Gay Worlds*. Boston: Beacon Press, 1984.

Greenaway, Jai. *Political Acts: Lesbian Theatre in Sydney*. Sydney, New South Wales: The author, 1990.

Grieve, Norma and Patricia Grimshaw, eds. *Australian Women: Feminist Perspectives*. Melbourne: Oxford University Press, 1981.

Harvey, S D. *The Ghost of Ludwig Gertsch*. Sydney: Pan Macmillan, 2000.

Hilliard, David. *Godliness and Good Order: A History of the Anglican Church in South Australia*. Adelaide: Wakefield Press, 1986.

Howard, John. *Men Like That: A Southern Queer History*. Chicago: The University of Chicago Press, 1999.

Hurley, Michael. *A Guide to Gay and Lesbian Writing in Australia*. Sydney: Allen & Unwin, 1996.

Jennings, Rebecca. *Tomboys and Bachelor Girls: A Lesbian History of Post-war Britain, 1945–71*. Manchester: Manchester University Press, 2007.

Jennings, Rebecca. *A Lesbian History of Britain: Love and Sex Between Women Since 1500*. Oxford: Greenwood World Publishing, 2007.

Johnson, Ken (Kandy). *Kandy: What a Drag!* Sydney: Vegas Press, 2009.

Johnston, Craig and Paul van Reyk, eds. *Queer City: Gay and Lesbian Politics in Sydney*. Sydney: Pluto Press Australia, 2001.

Kaplan, Gisela. *The Meagre Harvest: The Australian Women's Movement 1950s–1990s*. Sydney: Allen and Unwin, 1996.

Kaye, Bruce, ed. *Anglicanism in Australia: A History*. Melbourne: Melbourne University Press, 2002.

Kelly, Vince. *Rugged Angel: The Amazing Career of Policewoman Lillian Armfield*. Glebe: Fast Books, 1995 [originally published by Angus & Robertson, 1961].

Kennedy, Elizabeth Lapovsky and Madeline Davis. *Boots of Leather, Slippers of Gold*. New York: Routledge, 1993.

Kinder, Sylvia. *Herstory of Adelaide Women's Liberation, 1969–74*. Adelaide: The author, 1980.

Lake, Marilyn. *Getting Equal: The History of Australian Feminism*. Sydney: Allen & Unwin, 1999.

Martin, Sylvia. *Passionate Friends: Mary Fullerton, Mabel Singleton and Miles Franklin*. London: Onlywomen Press, 2001.

Martin, Sylvia. *Ida Leeson: A Life*. Sydney: Allen & Unwin, 2006.

Matthews, Jill Julius, ed. *Sex in Public: Australian Sexual Cultures*. Sydney: Allen and Unwin, 1997.

Matthews, Jill. *Good and Mad Women: The Historical Construction of Femininity in Twentieth Century Australia*. Sydney: Allen & Unwin, 1984.

McCalman, Janet. *Journeyings: The Biography of a Middle-Class Generation 1920–1990*. Melbourne: Melbourne University Press, 1993.
McGregor, Craig. *Profile of Australia*. Melbourne: Penguin, 1968.
Meeker, Martin. *Contacts Desired: Gay and Lesbian Communications and Community, 1940s–1970s*. Chicago: University of Chicago Press, 2006.
Mercer, Jan, ed. *The Other Half: Women in Australian Society*. Melbourne: Penguin, 1975.
Moore, Clive. *Sunshine and Rainbows: The Development of Gay and Lesbian Culture in Queensland*. St Lucia: University of Queensland Press, 2001.
Moore, Nicole. *The Censor's Library*. Brisbane: University of Queensland Press, 2012.
Moran, Herbert M. *Viewless Winds: Being the Recollections and Digressions of an Australian Surgeon*. London: Peter Davies, 1939.
Morgan, Robin. *Sisterhood Is Powerful: An Anthology of Writings from the Women's Liberation Movement*. New York: Random House, 1970.
Morgan, Robin. *Monster, Poems*. Melbourne Radical Feminists, eds. Melbourne, c.1970.
O'Farrell, Patrick. *The Catholic Church and Community: An Australian History*. 3rd revised edn. Sydney: NSW University Press, 1992.
Plummer, Ken. *Telling Sexual Stories: Power, Change and Social Worlds*. London: Routledge, 1995.
Portelli, Alessandro. *The Death of Luigi Trastulli and Other Stories: Form and Meaning in Oral History*. New York: State University of New York Press, 1991.
Pressley, Alison. *Living in the 70s*. Sydney: Random House, 2002.
Pride History Group. *It was a Riot! Sydney's First Gay and Lesbian Mardi Gras*. Sydney: The Pride History Group, 1998.
Pride History Group. *Camp Nites: Sydney's Emerging Drag Scene in the '60s*. Sydney: The Pride History Group, 2006.
Pride History Group. *Camp as a Row of Tents: The Life and Times of Sydney's Camp Social Clubs*. Sydney: The Pride History Group, 2007.
Pride History Group. *Out and About: Sydney's Lesbian Social Scene 1960s–1980s*. Sydney: The Pride History Group, 2009.
Radicalesbians. *The Woman-Identified Woman*. Pittsburgh: Know Inc, c.1970.
Reynolds, Robert. *From Camp to Queer: Remaking the Australian Homosexual*. Melbourne: Melbourne University Press, 2002.
Riley, Elizabeth. *All That False Instruction: A Novel of Lesbian Love*. London: Angus and Robertson, 1975.
Rose, Jon. *At the Cross*. London: Andre Deutsch, 1961.
Sedgwick, Eve Kosofsky. *Epistemology of the Closet*. New York: NAL Books, 1989.
Storer, Robert V. *A Survey of Sexual Life in Adolescence and Marriage*. Melbourne: Science Publishing Co, 1932.
Summerfield, Penny. *Reconstructing Women's Wartime Lives: Discourse and Subjectivity in Oral Histories of the Second World War*. Manchester: Manchester University Press, 1998.
Summers, Anne. *Damned Whores and God's Police: The Colonization of Women in Australia*. Melbourne: Penguin, 1975.
Symons, Beverley and Rowan Cahill, eds. *A Turbulent Decade: Social Protest Movements and the Labour Movement, 1965–1975*. Sydney: Australian Society for the Study of Labour History, 2005.
Taylor, Jean. *Brazen Hussies: A Herstory of Radical Activism in the Women's Liberation Movement in Victoria, 1970–1979*. Melbourne: Dyke Books Inc, 2009.
Thompson, Denise. *Reading Between the Lines: A Lesbian Feminist Critique of Feminist Accounts of Sexuality*. Sydney: Gorgon's Head Press, 1991.

Thompson, Denise. *Flaws in the Social Fabric: Homosexuals in Sydney*. Sydney: Allen and Unwin, 1985.
Tilgals, Kirsten (Powerhouse Museum), ed. *Absolutely Mardi Gras: Costume and Design of the Sydney Gay and Lesbian Mardi Gras*. Sydney, Powerhouse Publishing and Doubleday, 1997.
Wafer, Jim, Erica Southgate and Lyndall Coan, eds. *Out in the Valley: Hunter Gay and Lesbian Histories*. Newcastle: Newcastle Region Library, 2000.
Weeks, Jeffrey. *Sex, Politics and Society: The Regulations of Sexuality Since 1800*. London: Routledge, 2014.
Wherrett, Richard, ed. *Mardi Gras! True Stories: From Lock Up to Frock Up*. Melbourne: Viking, 1999.
Willett, Graham. *Living Out Loud: A History of Gay and Lesbian Activism in Australia*. St Leonards, New South Wales: Allen & Unwin, 2000.
Woollacott, Angela. *To Try Her Fortune in London: Australian Women, Colonialism and Modernity*. Oxford: OUP, 2001.
Wotherspoon, Garry. *Being Different: Nine Gay Men Remember*. Sydney: Hale and Iremonger, 1986.
Wotherspoon, Garry. *City of the Plain: History of a Gay Sub-Culture*. Sydney: Hale and Iremonger, 1991.
Wotherspoon, Garry, ed. *Gay and Lesbian Perspectives III: Essays in Australian Culture*. Sydney: Department of Economic History with the Australian Centre for Lesbian and Gay Research, University of Sydney, 1996.

Articles

Baird, Barbara. '"Kerryn and Jackie": Thinking Historically about Lesbian Marriages'. *Australian Historical Studies*, vol. 37, no. 126 (2005), pp. 253–271.
Baird, Barbara. 'The Role of the State in the Regulation of Sexuality: The Police and Violence Against Lesbians and Gay Men'. *Flinders Journal of Law Reform*, vol. 2, no. 1 (1997), pp. 67–74.
Boyd, Nan Alamilla. 'Who Is the Subject? Queer Theory Meets Oral History'. *Journal of the History of Sexuality*, vol. 17, no. 2 (May 2008), pp. 177–189.
Casuarina. 'Refusing to be a Woman: Being Not-woman, Not-man'. *Journal of Australian Lesbian Feminist Studies*, vol. 4 (June 1994).
Chenier, Elise. 'Rethinking Class in Lesbian Bar Culture: Living "The Gay Life" in Toronto, 1955–1965'. *Left History*, vol. 9, no. 2 (2004), pp. 85–118.
Chesser, Lucy. 'Australasian Lesbian Movement, "Claudia's Group" and Lynx: "Non-Political" Lesbian Organization in Melbourne, 1969–1980'. *Hecate*, vol. 22, no. 1 (1996), pp. 69–91.
Chesser, Lucy. '"A Woman Who Married Three Wives": Management of Disruptive Knowledge in the 1879 Australian Case of Edward De Lacy Evans'. *Journal of Women's History*, vol. 9, no. 4 (1998), pp. 53–77.
Damousi, Joy. 'Depraved and Disorderly: The Sexuality of Convict Women'. *Labour History*, issue 68 (May 1995), pp. 30–45.
Damousi, Joy. 'Beyond the "Origins Debate": Theorising Sexuality and Gender Disorder in Colonial History'. *Australian Historical Studies*, vol. 27, issue 106 (1996), pp. 59–71.
Daniels, Kay. 'The Flash Mob: Rebellion, Rough Culture and Sexuality in the Female Factories of Van Diemen's Land'. *Australian Feminist Studies*, vol. 8, issue 18 (Summer 1993), pp. 133–150.

Davies, Susanne & Andrea Rhodes-Little. 'History, Sexuality and Power: Deconstructing the "Lesbian Vampire" Case'. *Australian Cultural History*, vol. 12 (1993), pp. 14–28.
Douglas, Louise and Elizabeth Fletcher. 'Women in the Music Industry: "The Exhaust Pipe of Your Love is Enough to Keep Me Warm" – Women in Rock 'n' Roll'. *Refractory Girl* (December 1979), pp. 44–47.
Ford, Ruth. 'Disciplined, Punished and Resisting Bodies: Lesbian Women and the Australian Armed Services, 1950s–60s'. *Lilith: a Feminist History Journal*, no. 9 (1996), pp. 53–77.
Ford, Ruth. 'Speculating on Scrapbooks, Sex and Desire: Issues in Lesbian History'. *Australian Historical Studies*, vol. 27, no. 106 (1996), pp. 11–26.
Ford, Ruth. '"The Man-Woman Murderer": Sex Fraud, Sexual Inversion and the Unmentionable "Article" in 1920s Australia'. *Gender and History*, vol. 12, no. 1 (2000), pp. 158–196.
Hawthorne, Susan. 'A History of the Contemporary Women's Movement'. *Journal of Australian Lesbian Feminist Studies*, vol. 2, no. 1 (June 1992), pp. 71–79.
Holmes, Katie. '"Spinsters Indispensable": Feminists, Single Women and the Critique of Marriage, 1890–1920'. *Australian Historical Studies*, vol. 29, no. 110 (April 1998), pp. 68–90.
Jennings, Rebecca. '"The Most Uninhibited Party They'd Ever Been To": The Postwar Encounter between Psychiatry and the British Lesbian, 1945–71'. *Journal of British Studies*, vol. 47, no. 4 (2008), pp. 883–904.
Jennings, Rebecca. 'Lesbian Mothers and Child Custody: Australian Debates in the 1970s'. *Gender and History*, vol. 24, issue 2 (August 2012), pp. 502–517.
Jennings, Rebecca. 'Sandra Willson: A Case Study in Lesbian Identities in 1950s and 1970s Australia'. *History Australia*, vol. 10, no. 1 (April 2013), pp. 99–124.
Kiley, Dean. 'Look Back and Wonder: The Question of Our History: Contemporary Gay and Lesbian Historiography'. *Burn* (November 1993), pp. 44–49.
Kirkby, Diane. '"Beer, Glorious Beer": Gender Politics and Australian Popular Culture'. *The Journal of Popular Culture*, vol. 37, no. 2 (2003), pp. 244–256.
Luckins, Tanja. 'Pigs, Hogs and Aussie Blokes: The Emergence of the Term "Six O'clock Swill"'. *History Australia*, vol. 4, no. 1 (June 2007), pp. 8.1–8.17.
Martin, Sylvia. 'Rethinking Passionate Friendships: The Writing of Mary Fullerton'. *Women's History Review*, vol. 2, no. 3 (1993), pp. 395–406.
Martin, Sylvia. '"These Walls of Flesh": The Problem of the Body in the Romantic Friendship/ Lesbianism Debate'. *Historical Reflections/Réfléxions Historiques*, vol. 20, no. 2 (Summer 1994), pp. 243–265.
Matthews, Jill Julius. 'Doing Theory or Using Theory: Australian Feminist / Women's History in the 1990s'. *Australian Historical Studies*, vol. 27, no. 106 (April 1996), pp. 49–58.
Mim and Sue. 'On Holding Hands'. *Camp Ink* (Dec 1971 / Jan 1972), p. 10.
Moore, Nicole. 'National Parapraxis: Sex and Forgetting in Australian Censorship History'. *Australian Historical Studies*. vol. 36, no. 126 (2005), pp. 296–314.
Murray, John B. 'The Genesis of The Naked Bunyip'. *Senses of Cinema*, Issue 38 (February 2006), http://sensesofcinema.com/2006/38/naked_bunyip/.
Nestle, Joan. 'Butch/Fem Relationships: Sexual Courage in the 1950s'. *Heresies*, Sex Issues 12 (1981), pp. 21–24.
Phillips, Walter. ' "Six O'Clock Swill": The Introduction of Early Closing of Hotel Bars in Australia'. *Historical Studies*, vol. 19, no. 75 (October 1980), pp. 250–266.
Reekie, Gail. '"She Was a Lovable Man": Marion/Bill Edwards and the Feminisation of Australian Culture'. *Journal of Australian Lesbian Feminist Studies*, no. 4 (1994), pp. 43–50.

Reynolds, Robert. 'Confessing to Change: Gay Liberation and the Deployment of Therapeutic and Confessional Practices'. *Meanjin*, vol. 55, no. 1 (1996), pp. 138–152.
Reynolds, Robert. 'Writing Queer Cultural Histories'. *Critical InQueeries*, vol. 1, no. 1 (1995), pp. 69–83.
Sport, Kathy. 'Below the Belt and Bleeding Fingertips: Feminist and Lesbian Music in the Late 1970s'. *Australian Feminist Studies*, vol. 22, issue 53 (July 2007), pp. 343–360.
Summers, Anne. 'Marion / Bill Edwards'. *Refractory Girl* (Summer 1974), pp. 21–22.
Thompson, Denise. 'Feminism and Sexuality: The Political Lesbianism Debate'. *Journal of Australian Lesbian Feminist Studies*, vol. 1, no. 1 (1991), pp. 5–15.
Ware, John. 'Twelve Months Past'. *Camp Ink* (September 1971), p. 4.
Willett, Graham. 'Making Gay Pride a Reality: The Australasian Lesbian Movement'. *Gay Community News*, November 1981, pp. 27–28.
Willett, Graham. 'Marxists and the Gay Movement'. *Reconstruction*, no. 9 (Summer 1996–97), pp. 25–31.
Willett, Graham. 'Minorities Can Win: The Gay Movement, the Left and the Transformation of Australian Society'. *Overland*, no. 149 (Summer 1997), pp. 64–68.
Willett, Graham. 'The Darkest Decade: Homophobia in 1950s' Australia'. In John Murphy and Judith Smart, eds. *The Forgotten Fifties: Aspects of Australian Society in the 1950s*. Melbourne: Melbourne University Press, 1997 (a special issue of Australian Historical Studies, vol. 28, no. 109), pp. 120–132.
Willett, Graham. 'Australian Gay Activists: From Movement to Community'. *Radical History Review*, no. 76 (2000), pp. 169–187.
Wills, Sue 'Intellectual Poofta Bashers'. *Camp Ink*, vol. 2, no. 11, (1974) pp. 4–11.
Wills, Sue. 'Inside the CWA – The Other One'. *Journal of Australian Lesbian Feminist Studies*, no. 4 (June 1994), pp. 6–22.
Wotherspoon, Garry. 'Thirties Images: Images of Gays in Australian Writing and Films Between the Wars'. *Gay Information*, no. 14/15 (1984), pp. 46–50.
Wotherspoon, Garry. 'The View from the Novel: Homosexuality and Australian Literature'. *Perversions*, no. 3 (Autumn 1994), pp. 61–91.

Chapters in edited collections

Baird, Barbara. 'Lesbian identities'. In Barbara Caine, Moira Gatens et al, eds. *Oxford Companion to Australian Feminism*. Oxford: Oxford University Press, 1998, pp. 198–206.
Baird, Barbara. 'Putting Police on Notice: A South Australian Case Study'. In Gail Mason & Stephen Tomsen, eds. *Homophobic Violence*. Sydney: The Hawkins Press, 1997, pp. 118–131.
Bunch, Charlotte. 'Lesbians in Revolt'. In Nancy Myron and Charlotte Bunch, eds. *Lesbianism and the Women's Movement*. Baltimore: Diana Press, 1975.
Curthoys, Ann. 'The Women's Movement since 1970'. In Kay Saunders and Raymond Evans, eds. *Gender Relations in Australia: Domination and Negotiation*. Sydney: Harcourt Brace Jovanovich, 1992, pp. 425–447.
D'Emilio, John. 'Gay Politics and Community in San Francisco Since World War II'. In Martin Duberman, Martha Vicinus and George Chauncey, Jr, eds. *Hidden From History*. New York: New American Library Books, 1989, pp. 458–459.
Ford, Ruth. 'Lady-Friends and Deviationists: Lesbians and the Law in Australia 1920s–1950s'. In Diane Kirkby, ed. *Sex, Power and Justice: Historical Perspectives on the Law in Australia, 1788–1990*. Melbourne: Oxford University Press, 1995, pp. 33–49.

Ford, Ruth. 'Lesbians and Loose Women: Female Sexuality and the Women's Services During World War II'. In Joy Damousi and Marilyn Lake, eds. *Gender and War: Australians at War in the Twentieth Century*. Melbourne: Cambridge University Press, 1995, pp. 81–104.

Ford, Ruth. '"Filthy, Obscene and Mad": Engendering "Homophobia" in Australia, 1940s–1960s'. In Shirleene Robinson, ed. *Homophobia: An Australian history*. Sydney: Federation Press, 2008, pp. 86–112.

Gays and Lesbians Aboriginal Alliance. 'Peopling the Empty Mirror: The Prospects for Lesbian and Gay Aboriginal History'. In Robert Aldrich, ed. *Gay Perspectives II*. Sydney: University of Sydney Press, 1993, pp. 1–62.

Ion, Judith. 'Degrees of Separation: Lesbian Separatist Communities in Northern New South Wales, 1974–95'. In Jill Julius Matthews, ed. *Sex in Public*. St. Leonards: Allen and Unwin, 1997, pp. 97–113.

Luckins, Tanja. '"Time, Gentlemen, Please": The End of Six O'clock Closing and the "Post-Swill" Pub'. In Sean O'Hanlon and Tanja Luckins, eds. *Go! Melbourne in the Sixties*. Melbourne: Circa, 2005, pp. 174–187.

Matthews, Jill Julius. 'Reflections on Gay and Lesbian Activism'. In Robert Aldrich and Garry Wotherspoon, eds. *Gay and Lesbian Perspectives IV: Studies in Australian Culture*. Sydney: Department of Economic History and the Centre for Lesbian and Gay Research, The University of Sydney, 1998, pp. 20–27.

Melbourne Gay Women's Group. 'The Melbourne Gay Women's Group', in Jan Mercer, ed. *The Other Half: Women in Australian Society*. Melbourne: Penguin, 1975, pp. 441–446.

Modjeska, Drusilla. 'Introduction' in Drusilla Modjeska and Marjorie Pizer, eds. *The Poems of Lesbia Harford*. Sydney: Angus and Robertson. 1988, pp. 1–38.

Nutting, Eugene Barbara. 'The Shadows Also Compose: The Autobiography of a Tasmanian Lesbian'. In Robert Aldrich and Garry Wotherspoon, eds. *Gay and Lesbian Perspectives IV: Studies in Australian Culture*. Sydney: Department of Economic History and the Centre for Lesbian and Gay Research, The University of Sydney, 1998, pp. 194–222.

Paull, Marion. 'A Letter From Australia'. In Joan Nestle, ed. *The Persistent Desire: A Femme-Butch Reader*. Boston: Alyson, 1992, pp. 169–179.

Reade, Katy. '"Struggling to be Heard": Tensions between Different Voices in the Australian Women's Liberation Movement in the 1970s and 1980s'. In Kate Pritchard Hughes, ed. *Contemporary Australian Feminism*. Melbourne: Longman Cheshire, 1994, pp. 198–222.

Reynolds, Robert. 'Postmodernism and Gay/Queer Identities'. In Robert Aldrich, ed. *Gay Perspectives II: More Essays in Australian Gay Culture*. Sydney: Department of Economic History and the Centre for Lesbian and Gay Research, University of Sydney, 1994, pp. 245–274.

Reynolds, Robert. 'The Radicalesbian, the Effeminist, and the Engendering of Gay Liberation'. In Mark Baker, ed. *History on the Edge: Essays in Memory of John Foster (1944–1994)*. Melbourne: University of Melbourne History Department, 1997, pp. 268–292.

Ross, Liz. 'Escaping the Well of Loneliness'. In Verity Burgmann and Jenny Lee, eds. *Staining the Wattle: A People's History of Australia Since 1788*. Melbourne: McPhee Gribble, 1988, pp. 100–108.

Smith-Rosenberg, Carol. 'The Female World of Love and Friendship'. In Carol Smith-Rosenberg, ed. *Disorderly Conduct: Visions of Gender in Victorian America*. New York: Knopf, 1985.

Willett, Graham. 'Camp Melbourne in the 1960s'. In Sean O'Hanlon and Tanja Luckins, eds. *Go! Melbourne in the Sixties*. Melbourne: Circa, 2005, pp. 188–200.

Willett, Graham. 'Into the Present: Anglicanism and Homosexuality in the 1970s'. In Colin Holden, ed. *People of the Past: The Culture of Melbourne Anglicanism and Anglicanism in Melbourne's Culture: Papers to Mark the 150th Anniversary of the Anglican Diocese of Melbourne 1847–1997*. Parkville: Dept. of History, University of Melbourne, 2000, pp. 41–64.

Willett, Graham. 'Marxism and the New Social Movements: The Case of Gay Liberation'. In Carole Ferrier and Rebecca Phelan, eds. *The Point of Change: Marxism/Australia/History/Theory*. St. Lucia, Queensland: Australian Studies Centre, Department of English, University of Queensland Press, 1998.

Willett, Graham. 'From Vice to Homosexuality: Policing Perversion in the 1950s'. In Shirleene Robinson, ed. *Homophobia: An Australian History*. Sydney: The Federation Press, 2008, pp. 113–127.

Wilson, Emily. '"Someone Who is Sick and in Need of Help": Medical Attitudes to Homosexuality in Australia, 1960–79'. In Shirleene Robinson, ed. *Homophobia: An Australian History*. Sydney: The Federation Press, 2008, pp. 148–171.

Wotherspoon, Garry. 'A Sodom in the South Pacific: Male Homosexuality in Sydney, 1788–1809'. In Graeme Aplin, ed. *A Difficult Infant: Sydney Before Macquarie*. Sydney: UNSW Press, 1988, pp. 91–101.

Theses

Cranenburgh, Naomi. 'From Invisibile to "Menace": Lesbians in Australia from 1939 to 1965'. Honours thesis. Monash University, October 2010.

Ford, Ruth. 'Contested Desires: Narratives of Passionate Friends, Married Masqueraders and Lesbian Love in Australia, 1918–1945'. PhD thesis. Melbourne: La Trobe University, 2000.

Chesser, Lucy. 'Negotiating Subjectivities: The Construction of Lesbian Identities in Melbourne, 1960–1969'. Honours thesis. Melbourne: University of Melbourne, 1993.

Unpublished manuscripts

Geake, Joyce. *Shadows and Substance: Reflections of a lesbian*. Sydney: unpublished manuscript, 1973. I am grateful to the executors of the Geake estate for permission to quote from this memoir.

Willson, Sandra. Unpublished memoir. I am grateful to the executors of the Willson estate for permission to read and quote from this memoir.

INDEX

All That False Instruction 37, 38, 40–2
Amazon Acres 88
Arena Three 37, 46–9, 113
Australian, The 40, 43, 78, 92
Aversion therapy 14–5, 17, 20, 76–7
Bar scene xi, xxv, 9, 32, 47, 49, 50–74, 86, 96–7, 121–2, 129, 130–1, 133–4
Beverley [pseudonym] (interview with) 1–2, 3, 25, 30–2, 37, 55, 57–8
Binning, Virginia 28, 58–9, 66–7
Birch, Florence 118–9
Blackwell, Kerry 113–4
Bloye, Carolyn 59, 66, 108
Boyd, Nan Alamilla xxii
Brown, Karen 58, 60, 66
Butch/femme 61–6, 121–4
  butch xxv, 8, 9, 59, 61–6, 69, 96–7, 102, 112, 121–3
  femme 61–6, 123–4
Butler, Judith xxiii–xxiv
Byrnes, Paddy and Robbie 32
Cabaret clubs 51
van Camp, Laurie 8, 39, 44, 60–1, 62, 64–5, 96–7, 123
CAMP Inc. 9–10, 34, 70, 75–80, 91–5, 97–100, 102, 108, 125–6
Camp Ink 77, 91–3
Campaign 17, 35, 97–8
Castle, Terry xiv–xv
Censorship xvii, 17–18, 22, 23, 36–8, 45, 48
Chesser, Lucy xiv, xviii, 8, 10, 28, 51, 53–4, 55, 57, 65–6, 67
Chez Ivy 58–9, 60, 66
Church 21–4, 76–7, 93
  Roman Catholic xvii, 22–4, 31
  Anglican 1, 22, 23
Clark, Anna xv–xvi
Class xiv, 62, 69, 72, 80
  working-class xix, 23, 33, 36, 41, 60, 66, 119
  middle-class xix, 1, 19, 48, 63, 78, 117, 119
Clover (see also social groups) 34, 67–69
Coffee shops xxv, 50, 54, 58–9
Coming out xxii, 90, 93–8, 100

Consciousness-raising xx, 76, 80–81, 83, 84, 87, 124
Coral (interview with) 28, 53, 56
Cranenburgh, Naomi 4, 17, 18–9
Cross-dressing, female 8–9, 13, 14, 36, 52, 59, 61
Custody, child xi, 89–90
Daughters of Bilitis, the 46, 49, 79, 92, 99
Dawson, Graham xxi
Deborah [pseudonym] (interview with) 26, 30, 39
D'Emilio, John xxiii, 53
Deveson, Anne 42, 101–2, 112
Diana [pseudonym] (interview with) 69, 72
Double life xi, 29–30, 42, 95
Drag queens 50, 52, 56, 58, 60, 62, 65, 79, 86
Drag shows 57, 59, 60, 67, 79
Dress codes (see also cross-dressing) 8–9, 49, 52, 53, 56, 61, 64, 66, 89, 93, 97, 122–3, 130
Elizabeth 34, 63–4, 70, 99, 124
Elsie Women's Refuge 83
Employment (see also nursing and teaching) xi, xiii, xx, xxv, 1, 2, 6, 8, 9, 27–8, 29, 30–3, 35, 42, 55, 56, 72, 73, 82, 84, 88, 89, 90, 96, 97, 98, 105–7, 109, 110, 112, 114, 117, 118, 120, 122, 132–3
Falleni, Eugenia xiv, 13–4
Family, relationship with xi, xx, xxv, 1, 9, 11, 16, 20, 28–34, 35, 39–40, 42, 45, 83, 88, 91, 94–6, 98, 99–100, 106–10, 113–19, 126, 129, 133
Feminist literature 9, 34, 40–1, 72, 82–6, 88–9, 124–8
Film, representations of lesbianism in 27, 42–45, 70, 112, 121
Ford, Ruth xiii–xiv, xvi, xviii, 5, 14, 34, 51, 55, 59, 63, 99, 124
Foucault, Michel xvi, xxiii
Friendship networks xx, xxvi, 9, 27, 40, 53, 55–9, 63, 66–7, 71, 73–4, 77–8, 98, 111, 129
Fuller, Dennis 52, 57, 60, 72
Gay Liberation xv, xx, 27, 69, 75, 76–7, 80, 91, 94, 97, 98, 125, 133

Geake, Joyce 19–20, 29–30
Georgina (interview with) 55–6, 57–8
Goldrick, Diana 82–3
Helen (interview with) 59
Helen [pseudonym] (interview with) 29, 33–4
Hepner, Robbie 28
Higgs, Kerryn 37, 38, 40–1, 88
Homes, lesbian (see also houseshares) xi, 6–7, 32, 48–9, 61, 68, 71, 90, 107–10, 111, 118, 121, 122
Homosexuality, male xii–xiii, xv, xvi, xvii, xxvi, xx, xxiv, 2, 3–4, 10–15, 24–5, 28, 35, 36, 44–5, 50–3, 55–9, 65, 67–8, 70, 72, 75–7, 79–80, 90, 91–2, 95, 97–8, 102, 122, 129–30, 132–6
House parties 51, 53, 55–6, 63, 68, 70, 73, 123, 127
Houseshares (see also homes, lesbian) 83, 86, 88, 89, 94–5
Howard, John xxiv
Hull, Isabel xv
Humanism 76
Jones, Margaret xxiv, 6, 23–4, 31–2, 35–6, 49, 56, 61, 66, 78–9, 98, 105–6, 107, 109–112, 115–7
Kaplan, Gisela xiii
Kennedy, Elizabeth xxiii
   and Madeline Davis xxi, 8–9, 32–3, 51, 53
Kings Cross 52, 59, 61, 62, 131
Law, lesbianism and the xvii–xviii, xxv, 3–10, 14, 36–7, 40, 42, 48, 54, 93–4, 131
Lee, G.J. 2–3
Leeson, Ida 118–9
Lesbian feminism xxv, xxvi, 45, 82–9, 93, 94, 97, 121, 124–8, 135
Lesbian Feminist Collective 85, 87
Literature, lesbian and gay xvii, 17–18, 26, 27, 34–42, 45, 56, 83, 88, 124
Mackay, Sandra 69, 71, 83, 88, 94–5, 127
Mardi Gras 129–136
Marriage
   Heterosexual xi, xviii, xxiv, 1, 4, 16–17, 22–4, 32, 34, 49, 69, 82–3, 94, 96, 99, 101–4, 106, 107–9, 115–6, 119–21, 124–6, 129
   Lesbian 6, 52, 103, 110, 119–21
Martin, Sylvia xiii–xiv, 118–9
McInnies, Jan 68–9
Melmouth, Kris xi, 16–7, 60
Minnis, Diane 86
Monogamy, critiques of 124, 127–8
Morris, Rae 8, 56
Motherhood (see also custody, child) xi, xiii, xviii, 4, 17, 22–4, 34, 69, 81, 82, 84–5, 89–90, 99, 108, 115, 119, 125
Music 28, 32, 53, 55, 71–2, 83, 88, 103, 130

Newspapers
   Mainstream (see also *The Australian*) xiv, xvii, xviii–xix, xxv–xxvi, 14, 18, 27, 35, 37, 66, 72, 76, 92, 93, 98, 132–3
   Lesbian and gay (see also *Campaign*, *Camp Ink*) 9, 35, 40, 66, 81 n.17, 124
Nursing xi, 21, 32–4, 62, 72, 104,-5, 110, 113
Odewahn, Valerie 71, 73, 81–3, 96
Oral history xviii–xxii, xxiv–xxv, 51, 52–3, 59, 62, 65, 96, 101, 102–3, 110, 122, 126, 127
Park Inn 60–2
Parr, Colette 61–2
Payne, Harcourt xiv
Pearce, Chris 93, 110, 127–8, 130, 132
Plaister, Robyn 39–40, 78–9, 83–4, 89–90, 94–6, 130–3
Plummer, Ken xx
Police xvii, 5–10, 18, 20, 52, 58, 62, 75, 97, 103–4, 130–2, 135
Poll, Christabel 75–6, 92
Psychiatry xiv, xv, xvi, xviii, xxiv–xxv, 3–4, 5, 7, 10–21, 24, 29, 33–4, 76–7, 90, 93–4, 101, 104–5, 111, 121
Psychosurgery 17
Psychotherapy 14–16
Race xiv, xix, 80
Rachel (interview with) 45
Radicalesbians 86–8, 98, 125
Refractory Girl 40, 84, 86
Reynolds, Robert ix, xii, 11, 95, 97
Ritchie, Ruth 66
Richter, Ivy 60, 62
Riley, Elizabeth [pseudonym] see Kerryn Higgs
Romantic friendship xiv, 117–9
Royal Commission on Human Relationships 125
Ruby Reds 10, 72–3
School 2, 20, 22–3, 83, 90, 94, 108, 133
Sexual intimacy 1, 6–7, 9, 19, 21, 22, 23–4, 35, 36, 44–5, 47, 48, 61, 71, 81, 83, 85, 89, 103–6, 108, 110–12, 116, 117, 120–4, 126–8
Sex education 18–9
Sexism 79–80, 84
Short, Penny 21, 90–1
Silence xi, xiv–xviii, xx, xxii, xxiv, xxv–xxvi, 3–4, 24–9, 35, 39, 42, 47, 93, 101–2, 105–6, 110, 129
Social groups, lesbian (see also Clover) 34, 49, 51, 57–8, 65–6, 68–9, 73–4
Summerfield, Penny xxii
Sussex Hotel 60
Sydney Rape Crisis Centre 83, 88
Sydney Women's Commission 84–5
Teaching xi, 3, 21–3, 70, 78, 82, 90–1, 97, 133

Index

Television, representations of lesbianism on 42–3, 44, 92, 93
The Killing of Sister George (see also film) 43–4
The Ladder 45–9, 79, 113
The Naked Bunyip (see also film) 44–5, 112, 121
Trolley Car 60
Webber, Iris 5
Weeks, Jeffrey xxiii
Well of Loneliness, The xvii, 18, 36–40
Willett, Graham ix, xii, xvi–xvii, 3, 80, 97, 134
Wills, Sue 77, 79, 92, 94
Willson, Sandra xxiv, 6–8, 18, 20, 103–5, 111–4, 120–1
Women's bands (see also music) 71–2
Women's dances 71, 83, 88
Women's Electoral Lobby 70, 82, 135
Women's Liberation Movement xiii, xx, 55 n.15, 69–72, 80–89, 91, 97, 100, 124–7, 134–5
Wotherspoon, Garry xii–xiv, 57, 80